To Ralph S. Jackson
With sincere hopes that
you may enjoy my
Country-style story!
                    Viola Ebel Adlof
July 20, 1963

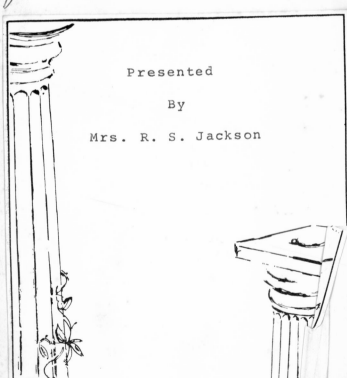

Presented

By

Mrs. R. S. Jackson

LISA'S
TEXAS
GRANDMA

by

VIOLA EBEL ADLOF

THE HIGHLAND PRESS
BOERNE, TEXAS

FIRST EDITION

———

Library of Congress Catalog Card No. 63-17463

Copyright 1963

by

Viola Ebel Adlof

Printed in Texas, United States of America

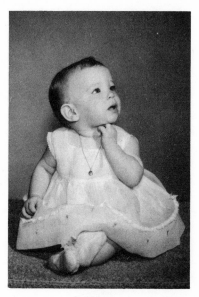

To Lisa,

my first grandchild, who even before she talked,
asked questions . . . with her eyes.

Prologue

Why have I written this book?

Even the one who has lived with me for 36 years of my almost 54 asks me why have you written this book?

I believe it would have been a great help to me to have had a written account of the battles my ancestors fought . . . not on the war battle-fields but on their everyday home fronts. I doubt their times saw as many drastic changes as did the period from 1908 to 1958 of which I have written.

If I shall encourage one little country girl to love the land and her man who tills it through good and through evil days . . .

If some person is helped to see around, over and through the molehills that turned into mountains and find the sun shining on the other side . . .

If I have encouraged anyone to continue to educate himself though formal schooling was out of his reach . . .

If a busy housewife comes to understand it is important to do church work, civic improvement work and yet to look fresh and sweet when her man comes home . . .

If I could teach myself to fully practice what I preach, realizing everyone preaches his own sermon daily, then that is why I wrote this book.

I have not told all the family's innermost secrets, for I have tried to write a book to prove that the plain, everyday little things in life are what most folk cherish.

From Model T's to jets; from straight rows to contours; from men to women Methodist preachers; from starched and celluloid collars to short-sleeved, soft sports shirts worn without ironing; from one-room country schools to consolidated county schools 1908 has brought us to 1958 . . . even in the brushlands of Texas.

Viola Ebel Adlof

Papa and Mama's
silver wedding anniversary

His photo and life were unfinished

The Arthur
who left us . . . and me

The twins dolled up
for Sunday School

PAULINE
My big sister, "Pena"

LYDIA
Quiet and so pretty, "Lucy"

PEARL
To her with my questions

OLGA
Papa called her the business lady

CECELIA
The stylish one

GEORGE
Best brother ever

Live Oak County Courthouse
where I covered news

Even the cows trust
his faithful care

Our Home before the
seven year drought

Ruth and Carolyn
get Shirley Temple hats

Women of Live Oak County
Centennial Celebration — 1956

Preacher Grandpa
and his three branches

Our wedding picture,
twenty years later

The big kids start to teach school

Doctor Carolyn starts
her practice

Septembers

"Today is October first and I am so glad!" was the way I greeted my family that bright day when we were all together once again. As I looked into the bright blue eyes of this wee, golden-haired girl baby all I could say was, "Yes, I am so glad!"

"Glad?" my husband asked in sheer amazement — though he was as pleased as I with the first grandchild.

I explained I was glad another September was allowed me. He knew, as did my whole kith and kin, about Septembers and how the month often treated me. I was glad another September was now history. Yet, quickly, I counted, one by one, the blessings Septembers had brought me. For not everything that came my way in Septembers was gloomy. Many glooms had brought their own bright glows.

"Really, I am wealthy. Not with money in my purse nor even in my bank account. I am wealthy in lessons learned from life. Life which has included fifty Septembers full of the light and the dark days."

"And now this little one who will be expecting you and me to be the best grandparents ever," Arthur added to my listing.

Fifty years it has taken me to learn some of the simplest lessons; to make thousands of acquaintances and cultivate many friendships; to know the real meaning of love and of life and to realize that each new day brings new assignments to be mastered.

These friends were not all made while days were bright and sunny. Many came to me while looking up into their faces from my place between sheets — bedsheets of my bed at home and of many hospital beds.

My "beginning" was in September so I was born in June, 1908. It was in a part of Texas where midwives and old-wives did not have an exclusive right to superstitions. Most folks have a few queer notions of their own. My mother thought it was bad luck to be born in June.. Yet, she and my father often shared my feeling that September is the best month of the year.

The two persons responsible for my birth shared my love of later years for the month of September. They were farm people in Gonzales where the fall months mean new beginnings. It could well be their appreciation for September was deepened by their association with merchants and friends of the Jewish faith.

One of these friends visited often with my father. I suspect, he often loaned Papa funds to see us through a year when crops failed. Mama said she thought maybe the man was just keeping an eye on his interests.

I recall it was once a very warm day when Papa returned with the eggs and cream. He had forgotten it was Yom Kippur, the Day of Atonement, an annual Jewish fast-day. His friends' stores were all closed when he got to town. That night, after chores were done, we sat on the porch as was our summer custom.

Papa taught us the lesson his friends' observance meant to him. "It is good to stop for a day to think and pray, to renew one's spirit for the start of a new year."

"If we would stop a whole day to think, who would milk the cows and gather the eggs and churn the butter and make the cheese and feed the animals," — Mama interrupted.

We all laughed; and when Mama got about half done with her list, we chimed in with her, and some of us kept adding on one chore after the other until Papa said, "Guess we will just continue to pray on the run."

In September, farmers begin to plow, for winter-grazing seeds must soon be planted. Many of the farmers begin to look for places to move for the next year. That is, they did at that day and time as share-croppers were numerous. Some would be evicted by greedy landlords. But mostly, tenants were evicted by Mother Nature.

Still others moved because they were able to buy land.

This was the case with my parents. They had lived several years near Sublime and dearly loved the area. Papa worked like a slave, was a good manager and established a good credit rating. So, he began to look for a larger place in keeping with his ever-increasing family. Not finding one for sale, he saddled his horse one day and rode into the next county — Gonzales.

Mama often told us how frightened she was when night came and Papa did not return. They had no way of letting each other know the day's developments, for there were no telephones in the neighborhood. For three days and nights, she kept reminding herself that Papa had said he would not return until he found them a permanent place to live.

He was weary of mending fences, filling gulleys and plowing extra deep just to be told to move. Twice, the owners' sons had grown up and wanted the land to start their families and homes.

2

This was right and good, Papa surely knew, but he was wanting a place to call his own.

Besides, the fifth child born just a year before was a son. A man must seek a better life when he has five children.

He found the very place, just north of the town of Gonzales and only two miles from Mama's father and step-mother. It was a very wet summer, and Papa's horse grew lame on the second day of his search. So he rode into the barnyard at Grandpa's for the night.

Grandpa was a "local" preacher. Papa, too, was an excellent speaker and could memorize pages and pages of Scripture and poems. Grandma never did really care too much for Papa, but she invited him to spend the night.

At supper Papa learned from Wesley, Mama's half-brother, about a farm being offered for sale nearby. It was actually not yet a farm as there were only five acres grubbed. Some persons from Ohio had it for sale as they did not like Texas after all.

Without even waiting to look at the place, Papa walked to town in the night to mail Mama a letter. The letter arrived the same day Papa returned home, but Mama treasured it all her life. She showed it to us many years later.

It simply told where he was and that he would walk over the land the next day. Then, he wrote in his very poor hand-writing, "Bea not dismay whatever betide God will take care of you and me and the chillen and Arthur."

The "chillen" to Papa were always we girls — the four before me and the one afterwards. Arthur was the son of the blessing meant by his letter. Later another son was born.

Today, fifty years and more later there is still a great lesson in Papa's words even though he could not spell them all correctly. Be not dismayed! Dismay — a sudden or a complete loss of courage was not our Papa.

It became our home — home for me to be born in the next June and for many ailing persons to find courage and comfort in the years ahead. A place to live and let live; to work and save; to weep and laugh. Most of all a place where Septembers always brought more blessings than sorrows . . . no matter how many the sorrows of the days.

Joys never to be forgotten by children who grow up on farms are the new buds and blossoms on the trees in the orchard; the pecans ripening in the fall; the big pumpkins and funny seedheads on dill and on the last onions in the garden.

The joy of gathering the best of everything to polish and dry for exhibits at the county fairs. The joy of birthdays when even though it wasn't Saturday night, we would make a freezer of ice-cream. The thrill of going to the woods for a Christmas tree and the smell of Koch-Kaese on the kitchen stove . . . of Kaffee-kuchen baking Saturday afternoons . . . and of swimming in the stock-water tanks when the fields were too wet for hand labor.

So, today is October first, and again I am glad! Glad for the strength — for the time — to write about all the blessings that have come to me and my people for the past fifty years. Fifty years that seemingly always found their climaxes in September. When that month is filled, it is usually enough conversation material for the whole fall. The family gathers for Thanksgiving and even more of the family comes together for Christmas.

It has come to be somewhat of a tradition for someone to ask, "Well, Ola, how are you coming on your manuscript? Will you ever let us read about ourselves?"

This year — after the question was posed so often — I bravely announced: "It is written, but will any of you have time to read it?"

I am not the only busy person in my family. Many people think we are somewhat "touched in the beezer" to rush about as we do. Seems there are always two committees meeting at the same time. Somehow, my sisters and I seem to be named to many of the groups.

Was it always so? It must have been in our family. I can remember when I was a small child that Papa would be absent from the after-supper circle around the dining table very often. Papa was not away in the saloons, not out coon-hunting or at any of the places some of his friends could be found at night. Papa would be in a farm meeting, a church board meeting or any way in a meeting of some sort to promote the welfare of the community.

Later, I resented the many times Mama, too, would be absent. Mama would be at a neighbor's — be they black or white. The next day or so, we would know without asking where she had gone . . . at least, we would know why. For she would wash her long, white mother-hubbard in the black iron wash-pot in the back yard and hang it on the line to dry for hours and hours. Sometimes when we were older, Mama would tell us a few — a very few — of the details of her night's work.

A few times, Mama brought home a premature baby; and for days and days, she would care for it. She loved each one as if it were her own. If we ever doubted Mama's love for children, we have only to recall the way she cared for these.

Now, as I reflect on the earliest events of my life, it comes to mind that these absences of Mama gave us longer evenings to look at the catalogues. Oh, the joy of mail-order catalogues! Each fall new ones would arrive from Sears, Roebuck and Company; Reuters Seed Company, and Montgomery, Ward and Company.

We would crease and mark, hoping the hints would be heeded when Christmas orders were made. But never did we tear out pages except the stiff ones which we often used for illustrations in our school work. (The rest of the catalogues were always saved for use in the little house out back.)

Of course, I only know what my sisters tell me about the year I was born. They must remember correctly for I did later hear Papa tell of his disappointment when the sixth child arrived in the female side of the family.

One person, however, tells with joy and with much amusement how he remembers my birth. He is my husband. He recalls often how his mother announced at their breakfast table one June morning that the Ebels (pronounced ables) "have another girl baby."

He tries to make me believe he was glad, even then. This I doubt as he was not quite eight years old. It could be, though, for he was glad to remain the center of attraction in the circle of men of the church. He was, they tell me, a beautiful child.

My Kindergarten Life

Through the years, I have not held against my parents their disappointment in my being just another girl. Nor would I say they neglected us for not taking the time to teach us, in so many words, about life — the birds and bees, it is referred to today.

We did not attend formal Kindergartens though there were several in operation. Gonzales has and always has had many wealthy families who supported these schools for their children. They had the best teachers available. Some of the churches even have these schools for the pre-school age children and for first graders.

There was never money for such extras as this in our household. Besides, we were always too busy. Even when we were small children, we had our share in the chores about the farm. So as far as the "birds and bees" education, we learned from observation.

Living on a farm and especially on a dairy and poultry farm, it is next to impossible to miss the sex lesson. In fact, children there often chance upon an excess of illustration. I do not recall ever asking my mother about anything that puzzled me along these lines. It was to my sister, Pearl, I went with all my questions.

About the first thing which I can recall of great importance in my pre-school days was the death of my brother, Arthur. It seems the thing I remember most about it was the grief of my father. I recall sitting on his lap in our parlor during the funeral services.

It seems I can still feel his tears dropping down my neck and shoulders. He must have held me close to him as he bowed his head and just let the tears flow.

The flowers were beautiful. The preacher sang all by himself. There were so many people in our house. They stood around the walls and cried. Everyone was so good to us. Today, I wonder why the people were allowed to come, for Arthur died of diphtheria.

I really don't know where the twins were during all this. They were only a few weeks old, having arrived the middle of December. It must have consoled all of us to have them, especially since one was a boy, my brother George Edward. The tiny little girl was also given a name for royalty that was popular in that day — Cecelia Elizabeth.

To a small child, sometimes grief brings with it great joy. I remember how happy I was over all the attention we received from friends; how beautiful were the potted plants in the east parlor window left after the funeral; how Mama and Papa stayed at home for months, never leaving to go to committees or to be a mid-wife.

The joys did not hold top importance in my memory though as I recall the results of the injections we received sometime that week. The doctor and Papa took us, one at the time, into the dining room and laid us on the dining table.

We were given our injections it seemed with a needle just like Papa used on the cows. But never did I see as stiff a cow the next day as we were the next day. Sometimes, in this day and time, when I go to the physician to have a "shot," I secretly pray that it will not react like that stiff-one when I was about four.

Pearl later told me that she thought to comfort Papa by telling him he and Mama should just have another boy to replace Arthur. She said Papa told her, "Nobody can replace any one else. If we have a baby again, it will be given its own place by God who gives everyone a place. He gave Arthur a place but it must have been too small and so He sent him on to his mansion in the sky."

Pearl said Papa also informed her we were not to discuss such matters of having other babies. It must have been the custom for parents to allow children to teach themselves many lessons. In our case, Papa and Mama provided a wholesome atmosphere for our learning. Not only were we taken to church each Sunday, to prayer meetings and to Cathecism when we were teens, but we had a family altar.

My parents were also very modest and never appeared in our presence in scanty clothing. Seldom did we see them kiss. Today, I would not approve of my husband's leaving for work in the morning without kissing me. Yet, much of yesterday's influence stayed. I always dress in privacy.

One evening late in a summer day, Pauline (my eldest sister) whispered to Lydia, "I bet we are going to have another baby."

The evening was very still and the bedroom we shared got even stiller as we caught the remark made. Now, forty-five summers later, I can remember her explanation.

" 'cause Papa is sure huggin' Mama out there in the porch swing tonight. 'sides he made us go to our room early. Papa was grouchy again today and . . . "

"What are all of you little outfits sitting up in bed for all of a sudden? Go to sleep!"

Odd how such little incidents influence a person for life.

Another strong influence of my pre-school days was the attitude developed toward persons of other races and creeds. This was learned in our daily family devotional periods. I believe the only things that would have prevented us from holding our devotions would have been the house catching fire or someone suddenly falling in a faint.

I can recall the very design of the linoleum floor-covering in the dining room where we knelt to pray. Papa had put the floor-covering in this room first for the very reason that we children, in our shuffling from one knee to the other during the prayers, had gotten wood splinters in ourselves. We were sure that we were now rich, having such fine things as floor-covering. We also had new curtains in the dining room and a varnished shelf for the clock. On this shelf, the Bible was placed each morning after prayers.

Papa had decided to go ahead and put the shelf where some day he hoped to build a fireplace. Most likely, Papa thanked God for the new things and asked God to bless our work so we could have the fireplace. Without a doubt, if he prayed for anything, Papa added, "Thy will be done."

I am ashamed to recall how often I wished Papa wouldn't pray so long. (And why did he have to tell God everything when Papa claimed God knew everything already?)

It shames me to think how often I wished the preacher would not have the prayer meetings so often in our house. Seems after we got the linoleum for our floors, we spent half of our week-nights on our knees.

Mama was sick a lot in these years and once or twice, maybe oftener, I suspected her of being too weary to kneel so long. I suspected that was her reason for rising later than we did. Papa might have thought Mama was "possuming," too. Soon, we would gather in their bedroom to read and pray when she was sick.

"I will sure be glad when you get well enough so we can read in the dining-room and get off of this old rough wood floor," Olga remarked one morning. Olga is the one who says what she thinks, bless her heart! You never have to guess what she thinks about you.

Today, many of my friends make tape recordings of such important sayings as family prayers, wedding vows, grandchildren's first words. Would that I had a recording of my father's prayers! Mama never prayed aloud in the family circle, even when we grew up and had to take our turn at doing so. I say "had to" for we knew when Papa said, "This morning you will pray," it meant this morning I would pray. And pray loud enough for Papa to hear. Papa was partially deaf.

I do not know why Mama never prayed aloud in the family circle. We know she prayed . . . she must have. She also sang as she went about her work, but she did not sing when we all sang together. She had a fine voice which all the church congregation enjoyed. There, she would sing with others.

Maybe, Mama was Papa's observer at home, listening to make sure none of us loafed through our duties. Seems Papa, even though he could not hear well, always knew within moments if I failed to say all the words of the unison prayers. Many of the Psalms and the Beatitudes were memorized.

There was one in our family circle who was excused from the unison recitations, for she could only speak German. She was about sixty when she came to America. She was Papa's maternal aunt. We called her Tanta. There was never a finer person in my life. But Tanta, even though she was up in age, was always among the first to kneel.

Tanta also took her turn at saying the prayers. We could all understand what she said though our parents encouraged us to always speak English to each other. Papa said we should use the language of our land.

Papa was born in Germany and came to the United States with his parents when he was four years old. On the long voyage on the seas, his mother had taught him to read German. Not many years after their arrival, his father died of tuberculosis. This left Papa to be the breadwinner for a family of five.

Little time was left for formal schooling. But Papa never ceased to learn. He studied every opportunity he had. In later years, he studied each evening when he was not attending some meeting. He would sit with us children at the long dining table, and together we would do the homework.

Mama had gone to all of grade school and was more help to us. Mama loved to read and saved Papa much time by reading to him as he did odd jobs about the house and farm. Papa learned so well that he later became a very successful insurance agent. This was our pride and joy.

He did so well at sales that he soon felt it necessary to have a desk. So he built himself one. It is really nice. Pena (our nickname for Pauline) treasures it in her home today.

The best part of the desk was the upper portion with two small glass doors on it. Here, Papa started our first home library. With his own knowledge, he selected two shelves of fine books to put there for us to read. For Mama, he also bought a hard-bound cook book which she kept in the kitchen along with a box full of recipes out of the Farm and Ranch. (Remember, these were the days before ready-mixes, frozen pies and TV dinners.) It was a real accomplishment to make a cake — starting with wood-fired ovens, sifting and measuring each ingredient, beating eggs with a fork and often having to substitute lard for butter. (Butter sold better than lard, and heaven knows we needed the money.)

Our large garden, our full supply of fresh meats and eggs and fruits from the orchards were all among our blessings. We even thought it was a treat to get to hoe in the garden or orchard where there were beautiful rows of vegetables or trees in bloom or in fruit.

It was much better than hoeing the long rows of cotton or pulling suckers off of the corn stalks; cutting hegari heads with butcher knives or corn-tops which were stacked for winter cattle feed. Papa did buy the first ensilage cutter and combine in the area, but many years passed before we had these to help with the heavy work.

With blessings come responsibilities. We learned this early. One day as we were picking cucumbers by the bushels to sell, Lydia said, "Maybe we should not have prayed so hard for rain. I am so tired of picking cucumbers I would just as soon they would dry up and blow away."

Today, I ponder the thought. Are we always willing to accept all that we pray for? What about asking God to bless the work of the commission on evangelism? Do I really want to go over to the west part of town today to tell them of Christ? Or had I better stop asking God to let His kingdom come on earth as it is in heaven?

Miss Ora Teaches Tanta and Me

When I went to visit in the home of our hired man today (to show his wife how to bathe their new baby) I explained to him the necessity of having kids vaccinated. I remember the September I started to school. My vaccination for smallpox had made me very sick.

The neighbors had come to call, which had only served to add to our fears . . . way back then. They had told in detail of the death of one of their children who had gotten his vaccination infected. There were no so-called miracle drugs in those days. Many people opposed small-pox vaccinations. So it was that many neighbors had come to call to plead with Papa.

Papa was on the local school board. There was talk of making the small-pox vaccinations compulsory and some of the people had come to beg him to vote against the new rule.

Usually, we did not know what callers wanted when they came to see Papa. They could be seen from the house, leaning against the wagon or a fence. Or perhaps, the man would have to walk way across the field, and then we would see Papa and him settle down on the furrow tops to talk.

Papa always had time to talk with a friend . . . Mama said even with all the peddlers. Poor Papa! He would buy things we just did not need when some salesman came along. After all, he had a mutual compassion for salesmen; and, too, he loved trying out new inventions.

He probably took up a lot of time telling about his family.

Several times, I can remember he used almost exactly the same words when he proudly announced, "We have six girls and each one has a brother."

He got so used to catching people off-guard with this story he would begin to chuckle before their reply. Usually the reply was, "You have twelve children?"

Naturally, Papa was telling the truth. We did have one brother . . . and he was George. We were as proud of him as were Mama and Papa. To add to our pride was the fact of his beauty. He has big blue eyes and blond curls.

11

Most of us girls have gray eyes and though some of us are blonds, none has natural curls. Lydia was born a brunette and her hair is wavy. My hair was as white as cotton and my eyes are undecided. With blue dresses, they appear to be quite blue; with green, they tend to look almost yellow; and when between white bed-sheets, you hardly know they have color.

Tanta made us conscious of our hair, for she took special pride in well-groomed hair. If one protested, a quick yank would remind her of Tanta's opinion. Tanta had a room of her own in the little lean-to made from part of the long, open back porch at the back of the house.

When I was a very young child, Tanta would arise quite early and help with the breakfast. Then she would brush the hair of the young ones who were not out helping in the dairy. It was a time we looked forward to as we could go into her room and sit on the little braided rag-rug in front of her rocker.

It was the only time we went to her room except by special invitation. These invitations came in the order of our ages, two at the time. Being an odd number, I got shifted from one group to the other.. I liked being in the room better with Olga than with the twins. If we were very naughty that day, Tanta would make us sit on the floor the whole visit while she read to us in German.

She thought she was punishing us, perhaps. But I know I enjoyed that most of all. Olga and I seemed to be the naughtiest so I liked going to visit Tanta with Olga. Then we would get to listen to her read.

Papa and Tanta also taught us to sing folk-songs in German. Tanta was a cheerful person, always singing at her work. Some of the songs she attempted to teach us were difficult; and some I never understood, just sang them. Yet, these songs became treasures to us.

One little song asked questions. Translated, it would tell us in English to ponder how many stars are in the sky; how many butterflies and how many clouds; how many children in His kingdom. The answers were that God, the Master, counted them all, knew where they were and called them all by name.

The song is in my little green book, inscribed, "To Viola Ebel, 1918," by our good and faithful preacher, the late Rev. John Streit. He was a native of Switzerland; and, true to tradition, he loved to sing.

For my German friends who may have lost the words during all these years, I type them here in English letters.

12

Weist du, wie viel Sternlein Stehen?

1. Weist du, wie viel Sternlein stehen
An dem blauen himmels-zelt?
Weist du, wie viel Wolken gehen
weithin unber alle welt?
Gott, der Herr, hat sie gezahlet
Das ihm auch nicht eines fehlet
An der ganzen grosen zahl
an der ganzen, grosen zahl.

2. Weist du, wie viel mucklein speilen
In der heisen sonnen-glut
Wie viel fisch-lein auch sich kuhlen
In der hellen wasser-flut?
Gott, der Herr, rief sie mit namen
Das sie all ins Leben kamen
Das sie nun so frohlich sind,
Das sie nun so frohlich sind.

3. Weist du, wie viel menschen-kinder
Frohlich auf der erde gehn?
Und weist du, wie viele Gunder
Bangend um erretung flehn?
Gottes auge ruht auf allen,
Und, wo wir auch immer wallen,
Halt er uns in seiner hand,
Halt er uns in seiner hand.

The last four lines became a lifetime inspiration to me. They say: "God's eyes rest on everyone; and wherever we wander. He holds us in His hand."

A neighbor came one day to tell us of his brother's death in a nearby town. The brother was killed in a saloon fight. Afterwards, Tanta told us the only way to keep from getting killed in a saloon is to stay out of saloons.

That was the way Tanta taught us. She probably learned the simple little lessons from her intense interest in others and desire to learn. As Papa always said, "You only learn when you want to learn."

Tanta asked Papa to explain why she could not go to school with me. Tanta knew why. But I cried and cried as opening day came. I wanted Tanta to go, too. I simply wanted her to go because I dearly loved her, and I knew she would like to learn to read our school books.

I wound up saying, "Why do we have to have laws for everything, anyway?"

Today, often I catch myself thinking the same way. It is a foolish way to think. I know that. Yet, can I help but think about it?

But with or without Tanta, I finally got to start school. We walked the mile and a half to the little one-room Reid Ward School on the hill. I had visited often and so I knew the teacher and she knew me.

Olga told her I had cried much of the way to school.

Miss Ora was disappointed. She thought, perhaps, I had cried about having to start school. Many children do. But not I. I loved school; I still do. I seldom miss visiting the opening day of school in Three Rivers or in George West.

I explained that it was because of Tanta I had cried. Dear Miss Ora! She always seemed to know the answers to all our problems. She said to tell Tanta she would get her a book with two translations, German and English, with pictures to illustrate.

We could hardly wait to tell her. She was thrilled but in a way, Tanta seemed to resent the fact that I had told she could not read English. "One should not tell everything from our homes," she said.

Before the week was out, I was sorry I had told it, too. For Miss Ora brought the book, and Tanta hurried through the supper dishes and went into her room. There we could see her with the new book. She forgot all about inviting us into her room for our visits.

It was Christmas week when one night Tanta joined us at the family circle where we were all studying our parts in the church-tree program. To our amazement, Tanta read to us.

"Dis is de American flag. It is red, vite and blue."

Papa reached up for the china-bowl that held the kerosene lamp and pulled it down closer so Tanta could see better. He just raved about how smart all his people were.

Now for one of her age to learn to read a new language is somewhat of a miracle. Tanta thought it not so. She told us in German, she could hardly help but learn with ten of us talking all the time (much of the time two or three of us at once.) You see, there were the seven children, Papa and Mama, and Mama's young half-brother, Wesley. He was not with us constantly but very often.

Pauline, Lydia and Pearl attended the town school by this

14

time. Even if they had not now been in advanced grades, it would have been necessary. They, and others in turn, drove to the school in town in a buggy so they could take the eggs, cream, milk, butter, and cheese. And oft-times there were plow-shares to repair or other erands to be run.

Two of them were in the same grade. Pena had had to skip a year while Mama was carrying me. Sometimes I feel I cheated poor Pena out of a year's advancement.

It turned out to be a real boon to them, though. For when Pena would be late to a class or have to miss a day to help with some errand or chore, Lydia would be there to get it all. Then, Pena could catch up on home-work easier with Lydia in the same class.

Vivid in my memory is the Reid Ward School where I first went. The one room building was about square. Windows on the east flooded the one half with sunshine in the mornings; and on the west, windows let in the sun in the afternoons. There were about forty students. We were seated in single seats in rows of about five to the row.

There were six grades. In my grade, there were six boys and I. One was my cousin, a year older than I, who was one of the three children who did not walk to school. His parents may have been wealthier than the rest of the folk, or they may not have been. But their mother was more "up-to-date," my parents said. She did not approve of her children's sitting in school all day long in wet or gritty shoes. And how would one get there afoot without having either muddy shoes or dusty feet? She had a point! Could be a large portion of my body is turned under for feet because of the need to paddle through the thick mud of the Gonzales farm.

Some children never wore shoes. When the weather was freezing, they would be absent. In warm days, they would be back in school. Fortunately, we always had shoes. Sometimes, they were third-handed. But who knew the difference after they were coated with black dirt or red clay? Papa had his own cobbler's repair box, and many nights we could hear him tapping away at a half-soling job after we went to bed.

At school, we had a recitation bench. When it was a class' turn to go to the bench, the pupils would rise and march like soldiers to the long wooden bench at the left-hand side of Miss Ora's desk. Each would read aloud, taking his turn at spelling words or answering geography or health questions.

If one missed an answer, he had to move down in rank on the

bench. I tried very hard and usually managed to stay at the head of the bench. Silly me! If I did happen to miss and had to move down, I'd be so upset over it that in a few minutes I'd have to raise my hand showing my pointer finger.

I always have had trouble forgiving myself if I fail to do what I set out to do. After all, with all the sisters older than I having had the answers drilled to them by Mama, there was no excuse for my missing. Mama would drill us in spelling and memory work as we dried dishes in the evenings or even in the fields when she came to bring us drinking water.

Being turned down on the recitation bench would so upset me that I would get a violent tummy ache and have to rush over to the corner of the campus. Several times, Miss Ora would send Olga or other big girls to see about me. Even today, failure to do what someone expects of me makes me ill. Like in those days, ill enough to faint while trying to keep on with a routine too involved for me.

One September, we started early to make Hallowe'en decorations. Miss Ora sent a note home with us for our parents to sign their permission to have a night program. The Jack-o-lanterns would be so pretty at night, she wrote.

It was almost unheard of for young children to be away from home at nights unless it was to church or prayer meetings (except in the summer months when we all visited kinsfolk and neighbors at night.) So to have a night-time school program was a big event!

Today mothers of school children sigh and say, "Oh, how wonderful! Tonight, for once, we don't have to go anywhere."

Their children sigh and say, "You mean we are all going to stay here at home a whole night together . . . just us! Could I have a friend spend the night with me in my room?"

I hope I shall always remember the school days, the joys that were ours. This time was extra special — my first time to see our school at night! Tanta brushed my hair until I thought she was scalping me. She gathered the long stuff into a cluster behind my ears and braided it halfway down as tight as "Dick's hat band."

In the braid, she plaited a strip of the material scraps from my dress. Tanta and Mama always kept the little strips for our hair braids. Then she tied a neat bow and let the ends flufl. She had wrapped it very tightly the night before on dampened corn shucks. Oh, my! I looked so pretty!

Soon, we were at the program. The lighted Jack-o-lanterns glowed over the entire building. The children sat on the floor in the front part of the school and the women sat in our usual seats. The men mostly stood about the walls and in the doorway. There wasn't enough fresh air left for a gnat to keep going, I'm sure. Mama fainted. Papa and my uncle took her outside, and Miss Ora asked everyone to remain quiet. She assured us that Mama would be all right. We opened a few more windows and went on with the program.

When I got up to say my piece in the recitation that spelled out Hallowe'en, letter by letter, I felt Tom, the boy behind me, tug at my hair. In a flash, I was on fire. He had stuck the fuzzy curled ends of my pigtail braid in the nearest lantern top.

Miss Ora beat out the fire. People were yelling. I smelled like a singed chicken. I saw Papa look in at the front double-doors of the room. Soon everyone got quiet again, and the program went on uninterrupted.

Just as our recitation was over, Tom's big strong Papa reached over my head and fairly yanked his son up into space! It was so frightening, and I felt so sorry for Tom. I just knew he would get the fire beat out of him, too.

It was a spooky ordeal. As we were about to leave, Tom's mother came to us and said, "Well! How long did it take you Dutchmen to rehearse all the put-on-the-dog you did tonight? Sure the new car twern't the cause of you to faint out?"

Could be the new car helped me to forget the rest of the evening. We left right after the program. Mama did not even want to stay to be sure she got her cake plate back. It was not only our first car but it was the first car on Dry Prong Road, now called Harwood Road.

Papa knew for sure that if it started to rain, as it was threatening to do, we would get stuck. Our new Model T Ford, shining bright with brass trims and even carbide lights mounted in a metal box on the running-board was far more exciting than a daughter's burned pigtails . . . or even Mama's fainting . . . or Mrs. Smith's insults.

Except to Tanta. She had stayed at home from the program. When we got home, I went crying to tell her about my hair. She was very disturbed over what might have happened if Miss Ora had not been so alert.

All the girls did not have aunts to help their mothers with the endless chores, with curling daughters' hair, and with making-over their dresses so they looked new, instead of third or even fourth-handed.

17

"What y'all want curls for no-how?" Nonnie asked us very often. Nonnie was proud she had been able to save enough money to buy an iron with which she straightened her thick black hair on Saturdays.

It took me years to learn why the other girls did not comment or carry-on about our curls or our neatly made dresses as we thought they would. The little girl next door explained it to me today.

She came over to ask if I would loan her mother a pair of my old blue jeans. They were going on a family picnic. Her Dad had brought his wife new jeans to wear as she had outgrown hers after her babies came.

"Mama has some new jeans, but she says some of my aunts will think she is "putting on" if she wears everything new. She said she won't tell them she borrowed some from you that have already faded."

Folks haven't changed in fifty years. Jeans still fade and mostly kin and kith get along better when they, like the jeans, have aged some.

Garlic, Glory or Gangrene

I was now nine, going on ten. Because the family knew of my outspoken dislike for garlic, even the smell of it, and how I fretted over failure to make perfect grades in school, it wasn't heeded much when I said I was ill.

Miss Ora moved the children each fall according to the grades. This year, I asked (right out loud, of all the nerve) to be allowed to sit where no one sat whose parents used garlic in their home-made sausages. What a way to make friends!

Naturally, the teacher frowned at me. But when in the afternoon, I became very feverish and red in the face, she knew something more than garlic odor was wrong with me.

She let the older girls keep order and hear the classes while she took me home in the buggy. Mama went to the field to get Papa. It was decided we should call the doctor. We now had a telephone which by turning a crank one long "ring" would put the operator on the line.

It was very hot that September afternoon. Mama bathed my face with cool water until Papa took over. She brought her mending in so she could keep busy and yet be near me when the doctor arrived.

The doctor now had a fast automobile and a Negro man to drive. At full speed of forty miles per hour (as the chauffeur was said to drive), Papa assured us it would only take a few minutes for help to come. But there must have been others who needed him worse. It was late that night before he arrived.

As soon as he came, Papa asked him if I could perhaps have the new disease, influenza, which was becoming an epidemic in Texas, according to the Dallas Semi-Weekly. Papa read that paper religiously.

It was not; nor was it what Mama feared — diptheria. I felt relieved, to be sure. But really, I do not remember too clearly when it was that the doctor said, "It looks like gangrene. We must operate her." My appendix had ruptured.

I had never known the word before. I learned it first-hand. This first time to surgery, with Papa to go along, didn't seem a

19

bit frightening. What we don't know cannot scare us it has oft been said.

Papa went with me as they laid me on the back seat of the doctor's car to go to the hospital in Gonzales, only three miles away. Mama was to come early the next morning. Pauline and Lydia could drive our new car, although Papa warned Mama about Pauline backing out of the car-house. (We call them car-ports now.)

Mama kissed me good-bye. I remember the few times my mother actually kissed me with real "squozzy-ness" like children are kissed today. She so seldom kissed any of us children. I wondered if she thought I would die.

On the way to town, I asked Papa (he later laughed many times about it) if I were going to die, if the people would all come again, would there be so many cakes and food again, would there be so many pretty flowers, would Tanta miss me and one question right after the other. I must have been delirious from fever.

The pains in my side, stomach and right leg had left me several hours earlier, and I had even told Papa to go to bed. I felt sleepy.

There were already four patients in the room where they put me. Several were on cots in the hall. This was influenza, no doubt.

I could see through a division in the dividing screen (made by hanging sheets on wires across the room) that the patient next to me was a young man from our church, Johnny.

When today I tell of this ordeal, my daughters doubt my memory. After all, I was delirious or something. But I am quite sure Papa knew what was going on, and he said I was given a large dose of castor oil with orange juice afterwards. I still seem to taste the oil.

Days wore on. Many new patients were brought into the hospital. I never saw the young friend again in the next bed. For the first few days, I knew no one. Afterwards, I learned Johnny went to the "place God prepared for him" as Papa always said.

My hospital experiences would give me something to tell my sisters and brother, I was just musing to myself one late afternoon two weeks later. I had been propped up in a wheel-chair and brought onto the hospital lawn. It was covered with colored leaves that fell from the huge shade trees, for fall was here now.

When Papa and Mama came that night after the chores were done, I boasted to them of how I would have something to tell the family. Then, Papa told me his brother was also in the hospital and so was Lydia. I call her Lucy. Another week later, and we all went home at the same time.

I still did not feel strong, but we thought perhaps it was from being in bed so long. In that day, it was thought by many surgeons that the patient should stay in bed for two weeks after an appendectomy. One was not even given water for three days and nights to avoid vomiting and breaking of sutures.

Many times, in later years, Papa recounted this year. It was one to remember . . . not only for our family but the whole land. Influenza had taken many lives; war was again with us and crops were bad. He had not gotten over the loss of Arthur, who would now have been sixteen.

Yet, Papa always tried to end each day on a cheerful note. He would not put the cat out at night because, in the first place, the cats had their own house. He would not think of retiring in his daily underwear as he said most men did; nor would he allow his children to go to bed without a bath and clean night clothing.

So he recalled many times how lucky we all were — even though we had hard rows to hoe, we had hoes and rows and strength to go!

He would declare his daughters should get good educations and be "something worthwhile even if it were only mothers." Then, he'd give Mama a gentle pat on the shoulders and say to her that she couldn't think of anything better, now could she?

Papa actually loved to tell about the time, the next time, I had to be carried to the surgical table just a year later. He had carried me in his arms. I wasn't heavy, "just a runty girl."

Papa even told the story several times later to my husband and two daughters. "Now, this little old runty girl with big caved-in grey eyes," he would tell, "looked up in the doctor's face and asked him if he was a Christian."

"Be quiet, lie still, breathe in, deep now," the doctor told her. But she fought like a wildcat and said it again. We could hardly keep the mask on her nose as she asked him again, "Are you a Christian? If not, let me out of here."

The doctor told her again to be quiet, and soon the ether helped the doctor win his side of the argument, Papa told. Then he would laugh as he would say with pride, "It was Viola's first conversion, and she won it with my help."

After my recovery, Papa went to call on this doctor about his soul's condition. The doctor assured Papa he believed in God and the college training he received only emphasized God's greatness. He even told Papa he never started a day's work without prayer.

Then Papa wanted to know why the doctor never attended church in any of the churches in town. Soon it was our privilege to see this doctor join a church — not our denomination — but another during a city-wide revival meeting. These were held each summer on the courthouse square.

Papa had won his point. He had told the doctor that Jesus taught that persons who are ashamed to confess belief in God before their fellowmen could hardly expect Him to witness for them to God.

Yesterday, I was named to the commission on evangelism in my church. Dare I speak today with such childish faith as when I was just a runty little girl looking into the face of a learned surgeon? Dare I not have such courage?

Will my children remember the pattern of the floor-covering in our home because they knelt on it to pray? Or will they know it from constant need for waxing to keep it as pretty as the neighbors?

Our Loves Are Pruned

It seems now to me that Papa was very quiet for a few years after this. Oh, he still helped everyone who came to him and there were many. He still attended the prayer meetings, and we went to church as regular as the weeks brought Sundays, both morning and evening.

We were working in the orchard one Saturday late in September. Papa was pruning the trees, and we children who were still at home were carrying the trimmings onto piles to be burned. It was a particularly trying day for Papa as Uncle Fred was sitting under one of the trees that had not shed its leaves . . . just sitting there and watching us.

Uncle Fred didn't normally just sit and watch any activity — whether it was field work, house work, cooking, even mending, or work in the church or school. Papa must have known his brother's thoughts. Uncle Fred was gravely ill, and the two brothers knew it.

Papa had taken Lucy, my pet-sister, to town early that morning as she had a nice position in the candy kitchen. Oh, she used to look so pretty to us standing there in that showcase next to the long arms of pink and white taffy pulling on the machine. Lucy is my name for Lydia.

As the afternoon wore on, Mama brought out a large black tin pan of freshly baked kaffee-kuchen. We all gathered under the tree with Uncle Fred to eat and rest a while.

They suggested we leave a piece of cake for Lucy. Maybe she would eat it, Uncle Fred thought. Lucy had recently broken an engagement which was a distinct disappointment to Uncle Fred and, I believe to Papa. She had gotten so thin worrying over it and over our uncle's illness. They tell me Lucy and Uncle Fred were as close as dew and dawn and that mysterious and tender.

It's difficult to say now if we grieve for years because of losses or if we also grieve over what might have happened to us. Papa was at the hospital a short time later when Uncle Fred died. It was a warm Sunday afternoon. His family had been with him all night and had been persuaded to go for some food when our uncle just slipped away to "The place God prepared for him."

Only a few weeks before this, the whole family had spent a

23

weekend with us. They lived only five miles away but we wanted to exchange summer visits. It was our custom. On a Sunday afternoon, during that visit, the phone had rung and a neighbor boy had called to tell us he could see some children on top of our new silo.

What a horrifying sight! The silo was still under construction by Mr. Arthur Neumann, the first concrete construction company in the area. That is, the main cement blocks were in place up to forty-two feet high, but there was not a roof nor doors in the side as when a silo is finished.

Mama and Aunt Selma had clutched each other in terror. What should they do? There were my three cousins and George away up there in the sky! The middle cousin, Arnold, was getting into a standing position on the rim of the cement blocks which were about three inches wide.

By now, we were all standing at the doors and windows, scared stiff. We were too scared to think and thank goodness! . . . too afraid to yell at them to come down.

Then Aunt Selma ran out into the nearby melon field to tell the two fathers to look. Papa thought to tell them all to keep quiet. He dropped to his knees to pray and was instantly joined by Uncle Fred. But Uncle Fred had a heart attack and fainted dead away.

By now, the neighbors came running and some even came racing on their horses. A doctor was summoned. The boys saw all the confusion and came down to see what was all the excitement.

Finally all was quiet again. All, that is, except the boys behind the smokehouse where Papa went with them. He wound up being the only one who cried so hard at the supper table, that he couldn't eat. Our Papa! He could be so mean and so stern and yet be so sweet and tender. Why, he even hated to prune trees or to dehorn cattle. And to brand his dairy cows with a red hot iron, heaven forbid! That was our Papa. The cousins boasted of their adventure up in the sky so high while Papa went down in gloom.

Now with his brother's death, Papa felt the pruning knife's blow. Mention 1918 today, most any place, someone recalls World War I losses. Few escaped its tragedies directly — none indirectly. Few families can undergo a series of losses as did our family and still remain cheerful.

It must have helped us to believe as Mama taught us to: "What comes to pass may not suit us, but eventually God will fit things together to work out his patterns." She never told us it was God's will that a person should suffer sadness or die; that it was God's will when our puppies were all born dead; or that it was God's plan for us to fail to make a crop or for the neighbor's barn to burn.

Mama simply explained that God constantly revised his plans to make allowances for man's failures and for losses caused by mistakes. God prunes his people sometimes, she said, but like trees . . . only after they show signs of dead wood, decay or growing into the wrong direction.

The crop failure left little money for Christmas spending. Yet, Papa bought the usual full box of store-bought apples (each wrapped in colored tissue squares), a whole hundred pound sack of sugar and a barrel of flour. We invited our aunts, cousins, grandmother Sturm and the preacher's family to dinner with us.

The apples were always put in the parlor days ahead as we did not have a heater in there. They would make the room smell wonderful by the time we children were allowed to go in on Christmas Eve, the time for our family tree.

It would be the first time the younger children would see the tree after it was brought in from the pasture and decorated. We would have helped to string the frosted cookies, popcorn ropes and made paper link chains. And every year, the angel would be on top of the tree along with other trims Mama stored in the long bench in the hall.

We had gone to Smith Creek pasture to get a red-haw tree. Papa had let us take the team and wagon so I also got to go along. This year, we had gone on Sunday afternoon and now Tanta scolded. She thought if we had done this on Saturday, George, Arnold, Elroy and I would not have fallen off of the wagon when we went through the creek.

When we neared the house, a new car . . . a real long shiny black deal with celluloid side-curtains . . . was at the front yard gate. Someone suggested it was Papa's step-brother returning from the Army. Gee! were we ever excited. I thought that would be he for surely no one else would have money to buy such a fancy automobile.

The mules were hurried along the rest of the way from the mailbox to the yard gate. Everyone jumped off and scampered into the house . . . by the front door (which we seldom did) . . . expecting to see our rich uncle. We probably even saw visions of gifts of candy and we could surely expect new books for Uncle Frank always brought us books.

Aunt Selma and her married daughter, Elvira, who had not

gone with us, met us at the door. We were hurried to the other side door on the front porch and into the house through the girls' big bedroom.

"Why doesn't somebody tell us what . . . who is here . . . how come we had to come in here . . . what are we waiting for?," the questions piled up as we stood aghast.

We did not even remember to seek sympathy for our bruises from falling off the wagon into the creek-bed ruts.

Not so, it was the doctor's new car. This time, it was Mama who went to the hospital. With Christmas only three or four days away, how terrible! Mama must have thought something could happen as she had baked and baked all manner of cookies the week before and had even helped us wash the windows just yesterday.

Papa explained there would not be a new baby now. Mama would be all right, and the doctor said he would bring her home on Christmas Day if it did not rain. When it rained, cars could never travel the Harwood Road in those years.

We truly polished and slicked up the house after that. We were almost afraid to hope so, but Mama got home on Christmas Day, just as we were to have our dinner — at noon.

Papa had polished each of us an apple, and there were plates of cookies, too, after we had eaten our turkey with all the trimmings. My sisters were helped with cooking by my aunts and grandmother.

Tanta was away this time, visiting with an old friend in Braslau. I remember Papa's putting her apple in her room so she would know for sure that we had missed her.

When it came time to return thanks, it was Lucy who volunteered to say the lines. Then Papa announced to us that Lucy was going to college at mid-term. It was a frightening thought, two of the sisters to be gone from home. Pauline was working in town and was only home holidays and Sundays.

Exactly what changed their plans, we are not too sure. But eventually, both were away at college. At first to junior college in Texas, and later both took deaconess' training at Bethesda Institute in Cincinnati, Ohio. It was awful to see them go so far away. We knew they could not come home often, maybe every two years or so. Travel money was and still is hard to come by for farmers.

Always life stays so busy and so full, though, that one can endure and even become accustomed to such events. Pauline left first; and naturally, I remember that most.

Mama was truly a master when it came to cooking and to

managing to turn out a feast with little spending of cash. In fact, Papa got so used to her saving ways, he was astounded when once in a great while she had an unusual item on her weekly grocery list.

He would be so puzzled. Perhaps, he would ask if she were to entertain the Ladies Aid Society soon. If so, Papa never complained over an extra cost on the list. Nothing was too good for the church work. Sometimes we thought he over-did his contributions and his interest in the church work.

I agreed with him then, and I still feel it is right to give the best one has to the work of the church. Especially should one give his time, his witness and his interest by attending its services. Many times I have had nothing but witness to give.

These winters seemed to be more of the same for me. Still a runty little girl, I was either making mountains out of mole-hills (which gave me frequent illnesses) or bearing the after-effects of the two operations. Days I spent trussed up like a turkey because of a hernia I'd developed.

Anyway, when winter came and the walking to school got wet and cold, I found the going rough. Morning after morning, Mama would start me off to school again; but when I got as far as the neighbors, I stayed for the day.

Olga was in the sixth grade this year and could have stayed in the country school. But Pearl needed help with the dairy deliveries. So for a time the folks did not know how often I stayed at the neighbor's home. Perhaps, with the bad roads and all, Miss Ora did not expect me at school.

If it were not for report cards, we might be able to get by with many such cheaty little things. There are always report blanks to make out or to help with, it seems. One is so tempted to write in more than was actually done — looks good on paper. Even reports to conference headquarters are tests of one's honesty.

Mrs. Ronshausen was such a dear person, though. She's bound to be in heaven. If not, there's no use in my trying, for I'll never be as kind and loving as was she to all us children. Maybe my family was right, I am thinking by now, to say that I was spoiled and lazy. But I surely did not agree with them those days. Neither did Mrs. Ronshausen.

I was scolded so severely that I still remember it.

I remember, too, that Tanta did invite me to spend the night with her in her tiny little room. She insisted on removing the truss from my waist herself and rubbing me with some sort of

27

balm. Later, many years later, Papa said Tanta gave him the money for me to return to the hospital to have the hernia repaired.

It seems impossible but the family Bible records the date of Tanta's death that year on Valentine's Day. Where was I? I recall our deep grief at her passing, but I have no recollection of the last rites.

The evening before she went away, we were making Valentines. The wrappers from our Christmas fruit would be carefully cut into fringe to go around the edges of the hearts we cut out of cardboard and colored with Crayolas.

It was my honor that year to make the box the whole school would use for the collection and then the distribution of all their Valentines. The whole crew around the table that night helped me as I was due to get to the hospital early the next afternoon. I still have a Valentine from that day. It came from the one who had drawn my name, but the writing on it and my memory have faded.

I studied at home for the remainder of the year, and I passed all my finals with flying colors. It was easy, for the family and all the visitors helped me with my homework.

Mrs. Ronshausen and other neighbors came often to stay with me while the folks went to church or worked out of doors in the garden. I had learned my lesson about cheating. With time on my hands and a love to write, I decided to send a short story to the Cousin's League page of the Farm and Ranch.

It seemed the next month's issue would never come. When it did, there was my story. It was a thrill I have never outlived. I have not been so lucky all the times that I have submitted work to publications. Seems I get rejection slips before my work gets there. But even today, it thrills me to see something I wrote in print. Then I know that one person, at least, thought it was good.

That day it was Mama who had walked to the mailbox at the road. She wore a huge slatted sunbonnet in which she tried to hide the Farm and Ranch when she came across the yard. But it was too wide and I spied it. In my excitement, I hopped out of the bed all by myself. Gee, now I was well sure enough!

Often when I go to visit with my brother these days, I see that same old mailbox with Papa's initials on it. It brings back a flood of memories . . . most all pleasant. All our family love to get mail, and we write to each other frequently.

Seems odd to me that with all the thrill, I lost the clipping. Sometimes I still wonder what the story was all about. It was so queer how it had shrunk by changing it from my large childish handwriting to printed letters. Last year when we were together for Christmas, it was again laughed about; and again we wondered if the story were not about Tanta. It probably was.

We wondered, too, if I would ever get this manuscript done. Lucy reminded me not to leave out Tanta . . . for Lucy, too, loved her dearly. Lucy is reserved and quiet like Tanta. Like Tanta, she always seems to have some money saved to help someone over a rough spot.

"What if I don't have the money to go through with the preparations for a full-length novel?" I asked the sisters.

George chirped, "Borrow it from Lucy, She still has some of her Uncle Frank's money."

"Don't start Ola off on Uncle Frank," they all said in one chorus.

The Soldiers Came Home

By the time I was eleven, the World War I was over. Of course, we did not call it War I. For surely, no one expected to have World War II. All of the soldiers in our immediate family returned. One was my Uncle Frank, Papa's youngest stepbrother. Also, two young men from our farm hands' families returned.

From our church and from our town, many did not return. We attended many memorial services.

We must have made good crops that year as it seems we were in the corn-crib half of our lives. We'd shuck barrels and barrels of corn for the animals and for cornmeal. Not only was meal ground in the mill in town for us to eat but for the Negroes, for the cats and dogs, and for the baby turkeys; and even one day we shucked a barrel full to be ground for Uncle Paul in Dallas.

We all learned how to work, and we also learned to enjoy work. The busier we all were, the more we sang and laughed. We learned to milk cows, to feed all the animals, to hook up a team of mules as well as to hitch the buggy horse. We learned to ride horseback. And Papa was the captain of our baseball team.

For that, we had the Buckholtz children to help us. There was never a shortage of them when it came time for a good afternoon of fun. Of course, the afternoons ended early for both families had dairies. Cows could fill their bags faster than we liked to work.

Papa was a slave-driver. He could work like a mule, and he never truly realized we were just runty girls. We were quite strong, however, and could put out a man-sized day's work.

I see all around me, day after day, the people who work the hardest are the happiest. They laugh the most and they seem to be able to take disappointments in stride. Could be, Papa knew that all along.

Uncle Paul was coming to see Grandma and us. I'll bet we had the house gleaming. We used to scrub the floors with soapy water, wash the woodwork, and shine the lamp chimneys and goodness knows what all every time somebody was coming. Those were the days we would wish we lived in the little Negro house down the hill behind the cane fields.

Grandma wrote Uncle Paul — or perhaps, she had my aunts

to write — that she wanted him to come help her write her will. When Papa told us that, I asked him to see that I got the china dish shaped like a chicken on a nest. I never got it, and I perhaps never will. But lately, I see them back on the shelves in the dime stores.

Papa probably scolded me for wanting some of his mother's things even before she died, for Papa reminded us many times that death had no age limits. Besides, we were not to covet other's possessions. My, it seemed every time one turned around, there was some way of breaking one of those Ten Commandments. The words of all ten were embossed in velvet on a black background hanging over our new shiny clock-shelf.

I had passed my eleventh birthday that June. Plans were back in my mind to return to school in September. School was to start late as crops were late and the school board, in those days, always asked the farmers when their children would be through with cotton picking.

Pauline was home for a few days. She had come, knowing our aunt and uncle were coming later from the city, and she could ride back with them that far.

Without a doubt, every extra table leaf was inserted, and many a chicken got it in the neck. Noodles were made and large sheets of them were put to dry for a couple of hours on clean cup towels placed on the swing and the tables of the two porches. Perhaps, I was put to cutting them. It's a neat trick to know. One first cuts the noodle sheet in half and then rolls the two halves up quite tightly. Then, like today we cut slices off of the long rolls of frozen cookie dough, one would cut the noodles. Only very much thinner would noodles be cut than cookies are.

Mostly, today we buy the noodles and the cookies ready mixed, cut and baked. Why not? With so many committees to attend, who has time to make noodles and cookies?

Mama could truly cook enough for Cox's army. And with Pena there to help, it is small wonder we didn't all pop. As it happened, it was only I who went back to the hospital. Luckily, the whole thing escapes my memory except for the fact that when Uncle Paul came to see me, he told me I should someday get Grandmother's china-chicken. Guess he forget about it though.

Papa told me several times later that it was to Uncle Paul I confided my desire to be a Methodist preacher. Uncle Paul did some preaching in Dallas; and too, my mother's father's sermons always fascinated me. He would preach on Sundays when the regular minister was away for some reason.

They probably thought I was what the kids today call "nuts." First I had wanted my Grandmother's things even before I was supposed to have overheard that they were writing wills. Now, of all the absurd desires, I wanted to be a woman preacher in the Methodist Church!

In those days, the men and boys still sat on the south side of the church in the mornings, and the women and girls — and the crying babies — sat on the north side. It was a kind gesture, for that way the bright sun did not shine in on the sleeping babies. It shone instead on many a sleeping man or big boy.

Papa said Uncle Paul was real proud of his account of the family doctor's decision to join a church, but he did regret it was the "wrong" church. Wrong in his opinion, not Papa's. For Papa thought well of all denominations.

Would that Papa could have lived until this writing! Now, the Methodist Church has voted to accept women into full-time clergy.

"Now, they would when it is too late for me to have a try at preaching," I remarked to my family when the news was published in a morning edition.

Both daughters were at home that weekend. They roared with laughter and the younger dared to say, "D.O.M., you can always keep on trying on us. We love your sermons." D.O.M. is her name for "dear old Mother."

I detected a hint of meanness in the remark and suggested, "Let's all laugh!"

I thought again of my maternal grandfather Menking. He always said we are all preachers by the way we act and by what we say each day. It is truly correct to remember this. Many times have I unknowingly preached a poor sermon.

Now, I have grown up enough to have no regrets that my church did not allow me to be a full-time preacher. Now, too, I am aware that each day as I set out to do my daily work, I must choose anew my text for the sermon of the day.

Dare one go to a Parent-Teacher meeting, cover a Chamber of Commerce, report a high school football game, attend a board session of the county fair, speak to a Student Nurses' Club or stuff Christmas seal sale-letters without a text? That text had better be inspired by God and adhered to — no matter how trying the day!

The family must have thought about my wish many times —

even this year when the news was read aloud about the conference's decision and the discussion ended with my remark, "Let's all laugh!"

Several days later, my husband teased me about all the money I could have made preaching. I am now sure he meant the remark kindly, but that day it made me very angry.

"You mean, I preach all the time anyway and don't get paid for it? That's really what you mean!"

He tried to smooth the whole matter over and made every attempt to explain. It took a while and a three mile walk that day, but then I understood. It is a battle I have to fight: don't advise, don't preach! It is sometimes better to let something go undone than to always come up with the advice on how best it could be done.

It seems I should have started learning that sound lesson even then, when I was eleven. When Uncle Paul and Aunt Nettie were there, Papa tried to reach our Uncle Frank to join the family group. Having just returned from Europe, we were all anxious to see and hear from him.

The day after the city family left, our soldier uncle walked in. He had walked from San Antonio. He still had on his uniform. He stayed with us several days, every day or so walking to town to spend part of the time with his mother and sisters. One day, after he had been gone longer than usual — perhaps a couple of nights — he came back and said he was leaving to go into business in Dallas.

Papa preached and preached to him. Uncle Frank was a brilliant school teacher before the draft. Salaries now were as high as $50 a month in many schools, Papa had read in the Semi-Weekly.

For years after this, we seldom heard from him. Papa went once to see about him as it had been so long since he had written. The other uncle did not write often either; so Papa got on the train in Harwood and went to see about them.

When he came back, he told us all about the lovely home of the one brother and family. He told, too, of his search for his soldier brother. The address had a "½" behind the number of the street. Papa said, "Now that truly is correct. Frank just half lives there. The other part of the time, he is busy helping others. The landlady says he is always taking care of some sick persons some place. He is in the insurance business, and teaches night school. Besides, he may be at college now as he also studies at the college. He walks there, and sometimes he doesn't get back for three days."

That's why, when last Christmas George teased, "Lucy hasn't

spent her Uncle Frank's money," it was really a great statement. Uncle Frank had his own text, and he lived to reach his aims. He did not forget us.

When I was just eleven I would much rather Uncle Frank had ridden trains, bought himself nice clothes and did like my friends' uncles did. He did not look just like an uncle ought to look, I often told Mama.

Many years later. George teased me about this by asking if I were still wishing Uncle Frank had used up all his earnings. He remembered his nieces and nephews just exactly at the right time — a time when we all appreciated a bundle from "heaven" so to speak.

George laughed and said, "It is just a pity we don't have uncles like him every day."

"For shame, you wouldn't want anyone else to have to die just to help us," Pearl remonstrated. Pearl and her husband were home for their vacation the summer we received word that our uncle had remembered us in his will.

"No, I would not. I did not mean to imply that remembering us killed him. It was an accident, the letter said from New York," our brother explained again.

Papa would have felt badly about this whole affair for Papa worried about his brother many times on cold days when we were children. He often mentioned him as we sat around the wood heater at nights. Sometimes, he would take out an old letter and read it again. Our Uncle wrote very seldom, but his letters were extremely interesting.

The letter I remember most was a source of embarrassment to me many evenings. Uncle Frank wrote to ask about each of the children. Of me, he wanted to know if I were still planning to be a preacher.

This urge to be a preacher kept at me strongly until in 1920. The Southern German Conference met in Gonzales for their annual session. It was in early November if I remember correctly. Crops were harvested and every nook and cranny was scrubbed at our church and in our home. Even the dairy barn did not escape a more thorough going-over than usual.

Papa had offered to be host to the Bishop E. L. Waldorf. Papa took a sudden notion to make this offer, not bothering to consult Mama about it. Papa was always that sure of Mama's ability to set a table that would be a credit to any husband. Mama was not always so thrilled about such wonderful ideas of Papa's.

If all 4,000 members of the conference had come to our house, we could not have been more excited. Seems it was just yesterday. I remember that the honeysuckle vines around the back porch trellis were in full bloom. The Marcheil-Neal rose at the front steps put on an extra crop that fall — surely just to please Papa.

I doubt if Mama ever saw the roses that week. Poor dear, with meals to get and children to push to get to the services every night and to school the next morning! The meeting lasted three days and nights. The night services seemed an eternity long. It was a real task just to stay awake.

Except the last night. The Bishop preached on the verse "What does it profit a man to gain the whole world if he loses his soul?" This is still my favorite text and most valued lesson. What does it profit a man to gain the world if in so doing he has lost his soul? Truly a man without a soul is dead. The lesson is as short and as simple as that. But it took the Bishop a whole hour to preach to us.

I was in my first year of weekly Catechism lessons that winter. I could hardly wait for Saturday to come when I would be going to class in the parsonage. We met there during the cold months so the big church would not have to be heated. Besides, some of our mothers would be in there cleaning and dusting for Sunday services.

I was all set to tell our pastor of my decision to give my heart to God. I told Papa, and I told my little brother when we were in the corn crib on Friday after school. It was the day after the conference had closed. I told Papa and George that I had decided to tell the preacher the next day of my decision to be a Christian. Papa was drilling me in the questions and answers of the Catechism lesson for the next day. He thought my decision was a fine idea.

It was during these years that everyone was compelled to speak the English language only. Our preacher could speak English very poorly although he read it well and understood full well what he read. His pronunciation was hard for him. We called it "Dutch" which of course is incorrect. People referred to all of us who were of German background as "Dutchmen." Perhaps, they could not pronounce *Deutsch*.

Preachers there who refused to preach in English were actually treated cruelly by some of the citizens. It was hard to understand then how anyone could be so intolerant, but have we not all some of these prejudices to battle in our own characters?

When I told the Reverend of my decision, I was not content to tell him only that I had decided to join his church. I must have

35

made a full three minute speech, adding much that I had not dared tell Papa and George. "I will be a preacher; and by cracky (Mama had said worse) the Bishop would stay in *my* house when I was the preacher! That is what parsonages are for, Mama said" . . . and I probably added a lot more.

"Vait, vait — yust von liddle minit, mine liddle poopel. It is wid much und berry deep heartfelt sorrowings I haf to dell you dat de Medodists don't have de vimmen preachers."

"Well, then I will just join the other church — the one where Nancy goes. I like the priest anyway and I could just as well marry a priest."

So it was that Papa always got such a bang out of Uncle Frank's wanting to know how the "preacher girl" was getting on in the family. I remember Papa's explanation about the priest's having no time for wife and family. The Methodists had no use for women preachers. I had heard of Papa's disappointment that I was not born a boy. There must be something wrong with being a woman.

Uncle Frank must have thought so, too. He never married.

Stumbling 'Tweener

Going into the teens — the age now often referred to as "tweener," between the tens and the teens — caught me as mixed up as a fruit salad. This time in a girl's age is usually a bit confused at best. I asked questions and asked questions without finding many who would give me direct answers.

Papa would say, "Go ask your Mama." She would say, "Why don't you ask your Papa?" My sisters were perhaps afraid they would be scolded if they told all they had managed to learn. Poor Mama, just the thought of having to listen to all our questions gives me a headache today, a headache she must have had rightfully many times.

They did try many times to be understanding and sweet about our questions by saying we would be answered tomorrow. Does tomorrow ever come? No! Tomorrow's actually only the day before day-after-tomorrow. Life moves that fast. One confession Mama did point out to us, though, many times was why she decided to marry.

She decided if she were going to have to wash babies and their three-cornered pants all her days, the babies and pants may as well be her own. She had before this been constantly at the washboard or over the black washpot for her young half-brothers and sisters. She kept her promise about keeping us scrubbed and our clothes clean.

Our mother seemed the happiest on wash days. She would hum and sing the whole day long. Many times she was not strong enough to do the rubbing or to even rinse the clothes. These days she would do the sorting, the folding, and the mending. We had a long, wooden bench on which three big tubs of rinse water were set. The clothes would be soaked in homemade lye soap and rain water overnight.

The next morning they would be put, a tub full at the time, into the boiling hot water over the fire. One of us would punch the clothes down time and time again with an old broom handle — the famous wash stick!

Then the clothes would be lifted out and drained and rinsed piece by piece through the three tubs of water. Extra soiled pieces

37

like Papa's overalls and long underwear would have to be rubbed on the corrugated metal wash board.

When Mama was sick, we would have one of the Negro women come to help us. Ofttimes my little brother and I would walk several miles from house to house looking for a woman who wasn't "swollen too much to wash on the board."

Papa would warn us not to engage any who were like that — too pregnant to be of help with the work. Papa never used the word pregnant. He simply told us to notice if the woman was swollen. If so, she wouldn't be able to reach over the washboard very well, and we should just go on to the next farm and try to find one that was all right.

This brilliant brother of mine learned early that to know things, one must ask questions. His motto must be, "If at first they don't answer, ask, ask again." It was a cold afternoon. We had a huge laundry piled up at home so Papa sent us out to find Mama a wash woman for the next day.

We came to a house on a farm on the Smith Creek Road. We had faced north all the way, but Papa had let us ride old Filly, the black horse. As we drew near to the house, about a dozen old hounds came yelping toward us. We rode right up to the porch and called out for someone to answer.

Brother was about nine. He was about frozen, too. When the door opened and this beautiful woman stuck her head out to say hello and, "What does you chill'en want with old Hannah?" we were glad. We explained our mission, and she invited us in to warm.

She was baking biscuits for supper and had corn hominy simmering with possum meat in it. Oh, it was the best smelling place I ever entered! She gave us each a nice dish of the stew and a good hot biscuit.

"Oh, my goodness, we should not expect you to wash for us. You are all swollen, too. Did you get hurt?" George asked her.

The woman roared with laughter. "Nope, my little white boy, your old aunt Hannah is all right. She jes' swallowed a pumkin' seed, that's all. You tell your Mama I will be there in the morning to hup her wid her clothes, the Lord willing!"

Questions — questions — why couldn't he leave good enough alone? He had to know all about the swelling and the seed, and bless her heart, the woman settled us down on the dirt floor by the stove and told us the first honest-to-goodness truth about the life of a man and woman.

I am sure Hannah came to wash. I am also sure George and I never told a soul about our new education. We did tell about the wonderful warm food and the love given us by the warmth of the nice, clean house — even though the floors were of earth and the bed covers were tanned animal skins.

With new education, I felt a great deal more confident. I was so glad that Hannah had explained that the statement about pumpkin seed was just an expression. In fact, I began to feel quite proud of being a girl. Maybe someday I could make some man as happy as Hannah was making old Ed.

My, now we were among the first again. We had rated first with our Model T Ford; with a mule-pulled row binder that not only cut corn and Fedrica off near the ground but actually tied it into bundles with twine; with a telephone that sometimes brought neighbors from way up at Clarkwood, five miles to the north, to use.

Papa had put screens on our windows, not just on the bottom half and nailed to the walls like some people did. But he made them on frames with swinging hinges of pieces of leather at the top so we could open them to clean the windows. (He had to do that, for if one of us was the least bit sassy, our punishment would most likely be to wash the windows come Saturday morning.)

But the first we scored about this time capped them all! Another salesman must have come to call, for Papa bought a washing machine. We filled it with buckets of the boiling hot suds from the black wash pot, then clamped down the lid (which had an inner lid with three short stobs of wood on it.) As we pushed a lever back and forth, the inner lid and the stobs would dash back and forth to remove the dirt from the soiled clothes that we had put in with the hot suds.

It is hard to remember which gave way first — the dirt in the clothes or the strength in the arms of us children. Oh, if Papa had just not been at home when that salesman came. No wonder Mama hated peddlers. It took away all the fun of hunting wash-women, and for Mama it meant scores of buttons to sew back on Papa's BVD's and shirts, our blouses and dresses. Remember, those were the pre-zipper days. Everything buttoned up — or in emergencies pinned with safety pins. Of course, one would not dare pin a dress or shirt with a safety pin if one was going any place other than the cow barn. Papa saw to that. Really, Papa saw to it that Mama sewed on the buttons until we were old enough to help.

That could be the reason we girls wore sack-dresses forty years before the modern style. The sack today is the sleekest . . . it's just like it was then, only then we called them one-piece dresses. Out loud we called them that. To ourselves, we called them about the same horrid names some of the young men call the things today — sloppy rags.

The next of our firsts we all truly adored was a bathroom. We had for years had running water to the dairy barns to hose down the cement floors and to water the animals, and we even had it piped in the milk house. But now, on my twelfth birthday, we got a full furnished bathroom in the house with running water (not just water in a bucket or hot tea-kettle while one was running to the bathroom in the lean-to that had been Tanta's room).

We even got so modern that we quit bathing two at the time. Or was it that now there were fewer of us to get ready when we wanted to go somewhere? It may also have been that with the running water, everyone took much less time getting bathed. We girls had always gone to the wash room two at a time. That was before we had a mirror on the bathroom door.

Seeing one's self for the first time in a full-length mirror stark-naked can almost take all the thrill out of being the first family in the whole community to have a brand-new three piece bathroom. At least, I had no idea a twelve year old could be shaped like what I saw in the mirror. I must have thought only my older sisters could have gotten so tacky.

Even Papa and my brother now had their own private turns at sprucing up on Sunday mornings and evenings to go to church. Papa, of course, bathed practically every morning as he began to be away more and more selling insurance or attending farm meetings. During the summer months, Papa would also do the milk and farm-produce deliveries. One of us would go along to hop out and do his leg-work.

It is now called leg-work, but we called it simply doing the deliveries. We usually made about twenty stops as we would take butter to our private customers, sour cream to the creamery, eggs to Stahl Bros., cottage cheese to a couple of cafes, and fresh vegetables and all manner of other produce to the hospital kitchen. Many mornings, we would also take of our abundance to the preachers — several of them, not only our own.

Yesterday while covering a dam construction suit in the Live Oak County Courthouse, a visiting attorney asked me if I was acquainted with Mr. and Mrs. Ross Boothe. I answered him in the affirmative, but at the moment I did not think to say, "I buttered his bread many times when I was a young country girl."

It is a good thing I did not say it, for the Boothes are wealthy and are so without any help from me. They simply bought Mama's butter, and I took it on many trips and placed it in their ice box. It was at our home that we spoke with pride about buttering the bread for several of Gonzales' best households. Today, buttering someone's bread seems to mean something entirely different.

Wanting to be a preacher did not make a saint out of me. I must really have been a terror at times, for my hindsides are still sore when I think of all the paddlings the folks had to give me. Curiosity was my undoing. And these home deliveries gave me a wonderful field in which to explore. I'd ask people all manner of questions; and I would tell, also, my own news from happenings at home. I'd have a rapt audience, but often I'd wind up with a sound boxing on my ears or a trip to the back porch at home where Papa's leather razor-strop hung. It was used for more than to sharpen his razor blade.

Some of the questions and their answers are still funny today even after getting a beating (which parents seemed to think was right) or as modern child psychologists say, "Maybe it is the punishments that cause a child to remember the affairs better." I am then glad, for the incidents bring me a chuckle every once in a while as similar ones happen these days.

It was one of these dull delivering mornings when I went to put the butter in a certain old bachelor's kitchen I found a beautiful red-headed lady fixing breakfast. I asked her if she had married Mr. Joe. Later, telling this to Mama, I pleaded my cause by explaining I had said, "Miss Mamie, have you married Mr. Joe? Then you will be needing more butter."

Miss Mamie turned around and swung the egg beater at me and jumped a foot high and screamed, "What are you doing in here? Don't you know to knock? Get out of that ice box. Are you a little thief?" It was then I had dropped the eggs right in the middle of the floor and the butter on the stove.

Mr. Joe came running in the kitchen without his garage-man suit on and I was running to the door. Only I did hear him say as I left, 'Honey don't run away. It is all right for you to come in. Bring us two pounds and two dozen eggs next week.' "

Perhaps, if I had left good enough alone, I would have escaped a whipping. But no! At the next stop, when I had had time to recover from my fright, I told the neighbors what had happened.

This was at the preacher's house; only the preacher was not there. Just a few women were sitting around the kitchen table making some things to send the mission station across the world somewhere.

I will never forget the hit I scored with these women. One of them even reached out and drew me against her warm bosom and into the circle of her arm, up toward the table. By then, having worked up the story quite a bit, as they seemed to enjoy my story so much, I had taken up entirely too much time; and Papa was really "sitting on the horn" (my tweener friends call it today). If you were fortunate to have lived in the Model-T Days, you will know what sitting on one of those horns sounded like. Buckholtz' ten herd-bulls could not out-blare our car horn.

Temptation to add to my story, which made it longer and caused me to diddly-dally at this last delivery, tipped Papa off to something I had done wrong. He was furious, and I knew I'd better make up some sort of excuse right quickly. A standard one of having to wait while the customer scrounged around in every purse and pocket for the money was again in error this time. Where were my wits? Did not I know that we never took money from any of our preachers for a dozen eggs and a pound of butter?

We girls often complained about such practices. Eggs were then eleven cents a dozen and our butter always brought a premium price — usually at least thirty-five cents. Hair-ribbon and lace for chemises or our camisoles was also about eleven cents per yard; and heavens, every girl wanted hers to be the prettiest when friends came to spend the night or when we were allowed to go to a slumber party.

Anyway, it all goes to show that it never pays to enter anyone's house — not even or especially not the kitchen door — without knocking. Had I knocked at Mr. Joe's, I would have saved myself a whipping, no doubt. Yet, think of all the fun and disturbance I would have missed. Besides, it felt good to have that sweet smelling lady put her arm about me and draw me into their circle. I still love circles of ladies around a table making things for mission boxes.

On another occasion when curiosity was my downfall, it happened in our home. Another dumb and stumbling tweener from our congregation came home with me to spend Sunday afternoon. She told me while we were changing from our Sunday dresses to our play clothes that she had just learned a world of new things. She knew exactly where one could get all this information. We whispered and whispered to one another until the call came for dinner. (We called our noon meal dinner.) I could hardly wait, for the plan we had formulated seemed perfect in our situation.

On Sunday afternoons, Mama and Papa would stretch out on their big bed and between them would be a pile of the week's mail. We would hear one and then the other reading portions of *Der Texas Stern* or *The Farm and Ranch*. Sometimes we would hear them get into some heated arguments; yet often Papa would roar with laughter at something.

I said we were not hungry even though my little friend seemed reluctant to leave the table early. But we had it planned that way . . . Surely she wouldn't back out now. We excused ourselves; and, as usual, the folk seemed glad to get rid of two extra chatter-boxes.

We softly crept from the bathroom (where we knew we must first go to wash our hands) to our parents' room. There we lay down flat and rolled under the big bed. Sissy was a real chubby girl and she had a time, but finally we were in place under the center of the bed. Imagine two twelve year old girls doing such a silly thing . . . and in broad open daylight.

My twelve year old neighbors today are out on dates, rushing from school and band practice to the skating rink, the whole gang seemingly "sitting on the horn" at about sunset raring to get to the movies. Imagine them having to hide under their parents' beds on a Sunday afternoon just to take a chance at hearing some choice bit of new information.

This time, like criminals, we again made mistakes. We forgot to take off our Sunday shoes, and soon they began to pinch. We also had swiped some of Pearl's new perfume her lover had given her and put it on our ear lobes, very generously, when we were in the bathroom after dinner.

It seemed an eternity, but at last Mama and Papa came in and settled down to their reading and naps. Soon Papa spoke up. He sounded rather cross as he said, "Don't you know better than to use girl's perfume — a woman your age? You did not have that on in church this morning, now did you?"

Mama said she did not use the perfume, now or ever. Papa insisted he smelled it. Mama was probably tired anyway; and before we got to hear anything "juicy," they were in a heated argument about the use of perfume. Then we saw Mama's feet hit the floor, and at about the same time a folded quilt and her pillow.

She said she would just rest on the floor if he did not like the way she smelled; after all, clean people always smelled good unless, of course, they were fool enough to smoke. That alone, then and today, would have been and is a remark to open fire in any of our households.

He must have seen her act this way before, for he did not even remark about her getting off on the floor. Then she sat upright with haste and said she, too, smelled perfume. *What* made her look under the bed? Why do I always look under the bed when I come home to find the whole family out someplace?

In our haste to get out, Sissy raised up and cut a big gash in her forehead on some part of the bed springs, and I tore the strap of my Sunday slippers. Quick as a flash, Mama grabbed up the slipper. As I was backing out, she was paddling me with it. Then she realized from the blood on Sissy's dress that she was hurt, and what else could Mama do but faint? Our Mama!

Years later while visiting in Houston, my husband and I called Sissy to come have lunch with us. We recalled the day we hid under the bed and laughed until the waitress gave us a querulous look. Maybe she thought we were tipsy. Sissy was always the most thoughtful person. When she came to eat with us, she was well aware that we would again recall all those funny Sunday afternoons when we were children. She even remembered to bring me a little gift — a bottle of perfume. Quickly I unwrapped it. Another dirty look from the waitress while we laughed and laughed!

"Be quiet, people will think we are from the sticks," my husband warned.

"Oh, now, you just get your little old quilt and pillow and get out on the floor," Sissy said to him. "You know, we never did get to hear a thing. We didn't learn anything, and all I got out of it was this old scar. That's why I always wear bangs. And I guess you had to wear that slipper with a patched strap all that summer. What irritates me is that we were so dumb in the first place!"

"Why be irritated? What you learn today you have to unlearn tomorrow, old Mose used to tell us down on the Gonzales farm."

Silver Wedding Days

Another salesman came on the scene, and this time Mama was the one who bought. She had wanted us to have a piano, a new piano all our very own. Besides, she explained they would be having their silver wedding anniversary and folks would need the piano to play for those who sang on the program. Mama could play the piano by ear. She had never taken lessons. I can still hear her playing and singing, "Trust and Obey." That was Mama's theme.

She sang it over and over as she would sew or mend, churn or mold butter pounds, bake cookies or gather in the eggs. If any of us joined her in the song, she would be silent. Could it be she wanted us to each take it for our own theme? She wanted us "to trust and obey, for there's no other way to be happy in Jesus."

The approaching wedding anniversary was the talk of the household. Yet, the daily work must go on as usual. On a dairy farm, cows don't ask but demand attention. It is not like on a Live Oak County ranch where range cattle can often be left unattended for a week. That is, they can if the stock-water pond is full and the rains have also brought good grazing.

We were carefully folding away our summer clothes. We would put layers of paper around the white things and all around the edges of the huge shipping case in which we stored our out-season clothes. Mama put in mothballs. As she put the clothes away, she would predict which dress would fit whom by next summer and maybe how she would make it over a bit so no one would remember it.

Mama was a genius at remodeling our clothes. But alas, she must have had a sinking feeling when she looked at my scrawny figure with bumps coming here and there. Pauline looked so like Mama, and by now they wore the same size. So sometimes we'd forget whose was whose. Pauline could sew much neater than Mama, but she usually chose darker materials. Mama loved wine, red and rust. She did have one grey wool dress. It was beautiful. But Mama seldom wore it.

So this was the very time to "get shed of it." Mama decided since Pauline must have a new outfit to come to the celebration, I could have the beautiful grey wool. I protested. After all, Lucy was next in line. She should have it. Besides, wool scratched me and made me "erp." For that word, I got a slap. Of that I am positive.

Lucy would not be coming home as it was too far. By now, Pauline was closer home, in Dallas attending Southern Methodist University and working for Trinity Methodist Church part-time. Pearl revolted as she would not be caught dead in grey; and Olga, even more outspoken about the color, did not have to wear it either.

After all that, I got the dress. Mama was real sweet about it though. She went to all the trouble to completely rip it up, press it all out and recut it into a different style. After all, there was much more than enough available material in the separate skirt, vestie and cape like she had worn them. If only I had carried out my plan! I had thought many times during the summer of taking it out and burning it when I would be burning the trash on a Saturday afternoon out by the washpot. I hate grey dresses.

But Mama did not wait long to get started on the fall sewing. By September when school started, she had made our new cotton dresses and was ready to do my "precious" silver wedding dress.

"It is not my silver wedding, why should I wear silver color?" I continued to protest. I suggested dyeing the material, but then Mama said she had already bought pretty, bright red Sansilk to trim it and was going to do red feather stitches along the princess line seams. Just the long cape was all she had needed to make my dress.

I guess I just resigned to the idea. It did look beautiful and she did work far into the night on the stitching. Aunt Lou, Papa's crippled sister, had come to spend a few weeks with us to help make new curtains and other things to spruce up the house for the silver wedding day. In all the hustle and bustle, I never did see what they made out of the rest of the grey wool until December the third. It was the morning of the big event and guests were beginning to arrive for dinner.

As I went through the parlor, I spied the grey. Lo and behold! .The meanies had made new sofa cushions out of the rest of the grey material and had even stitched them with the red Sansilk. They were beautiful. But I was just killed. Of all the people I ran to for consolation, I could not have picked worse. It was to Mama's father I ran and cried, "The sofa pillows are grey and stitched just like my dress, and it makes me so mad that I am going to the barn and stay there all day!"

Grandpa had the palsy somewhat, or maybe I bumped his elbow and hit his coffee-cup. He spilled coffee all over my dress front. I told him it was all right as I was going to the barn anyway. Being wool, the dress did not absorb the coffee quickly enough. The coffee mopped right off, and I had to stay. Grandpa saw to that. In one quick trip to the parlor, he picked up the two new cushions and carried them to the back bedroom where he shoved them under the bed in the corner.

That is why I picked the wrong person. He saved the day for me; but, alas, the day after! Mama found the cushions under the bed. To her dying day, you could not have convinced her that her father was the guilty one.

The silver wedding was otherwise a shining success. Everyone from our church must have been there and many other friends. The kitchen was filled with willing helpers, most of them our Negro friends. Papa had confidence in his friends, I guess, for he had bought a new glass-fronted china closet before the day of celebration. And it was filled when the party was over with all manner of silver gifts, most of which we never actually used.

As I think of it now, Papa was always confident of the future. He knew the people would come to his home when invited to partake of Mama's turkey dinner. He also knew she need not bake cakes and pies, for any good neighbor would see that they would be amply brought along. Just like he knew the china closet would be an appropriate gift to Mama on their silver anniversary even though we only had everyday dishes up until then.

After everyone had eaten and the big tables that were made out of all the doors in the house laid end to end on saw-horses had been cleared away, the elderly folk gathered in the parlor and the children went to the bedrooms to play. Pallets were made in every available space for the babies; and as quickly as the mothers could get them nursed and put down, the program started.

My day to embarrass myself was ripe. The speaker rose to call everyone to order and to say something about their having some special music, a prayer season, and then some toasts.

"Toasts? What for? Haven't we all had dinner? Who wants any old toast?" I said right out loud. Everyone looked at me. But not everyone laughed. What made it so bad was that it seemed to me only the town people laughed. Grandpa and Grandma, Mama and Papa and some of the other older "Dutchmen" just stared at me. No one answered my questions. The program went on; and at the end of it all, after I had nodded and dozed several times, I

47

suddenly heard the speaker say again, "Now, we shall have a toast to the happy young couple and their fine children."

Whoever heard of such foolish ideas among grown people, I thought. I also thought to keep my mouth shut this time. Toast to me was toast with milk or toast with hot water and pepper for stomach ache. My life had been too full of toasts of every sort, light brown, burnt and soaked to get any joyous significance out of the word.

Several other couples celebrated their wedding anniversaries about that time. At first, Papa and Mama seemed happy to be invited to these occasions, but later I believe they were tempted to ignore the invitations. One came from people they had not ever known except that Papa admitted he did try a whole morning to sell them some insurance. Maybe they thought we owed them a gift. Papa suggested we take one of the things they had received for which they found no earthly use whatsoever. Mama would not consent to this but came up with the suggestion of giving them one of the pretty grey cushions.

"After all, no one even got to see them, remember?"

"But they may think they were made out of my dress," I objected. That was the clincher. We would go and take the cushion, and I would wear the dress so they would know the cushion was not made out of my dress.

We went. Just like Mama suggested. It was a hard winter and Papa said he had spent much more on getting ready for the silver wedding anniversary than he should have. He was having an awful time paying off on the doctor and hospital bills. For a few months now none of us had been sick, and we thought it wouldn't happen again, I guess. Of course, Mama also took a nice big cake along.

This cake she let me bake. It was meant to be a compliment to make up for the apparent hurt of having to wear a dress to match the gift cushion. The cake turned out to look better than either the cushion or me. With raisins, I carefully spelled out "Happy Anniversary" on the top of the thick, chocolate fudge frosting. It took me most of the Saturday afternoon to get this done, starting with splitting some kindling for the stove fire.

It was at this party among many new people whom I had never seen before that I had the first inkling of a queer sort of feeling when talking with a boy. I still cannot describe it. I was neither glad nor yet was I afraid. It was mostly a good feeling to talk with someone who seemed not to have the least idea that my dress was made over, that I was called Dutchman at school, or even that Papa was disappointed when I was born.

But he was not a new acquaintance. I had always known him and he had talked and played with us many times. This day at this party, only six miles from both of our homes, it seemed to me I had never seen Walter before in my whole life. But I had. He was the eldest of the Buckholtz children and we had played and talked with each other all our lives. He was now about nineteen. Handsome! Teens today would describe him as "the most."

Yet, in all my new excitement, I became very angry with him when he said to me at the refreshment table that some day he and I would celebrate our silver wedding together. On the way home, I told Olga what he had said and she threatened to pinch my head off if ever I pestered those boys again. After all, I was only twelve and as ugly as Aunt Frieda's old grey horse, Cora. Poor Olga! Later I realized the seriousness of my foolish statement.

Even so, it only tended to make me think of the whole matter more seriously. As it happened nothing serious came of it except my thoughts, for we all continued to be good friends and the two families ran back and forth many times a week over the half mile of road between our dairies. Besides, at silo filling time each summer we took turns helping each other. That way, the two farmers needed to buy only one set of ensilage cutters and row binders and could use all their combined teams, wagons and hired hands. The hands, also, like their own dozens of children, were not considered puny, tired or ill during the harvest season unless a raging fever or something worse overtook one.

We had hardly recovered from Papa and Mama's house-cleaning spree, the other wedding anniversary parties, and the summer harvest when it was time again for school to start in September. This year all of us would be going to town to school. There were to be only three grades at Reid Ward. Even the twins were now as high as the fourth grade.

Cotton scrapping must be finished real quickly now. School clothes must be gotten in order. We would all go to town Saturday and buy some new shoes. Papa had an account at T. J. Knight's store and they kept good shoes that a farmer could afford to buy.

Papa had rented a cotton field a mile from home over by the railroad tracks behind the Buckholtz place. Each day during early September, when the earth would get so hot that we had to walk behind the cotton stalks where the shade was, he would send me home. After the walk home, I would help Mama get the noon meal on the table for the rest of the family and for several extra hired men.

Sister, as we call the girl-twin, usually stayed at home with Mama as there was just too much for one to get done. She was good to answer the telephone and write down messages for Papa. People would call to order produce; to cancel orders; to tell him of meetings and other things. We had our wall telephone in the hall with the mouthpiece up to where our six-foot-two father talked into it. There was a chair for us to climb on when we answered.

Of course, Sister was also good at listening in on the club lines. It wasn't exactly something she should be blamed for as we encouraged it. As we grew older, we tried harder and harder not to do this, but it also became more and more of a temptation. We just had to keep up with who was calling who for dates. Besides, when Mama would get caught listening in, she used the excuse that "somebody may be sick and need our help."

It was by listening in that we found out many things we might have been much happier not knowing. If sick persons had needed our help, they would have called us.

Mama said the next day after she listened in on Mrs. Buck-holtz talking with a friend that we were not to go there for a whole week.

That prompted me to go the very next day as I was to come home from the cotton field. I found my neighbor cutting out little blue chambray shirts; some were for the young ones to wear to school, and some were for the youngest two to wear when she took them along as she delivered the cream to town. She did not know that I had been told to stay away. When she offered me 25c each to take the shirts home to sew up the seams, I just had to accept. After all, I could sew real well, and I figured I'd get Mama to make the button holes. Mama was a whiz at them.

So I trudged home with an armful of work. Mama was so pleased with the whole idea, she forgot to scold me for breaking my promise to stay away from the neighbors. She was always so kind to the neighbors that she wouldn't think of accepting pay for making the button-holes. But if Papa agreed, then I could take the 25c for sewing each of the shirts.

It was all right with Papa so long as I gave a strict tithe of my earnings to the church. The rest I could save up to pay for the piano lessons I wanted when I started to school in town. I was glad to get the start at that. Yet I wondered why I had to do all that with *my* money. Didn't Papa use some of his money for tobacco? I began to wish for the day when I could be my own business manager. I must have been nuts!

It took me until almost time for the Buckholtz silver wedding in late fall to finish all the shirts, not just those I took home that first day but others she cut out from time to time.

Earning, Learning, Churning & Yearning

It was a start in business for me. Again, it was illness that overtook me. Again, the doctor and the folk thought most of my trouble was imagination. They were perhaps correct to a large extent. When a person thinks he is sick, he really is sick. The first year for me to go to school in town, my teacher refused to call me by my first name, Viola. She gave no reason. She just asked me, "What is your middle name?"

"Louise."

"Then from today on, I shall call you Louise and I don't want to hear anyone in this room calling her Viola. Understand!" That was all there was to it.

My teacher was beautiful — tall, large, and had auburn hair. I loved her until I got to thinking about the name change. I was afraid to ask her, even at recess, what was the matter with the name Viola. Sure, I had been teased about it being a "nigger-name," but so was Louise, I reasoned. On the way home, as I was riding in the back seat, I stood up as high as the tall car top would allow and announced," I am now Louise Ebel."

"You are no such a thing. Aunt Lou is Louise Ebel, and your middle name doesn't count that way," Olga yelled back from the steering wheel. I tried to explain, but they just couldn't believe me. We had such an argument over it that by the time we got home, everyone was yelling at each other.

Papa 'phoned the teacher that night. He explained it would be most confusing for us all. But when my report card came, it was made out "Louise." And "Louise" I became so consistently that many who were in my class that year and the next will greet me that way on the few occasions we meet these days.

Papa and the teacher wore a hole in the top of my report card that year. Each month he would erase the name and write in Viola, and each month she would erase Viola and write Louise. Mama suggested to Papa he could, at least, use pencil instead of the ink-staff and pen — easier to erase!

I hate to climb stairs. They put me in an upstairs room at school, and I'd hang on to the bannisters like a person drowning as I'd shut my eyes and climb, trying hard to stay in line. I'm sure everyone thought me lazy but actually many times as soon as I reached the top, I would flop dead away on the floor. Often, I would have to rush to get to the restroom; and there, after vomiting, I'd faint.

There was a service elevator in one corner of the building. It had to be manipulated by pulling some ropes by hand. That was as impossible as climbing stairs for me. Anyway, thinking I was just lazy or so bent on having things my way, the teacher (whom I will call Mrs. Smith) would hear of nothing different for any of her students. "We are all old enough to be in the sixth grade, and it is time we act like it," she said.

One always finds friends if one does not get impatient, I learned that year. Several of the girls from town families just loved the good home-made bread I would have in my lunch pail. So one after the other became my close noontime pals. One day a girl named Frances suggested a plan to cure Mrs. Smith of her idea that I was just "putting on."

When the bell rang, nine of the girls clung to the stairs and shut their eyes just like they had seen me do. They climbed along as slowly as I did. Then just as we all got to the top floor, which was a hall leading to our classroom, we all flopped out. And we truly gave a good act. Mrs. Smith never found out that we were just putting on. After that, all nine of us were allowed to stay upstairs during the lunch period.

She even let us bring our sewing to school. I was making doll clothes to sell at our church bazaar. Most of the girls still had their last dolls — the last ones that parents would be giving girls big enough to be in the sixth grade. They all wanted me to make them some clothes to put on their last dolls so they could set them on their chests in their rooms. I had made my last doll a beautiful outfit out of some scraps which Mrs. Neumann gave me. I had hung my doll on the wall a year ago now.

They brought me entirely too many scraps and dolls to dress. I would take one at the time home with me and Mama would help me make the clothes after our homework was all done at nights. For a while, Papa objected. But as he realized I was earning more than my music lessons and paying my tithe each Sunday, he even pinned the patterns down a few times for us.

Mama could lay a doll on a piece of newspaper and cut out a pattern that fit every time, almost. Later, during an extended illness in the spring months, I was able to make doll clothes and keep up with my studies at home. Mrs. Smith was then very kind to me. Each day she went to the trouble to write out my assignments and send them home with Olga or with the twins.

I kept this doll clothes business going until I had two real live "dolls" of my own. Now, it won't be too long until the granddaughter will be asking for Nanny to make doll clothes. I hope to see the day.

One day one of the girls asked Mrs. Smith if she liked to sew and if she ever made doll clothes. She told us she had lost all her dolls, all her family, and all her possessions during the war in Germany. She had married an American soldier and had come to the States with him. He disappeared in New York while they were attending a movie. It was a likely story, Mama said when I told her of it. She warned me not to ask her any other questions about it. Many persons have such tragedies in their lives and when they rise above them to make good school teachers or other good people, we should not be concerned about their past. What if we did not know her true name! What was it to us that she claimed to have no relatives anywhere in the world!

Maybe Mama was trying to tell me it was none of my business why my older sisters had not married, why they had chosen to go into professions themselves instead of making homes like she did. Maybe she was telling me it was none of my business to know why she often said she hoped we would all stay single.

Maybe, she was saying not to pry. But I asked her anyway. Not that she answered me. I even asked her if she were afraid for us girls to have babies. I'm sure she did not answer; she never did when we asked such as that.

One of these spring days while I was recovering from a siege of some sort of fever, I was told to water the front flower beds. I had only to hold the hose and with my thumb on the end of it, make a spray of water for the plants. We had a great big ram which Papa staked on the lawns to mow down the grass and weeds.

I thought it would be real funny to spray this old goat. I really gave him a bath. He pulled and pulled at his chain to get away, but I kept at him until he was about as mad as a hornet. It was a very funny sight.

As I turned around to go back to watering the flowers, he sneaked up behind me and with one big yank of his head just as I turned to look, he cut the front of my left leg open to the bone, from my knee-cap down about six inches. I yelled bloody murder. Mama had to go down to the field to get Papa, and then they had no car in which to take me to the doctor. Our only car was at school. We're still a "one-car" outfit.

Mrs. Ronshausen came in her new car to take us to town. After all the commotion was over, Papa sold the ram and in a few days I was sent back to school.

"With the leg like that you can't climb the stairs, but maybe they will let you go into the next class downstairs," he reasoned. He probably thought if I were that mean, I was well enough to go to school.

That's how I got promoted a half year all of a sudden. I finished with the low seventh grade and passed at the top of the class that May. Goodness, I felt important now. I was head of my class and I had paid for my own music lessons. Why, I was earning several dollars each month. There were no deductions, no income taxes and we never heard of such things in those days as United Fund and appeal letters for all manner of good causes. If we paid out our own church tithes, we thought we had been good citizens. Child labor laws were kept strictly, even though oddly.

Summertime brought the problem of how to get to my music lessons. I could ride along with whoever took the cream to town, but I would have to find a way back home. I could not walk the whole three miles. Finally, Papa hit on a big idea. I could take my lessons on Wednesdays, work several hours at the parsonage, and come to the cottage prayer meetings with the preacher and his wife. That worked on the days when the prayer meetings were in homes in our area. Walking would have been a snap!

Other weeks, I just had to miss. I did not stick with that idea very long; for soon after school was out, the music teacher's son came home from military school. One look at him and everything turned to music. He was as handsome as Walter . . . maybe even more so in a certain sort of way. I would just have to take my music lesson every week. I'd just walk home, that's what I'd do. And I did! If you have ever walked three miles about noon on a gravel road in Texas, you know what a nut I was. Can't imagine why my parents even allowed me to try.

I would first stop at Grandma Sturm's and rest a bit and have a cool drink of cistern water from the bucket (hanging under the chinaberry tree) wrapped in wet cloths. Then, another mile out from town, if I were very thirsty and tired, I could stop at Grandpa Menking's front porch and pump up some water from the underground cistern. I must have been insane to walk in all that heat

55

for no better reason than to take a piano lesson from a teacher who had a handsome son at home for the summer.

Wouldn't you say I was real touched in the head! Really!

With so many attractive girls in town and with his mother taking him each evening to the theater where she played the piano accompaniment to the silent films, I was stupid to think he would ever give me a second glance. Yet I made a desperate try.

Near the end of the summer, the music pupils were ready to give a recital. It was going to be in the theatre building on a Sunday afternoon. At first, my parents said absolutely I would *not* be allowed to play on the theatre piano and most assuredly *not* on a Sunday. However, the Baptist preacher's son and daughter were also in the class; and when their parents said it would be all right if the recital were in the afternoon and every light was turned on in the building, I was also allowed to be on the program.

When the day came, our whole family attended. It was the first time most of us had been in the theatre, and Papa enjoyed seeing the highly decorated ceilings, walls, rugs and lights.

There was a large attendance, for our teacher was very popular. People came from everywhere during the week nights to hear a person who could play tunes that exactly fit the scenes as they were shown on the screen. Her music could "walk, talk, cry, bang away or fall off a horse" at a moment's notice. She had no time to change pages during the movie so she played entirely from memory. We were shocked when during the refreshment period, the minister asked her to play a number describing some familiar story. He was probably shocked even more when she responded with the crucifixion story and the resurrection, singing several lines from hymns to give the proper effect.

While she was doing this, I was putting her things into a box for her. I saw a picture of her son fastened to the inner side of the box lid. I stole the picture . . . right then and there. Just as I was rolling it up to hide it in my bloomers, he came around the end of the piano and saw me tucking up my stocking garter.

"Excuse me! I did not know you were changing back here. Don't you know there is a ladies lounge?" he asked. He did not really see what I was doing then, I decided.

I was so angry I could have killed him but I did not put the picture back. It was not until later, much later, that I brought it back to his mother.

He went back to school in September. Oh! Septembers! Seems every September brings some terrible blow to my life plans.

56

This September was what we now call a "wing-ding." But it was also one to remember with joys as well as sorrows. Aunt Frieda came down with rheumatism, and I was to stay at their house for a while to deliver her "plunder" (Papa called it) with her buggy and Cora, the white mare. Could anything worse befall a person than to make old Cora move? She was as lazy as lazy can get . . . it would about take an act of God, like lightning, to speed her.

The plunder consisted of ten cents worth of some sort of fresh vegtables here and ten cents worth there from house to house. I had learned my lesson about knocking before entering houses, but I had no training in prodding so near-dead a plug, climbing out of the buggy a jillion times and still get to school on time.

The joy of serving that fall and winter for my aunts and my aged grandmother first came to me many years later. When I was young, I did not fully appreciate their efforts. My aunt Lou was crippled from birth in body, but not in mind and certainly not in spirit and courage. She had what some folk call "a green-thumb;" only in her case all ten of her twisted fingers must have been specially gifted in making things grow. Not only their little strawberry patches, their rows of vegetables from which they made their most income but a whole pit, sort of a half covered cellar, was filled with gorgeous potted plants.

Flowers, ferns and fruit trees rubbed elbows all over the front of the two lots. Cora supplied plant-food the best she could. Large compost heaps helped to keep the gardens fertile and Aunt Frieda never seemed to tire of wrapping things up to protect them from freezing or making shade for plants in the summer. She would actually take a quilt off of her own bed on a frosty morning to cover a tubful of early spring blossoms . . . blossoms that she needed to take to "the sick folks in town."

Nothing was ever wasted in that household. I found it hard to decide when cottage cheese was past selling stage and yet not good enough to give away . . . still not quite "ripe" enough to cook for smear-cheese. We call it Koch-Kaese.

Grandmother always wore a small quilted cap to keep her head warm and a tiny quilted bonnet to keep cool in summer. One night, I happened to see her unwinding her hair to brush it. I was surprised to find she had such beautiful hair and I told her so.

She was so pleased that I noticed. She kissed me warmly and said, "Ich liebe dich, Ich liebe dich."

"Und Ich liebe dich, Grosmudder!", I responded. Then Aunt Lou laughed and Aunt Frieda advised we better get some rest. First though, we all knelt to pray . . . even Grandma who was old and surely tired.

Aunt Frieda is a very religious person. She had a Bible on the buggy seat and many passages were marked. On a scrap of paper, she had written, "Yea, though we walk through the valley of the shadow of death, we will fear no evil." I knew, of course, that this she took from the twenty-third Psalm, but I noticed the plural. Who in all the world could she mean by WE? Did Aunt Frieda have a lover?

I read and thought of that so often — and even do now more than thirty-five years later — until I finally realized, it was that old horse Cora she meant by "we." For surely she must have known that someday she would get vexed enough at that old gray plug to shoot her. While moving at her snail's pace, one could have studied all the lessons assigned by even the meanest school teacher if one had not had to yank and prod and constantly say "swoop-swoop" like Aunt Frieda always did. Cora just would not move without hearing that constant melody.

I yearned for the day when either the horse would die or Aunt Frieda would get well. If the red-haired crush of mine had stayed on to go to our school and I could have seen him when delivering at the Ollre's, even Cora would have been endured as the valley of the shadow of death. Everything comes to an end that starts: there are two limits to everything — the start and the finish.

It was sad when both Cora and the young man died that fall. I cannot recall Cora's undoing, but the young man was accidently killed at Military School and his body was laid to rest at nearby Harwood.

His death set my thoughts to churning: they tumbled from side to side in my mind like the sweet cream that Mama would pour into the large wooden barrel on the back porch. She would sit there hours on end and turn the crank that churned the cream. When it was whipped to a beautiful stiff batter, she would open the lid and take out a large amount to put in the icebox for us to eat as whipped cream on our rice puddings or home-made gelatin or just to spread on our bread for supper. This act of opening the churn would also tend to let in some warm air and might have hastened the butter to form. But like as not, she would still be churning when Papa would come home for a cup

58

of coffee in the middle of the afternoon, or sometimes it would be at noontime.

He would take over. And sure enough, in a short time, butter would come. He would always tease Mama about that. He thought she should get fun (we call it a kick) out of the matter that he could get butter so quickly when she could not and had churned all morning. That's the way it was with my thinking those days. I even began to blame myself for being wrong to so secretly love this young man. After all, I had no right to even think of such matters this young. I was only thirteen.

It grieved me. I could not talk about it to anyone. Things one must keep entirely to one's self often are the things that cut the worse. I found later it was much easier to forget those things, though, than the matters one has talked over with others. I have not forgotten him, still adore auburn hair and tall young boys, have a forgiving spirit toward those who have killed someone through carelessness, and know also, I would soon have forgotten him as a lover.

He set my mind to yearning, nevertheless. Yearning to grow up and to be big enough to be allowed to enter the discussions going on when groups of women gathered here and there. One could find them in huddles everywhere, it seemed. No sooner would church be over and there would be a group circled around under every shade tree in summer or down the aisles in the building during bad weather. If one of us teenagers poked our heads anywhere nearby, it got very quiet for a minute or so; and then the conversation usually went on with such matters as quilt patterns, setting hens, and headache remedies. Did they not have any remedies for aching hearts among their teenagers? Do we?

Mama's Idea of Shadow

Shadows, the dictionary tells me, can be one of many things. I largely remember how Mama regarded the cloud or shadow that can be on a friendship or reputation. When I was young, though, I first had thought she was speaking of shadows caused by the clouds coming in front of the sun. These were the shadows we learned to love, for on hot days these traveled to and fro across the fields in which we worked.

It was when the sun made certain shadows that we knew it was time we could go home for lunch or that we realized how tired we were. I recall wondering why Papa's shadow seemed to have a smaller head late in the evenings. When one leans forward as Papa did when he was very tired, the head seems to melt into the shoulders of the shadow image.

Mama often spoke of shadows on friendships and reputations; and to me, thinking of the welcome shadows meaning entirely something else, they were not so important. Therefore it was next to impossible for me to see why Mama did not like my music teacher as much as I felt she should. Mama said she had the shadow of divorce, and she hoped I would understand that was bad. Bad for whom? Mama forgot to say.

This subject led me to one of the longest conversations in private I ever had with my mother. It was September again, and I had come back home from staying with my grandmother and aunts in time to help with the harvest work. There was much less delivering for Aunt Frieda to do in the middle of the summer. And too, she said her rheumatism was over again. It *would* be just when there was so much field work at home. Now it would have been more pleasant to stay in town and to enjoy playing with neighbor children there. One of these was Elvira Neumann. Mama thought it best not to get to visit there so much as the shadow of their wealth would perhaps make me unhappy with our simple, hard farm life. Mama seemed to think of everything like that.

This long conversation between Mama and me came about as we were canning tomatoes. We grew them by the bushels. They were gathered each day at noon, while we were resting from the field work. Resting! The vines would not be wet from dews at this time, and we would not get so stained. Besides, Mama and Papa had heard that it was not good to touch the tomatoes and beans while they were wet. Maybe it was not good for us either.

We would set some aside on sheets of paper all around the edges of the huge, back screened-in porch to send to the stores the next day. Sometimes we were real lucky and got as much as fifty cents per bushel for choice tomatoes. The bruised or ugly ones were used for canning and for making preserves. This was always a long and wearisome task. But when Mama helped and she got to talking, it was a rare treat.

The word shadow came into the conversation through my question, "Mama, why have you such dark shadows around your eyes again?"

She explained that many people thought that indicated illness but that she felt better than usual and really she thought they did not mean anything. She was not well at all and neither was I so I always felt very sympathetic toward her and watched her closely. Eating bites of the fine tomatoes did not improve our diarrhea either. It is a wonder tomatoes did not sprout out of our ears and noses.

It was a bit disgusting to us both that we were usually quite rosy and healthy looking. In fact, Mama was always the picture of health. She was a beautiful woman with soft, long hair and few wrinkles in her rather small face.

"It is not the shadows under your eyes that you need to worry about," Mama said. Then she confided that it worried her that she did not want any of us to marry — "not never, ever," she added. She said she knew it was wrong; for when she saw her friends enjoy their grandchildren, she was almost — not quite — envious.

Soon I would reach fifteen. Mama must have sensed how I had suddenly became aware of the male sex about us. She must have wanted to warn me that she would oppose any courtship I'd get started. She even went through days and days of being so cool toward Papa that the house had the air of being empty or something.

"Mama, if you are afraid of being alone and no one else will stay with you this year, I will stay home from school," I volunteered after hours and hours of talking about fears and shadows and burning two pans of tomato preserves. That night I cried until I heard the alarm clock go off for five a.m. milking time. I just could not understand why I had ever offered to stay home from school. Yet I knew it was because I loved my mother dearly and felt she should not be alone with all those shadows.

Pearl was teaching in the Mexican School in Gonzales with Miss Rosemary Morrison. On several occasions, when Pearl was out for illness, Miss Morrison let me substitute. I especially enjoyed the hour of class when the children had to write little essays. I also wrote some along with them. I asked Miss Morrison to let us take the class to the Gonzales Inquirer printing office on a field trip. This proved to be most inspiring, not alone to the young pupils but to me also.

The paper carried a story or two for several issues. The students were very happy. With pride, I announced that someday I hope to be a journalist.

We found an advertisement in the Farm and Ranch for a correspondence course which we ordered and I studied diligently. That is I studied when I was not ironing for Papa, Mama, Pearl the teacher, Olga the high school senior, myself and the twins who were now eleven. When the ironing was done, there would always be cows with well-filled bags to relieve, chores by the scores, and three times a week music lessons to practice and senior lessons in Catechism to learn.

It was a full life which proved to be as good an education for me as anything a college could have taught. Friends today sometimes ask me how I manage to do so many civic things: surely I must have a full-time maid! I do not, and never did we have such at our home. We learned early to overcome shadows. Not Mama's shadows only but the actual problems that will come in every person's household.

As I ironed by Mama's rocker or often by her bed so she could stretch out her aching legs, she would take each piece and sew on the missing buttons or mend it. She had the washtub of dampened clothes next to her; and as I was finishing a piece, she would pitch me another piece. Then she would fold the shirts, blouses and most everything else except our best dresses. We had not much closet space and so many things were neatly put into dresser drawers and on shelves.

Cooperation and scheduling our work was wonderful training. Some people think they have come upon a really modern idea to have date-books, calendars and shopping lists going all the time. All my life there were rings around certain dates on our calendars and a list hanging by the door in the milk house; and every one of us knew such standard things as potatoes were planted on Washington's birthday (unless it came on Sunday) and prayer meeting was every Wednesday — rain or shine. If rain, then we observed the time at home quietly.

Being at home so much more than the others, it is possible I noticed more than did they the chasm that seemed to be growing day by day between my parents. Finally I asked Mama about it. She assured me I was imagining things. She would never have such a thing as divorce in her family . . . no, never!

"But Mama, could you not have dressed and gone with Papa last Sunday afternoon when he wanted to go see the Watsons? After all, they are strangers among us. Besides, if you all had gone, you would have gotten away before they came here with all those brats who ate up every cookie we had on the place."

Mama scolded me about being selfish about our cookies. After all, we could bake more. How well I knew that! Mama's cookie recipe is so large that it starts off, "Cream together three pounds of sweet cream butter and six cups of sugar." In German, Tanta wrote in the book alongside, "Drei tasse smaltz and seben malase." I am sure she meant to spell molasses. Papa made it in a large vat out of homegrown sugar cane.

Years afterwards, my daughters decided they would surely like to have their grandmother's cookie recipe. She sent it as she had it, and they and their two friends rolled cookies far into the night.

It worried me that more and more Mama would not dress up. She loved pretty colored dresses and always had as many as any of her friends. Papa would ask her to go out oftener now than ever before. After all, I was there to answer the telephone and take the orders, keep the "home-fires burning," and bake the bread when it was well risen.

Mama just would not go. Papa was not well either and he so needed her to go along. Could it be she was weary of well-doing? Could it be she felt unwanted and not needed now that roads were better and more people had doctors to deliver their babies? Or could it have been Mama knew best not to leave a teenager at home alone in a ten room farm house with seven outside entrances which were never locked, day or night? Just think of all the cookies and kaffee-kuchen we could have saved if we had gone before company came. Why most every Sunday night after church we would wash dishes for hours. There was always some family in for Sunday afternoon. Many of these were our young friends and neighbors.

We would use the pretty dishes out of the China closet in the dining room when grown-ups came. That is, we used all except the very best pieces. After all, some had to stay in there to look pretty from where we sat at the table.

It was on one of these Sundays as I was bringing in refills of our coffee, I heard Papa tell how happy he was when I had volunteered to stay home from school for the year as it saved him from having to make me stay. It took the joy out of my sacrifice. I would have had to stay even if I had not thought to offer to do so. Oh, how hurt I was to hear that remark!

I told my father about it the next day as we were hauling fertilizer to the orchards — not the nice clean stuff we haul home these days in the trunks of our fine automobiles. It was just the sort of work and stink that would bring out a complaint in most any teenager having to sling shovels of the stuff onto the mule-drawn manure spreader.

He cried. Great, wet tears rolled out of his big grey-blue eyes that had drooping lids. I wished I had not complained. After all, all I would get out of doing so would perhaps be a vomiting spell or a siege of diarrhea. We then never fully knew — although now I do — if it was the extra rich food such as whipped cream, the fresh yeast breads, or the going about people that made me sick.

Papa had a heart of gold, sometimes in the molten stage and sometimes hard cast. Don't we all? He sent me home that day to see if I could help Mama. He also told me I was to start taking my piano lessons again. Besides, I might just as well take voice lessons while I was in town anyway. I could ride along to town in the mornings and get back home somehow . . . the somehow being the walks like the summer before I had stayed at my grandmother's place.

It was a great break for me — the one that completely changed my life. I did not become a concert pianist and singing was only made more of a personal joy through my training. Perhaps I was easier to listen to at home and later in the church choirs. But the walks brought new experiences most rewarding to me.

As I write this chapter, I am reminded of my doctor's orders here in the middle of 1958 — walk three miles a day! "Nothing you can do will help to tone your weary heart and body all over and even your mind and soul," the fine heart specialist in San Antonio said.

As I would walk home from town, there were always new things to observe. When I came to Papa's folks, I would usually

64

find my dearest aunt, Louise, in the garden with her tiny short-handled hoe. She was very crippled and could work only with these special tools that Papa made for her in his farm shop. Or she would be indoors on a wet day, stitching beautiful garments for the Neumanns or other of her customers. Grandma would either be stirring up a bit of dinner by the little wood stove in the kitchen or be seated by the east window reading. She was a very quiet person, perhaps having learned long ago that Aunt Frieda knew all the news to talk about, having so many contacts and such an unquenchable desire for knowing everything that went on in the town. She should have worked for the Federal Bureau of Investigation.

If Aunt Frieda were home, I'd be thirty minutes late getting home, and I could see my mother standing on the front walk a mile or more before I'd get there. Mama was wise enough to know the dangers of girls walking alone on country roads.

It was exciting to see the neighbors' work. Some would plow neat rows as straight as a bullet shot; some rows were really slouchy looking. Those were the days when one's farming was judged by how straight his rows were — except Papa's. Mama scolded and scolded with Papa when he first planted rows "to catch the water." This was after the terrible drought of 1917. Later, Papa plowed some sort of way to drain the water out of the fields. Farming is fickle!

Some of the neighbor men would wave. Some would even whip their mules up a bit to be at the end by the road when I'd get there. These were those I thought were jealous of us. After all, Papa was always way ahead of them in buying new gadgets and in using new row-crop seeds; and we painted our house *inside* and not only on the outside.

It was Papa's fault that I thought this as he had told me the summer I accompanied him to take the area census in 1920 about our neighbors being jealous of his new things. (I must have been quite well that summer. Or either they thought it easier for me to go along and open wire gaps, file papers for Papa, and spread lunch with him than to work in the fields.)

It was the wire-gaps that I couldn't open that made him say such awful things. Most of the gaps were made "sloppy loose," as most people had their children hop off the wagons or cars to open them. When we found a real tight gap, Papa would say, "There won't be any children to register here." He said, "If we had gaps instead of painted lumber gates, we would have more friends."

65

"Good heavens, more friends to bake cookies for on Saturdays," had been my reply.

Some of these men would ask me what Papa was doing these days, was he done with spring plowing, had we planted our potatoes, did I know if Papa could come over tomorrow to help dehorn calves or pull well-pipes. I would think to myself about Papa wondering if we had enough friends. Seemed to me, everyone was his friend and appreciated him and the use of his good supply of tools.

Soon, I began to notice the young Adlof man who farmed along the way would also wave at me. Yet, he never stopped to talk. He would even wave if he were already half way back up the rows away from the road. At this portion of the Harwood Road, the hill is rather high; and at that time, there was quite a deep barrow ditch. The horses people rode or the single-hitched buggies would use a little side road, here where there was no gravel hauled in, for their dry-weather travel.

One day as I was walking down in this low trail, I came upon this young man sitting at the side of his plow, shaking the dirt out of his high-top laced boots. I spoke, and he jumped up as if he were shot with a B-B gun. He returned the greeting and said he didn't see me. We both laughed as he apologized for being barefooted. He didn't look over the row of tall purple thistles blooming on the shoulder of the public road so he never knew I, too, was barefooted. I had taken off my shoes at the bridge in the valley as from that point, there would be this deep, soft black dirt on which to walk home.

Though we had known each other all my life, it was the first time we had actually met on common ground — both with our shoes off and completely off guard. A few weeks afterwards, he picked me up on the way home from town and took me as far as our mail box. He would have taken me all the way but I refused to let him. I was afraid, not only of what Mama would say; after all, I had a raft of older single sisters.

I tried every way possible to get to talk with this most wonderful creature again in the next few months. We went to his farm for plums, but he was nowhere around their orchard. Later we hoed cotton for him, but he managed to be away back in the far west field that Saturday. Even one rainy day after I had been sick again and Papa, not needing Filly for field work, let me use her and the buggy to go to town, this neighbor was not in sight. Absent, always absent!

This day, Filly kicked up so high she got her hind legs in the buggy and broke eggs all over the seat, me, and my music books. I was scared half to death. I jumped out of the buggy and crawled through the wire fence right where I had first caught him with his boots off. I ran across the field to their house and yelled for help. His stepmother was at home. She suggested I telephone my Papa to come to get me out of my trouble.

I was too scared to talk so she called our home and she not only told them of my dilemma but told Mama off about letting girls drive horses alone — especially horses that had eaten green feed, which made them kick.

This lady was also one of Mama's shadows. Mama felt sure we could all have done better if we had not had this most refined woman move among us. It was just that we did not understand her ways. She had worked for many years as a social secretary in a mansion in Oklahoma before coming to our neighborhood as the second wife of Carl Traugott Adlof. Papa warned us that we were comparing her to the first Mrs. Adlof, whom we children thought of as an angel, before death as well as afterwards.

My sisters were all at home for a brief vacation one weekend. Lydia had completed her deaconess' training and was now stationed with a church in New Orleans. Pauline was also holding a position which included religious education for the church school. We had many interesting things to try to pack into one brief visit. Even with the busy hub-bub, someone noticed Mama's blues (depression, the doctors call it today — depression then meant only lack of money as far as I knew.)

Papa talked to the doctor about Mama, and the age-old advice was to have a change of scene by taking a trip. Papa knew the advice to be sound as he had attended a world's fair in California, a trip he had won through his ability as a salesman. He also valued the many little trips he was constantly taking. Even the taking of the census was inspiring to him.

It took a lot of planning to get away from a dairy, especially since we had new hands on the place this year. Nonnie and her brood had an opportunity to move to town and get work so we had to take on some new Negroes.

When the girls returned to their positions in the cities, they wrapped and mailed back their empty suitcases. After all, postage was cheaper than buying new cases. Our parents needed travel bags so seldom that we had none except those Pauline and Lydia had needed.

I told Papa I was going to write about their trip to the local paper. After all, such excitement was not an everyday event even for town people. He warned me not to write the first days as he did not want it published before they returned. It might hurt the butter business, he thought. Mama said no one need know that I would be alone all day in the house while the others were at school, either teaching or in classes.

I promised, but I had no intention of obeying. After all, Mr. Ollre would always give me a nickel for telling him some news. He delivered the papers from door to door in Gonzales, and he would take along a pencil and a piece of plain newsprint and jot down things he saw or was told on his daily rounds.

When he came along the next day or so as I was starting home from my music lesson, I handed him the neatly written story about my parents' trip. To make it longer, I had told about everything — suitcases had to be secured, we had new milk-hands doing the work, Mama was blue, and all sorts of inside publicity. Thank goodness for editors who cut out the details. Papa would have roasted me alive.

As it happened, I got a real stropping when they returned for having turned it in early. It showed by the date line of the paper just how early I had reported.

It stands out even today as one of the most exciting weeks of my whole fifty years to date. Two women came one afternoon in a new shiny car. They even had on beautiful white gloves and the pretty dusters that most town-women wore those days in their touring cars. They were collecting membership dues for the Parent-Teacher Association.

"My goodness, did you not know that Papa and Mama are gone to New Orleans this week? Don't you all read the papers?" were some of the things I must have popped at them through the front screen door which now had a hook and eye on it.

I explained that I could not sign anything for my parents. We knew better than to sign for them. We never opened mail addressed to anyone else than ourselves and we never made promises for others. I had trouble enough keeping my own promises and taking whippings for those I broke. But they insisted on getting somebody's money. It was my quarter-dollar they got, and it was I who became a member of the P-T-A when I was only fifteen.

It was a good shadow. Today though my children are through

college and belong to P-T-A themselves, I am still active in the membership of this most worthy organization for the promotion of the welfare of children and youth.

Ready or Not I'm Coming

Like the players of a hide-and-go-seek game cry out, "Ready or not, I'm coming!" so life came at me those days. It seemed to have its upstart during the week that my parents were away, or maybe it was then in my loneliness that it was more apparent. It seems each day was a week long. We arose extra early to make up for the things our parents would do when they were home. By seven, the car would be loaded and Olga and the twins would be off to school.

They would be late coming home as they had to pick up cream cans after school. Olga was very popular in school and often stayed for class meetings or to take part in some sports event. The twins had their hands full, too, trying to enter as many contests as possible in the county meet. So when I had the day's work of washing milk vessels, baking bread, ironing and sweeping done, I went to the crib early one afternoon to start on the week's corn shucking. I was just a-going after the corn, when the crib door closed behind me.

In a flash, the worse came to my mind. Could it be he was as strong as that other boy yesterday, I thought, as I saw this giant man standing at the half-shut crib door? I could think of no other escape than to jump out of the open "loochie" (hinged wooden window which has no glass panes) at the top of the heap of corn ears in the crib. In another flash, I scampered up to the opening and jumped out flat-footed. When I hit the ground, I just kept running.

I never stopped until I got to Buckholtz. It never occurred to me that I was running right back to where I had battled with the same imaginations and fears just yesterday. There was nobody at home there either and I just kept running. Why was I so frightened anyway? When I got to the road again, my sisters and brother came along and I got in the car with them.

I dared not tell them that this was the second day I had been frightened out of my wits. The day before, it was as much my fault as it was Walter's. In the first place, I was told to stay at home behind those hooked screen doors after Fanny, our new woman helper left the house and milk-house each morning. It was a crazy thing for me to do, but I did so want to take Walter some

70

pretty flowers while he had the chicken-pox. I should not have sat on his bed. After all, he was most nigh twenty now and we got into a real fight before he would let me go without kissing him.

"Did you get that scratch jumping out of the window?" George asked when I cautiously related my corn crib scare. I had a deep scratch on my hand where Walter had held me too tightly with his strong hands and good nails. George had evidently not noticed it the night before.

I thought George was too young and innocent to know what I had feared in that corn crib but he said, "Was you scared that Clarence would do you like that woman they found behind the oil-mill last week?" When we arrived home, we crept very quietly up to the crib, slid back the door, and there was Clarence just finishing filling the shell-corn barrel. Bless his heart! He had come for no other reason than to help with the work. He had even "gone the second mile" and shelled the corn we always waited until Saturday to do.

I was ridiculed and teased as we went into the house. As this was enough, I wouldn't tell them of my other fright. To our utter amazement when we went into the kitchen, supper was almost ready. Fanny had made the fire and had a long pan of biscuit, like none other than Negro cooks can bake, ready for us. She even brought us most of a cake which she had cooked at home. Oh, what an angel!

"Oh, Fanny!" I hugged and kissed her. "I am so ashamed that I ran away, and all this time I could have been here in the kitchen with you!" It seemed like a halo glowed around her kinky black hair and her big eyes shone with joy.

"Y'll chillen best et your vittals now and get to milking if y'll want me and Chauncie (Clarence) to hup y'll. He and Mose done got the beasts in the clip-stalls and we'se in a hurry 'kase we'se got preachin' tonight."

With all the help, we got through early and when they said they were going on to church early, we said we wished we could go along. And we did. Only they went with us. Pearl was at home that night, too, and she was the best driver so we all piled in and headed north to the little church on Smith Creek Road. The Lord was already there when we got there and the pastor preached, "Lo, I am with you always even unto the end of the world."

"Even in the corn-crib and on my neighbor boy's bed," I thought, "He guarded me." Even to this day, I treasure the sermon from the little preacher in the tiny wooden church in the country.

Count One By One

I learned a valuable lesson that week: people are never counted in groups if one wishes to evaluate people. They stand one by one. Even groups depend on one by one to make up their number. Perhaps the text of my most frequent daily sermon, by word or example, is based on this knowledge. Never judge people by races, by nationalities, by groups of any type. If at all you need to evaluate people in order to know what to expect of one or to try to understand one's actions, set him in your mind as an individual.

It was no more Walter's fault that he should have made improper advances than it was my fault to sit on his bed with my long, blonde hair falling over the shoulders of my blue chambray dress. Had he not teased me often before about being his girl? Also, I had no right to be afraid just because Clarence's face was black.

Nor should it ever have been fourteen years before I was privileged to hear the pastor of the Negro Community Church sing, pray and preach. We should have heard him often for he surely could make one know the presence of God. Neither did I have the right to assume that the Adlof boy, really he was a grown man, came to see *me* the next day at noon. Not everyone thought my beautiful blonde hair was an attraction. Mostly, it was Elvira and her father in town who adored my hair. She would sit by the hour and brush it for me. I loved being loved. Don't you?

But he came, Arthur Adlof did. It was during the noon hour while he was letting his mules, Beck and Judy, eat and rest. I knew their names. I knew most all the farmers' mules names, and I even knew what else many of them called their mules as I walked by unnoticed some windy days. It was Saturday and I was sure as sure can be that he was coming to see *me*. Of course, Pearl and Olga knew better. There was to be an Epworth League meeting in the church that night. He surely was coming to ask to take *them*. At any rate, there was his pretty new Overland touring car at our yard gate.

I'm sure they went to the door together, knowing all the time if one was asked the other would go along. I'm sure they were nice to him as we were all taught to be courteous to our neighbors and other callers. I'm sure it was a warm day, or something really had me in a sweat. I was also sure I was going to be asked to go.

I got fooled. He did not ask anyone to go. He talked about the weather, the meeting to be that night, what the next rally would be about and a dozen or more short sentences like that — all short as he was most bashful. I was shoved back again and again from the doorway; and when the telephone suddenly rang, it was I who had to answer.

Imagine that! Me! Answer the phone with two eager older sisters waiting for dates to call. They always did call, first one and then others. Little did we know that day what Arthur came to see us about. He came and left; that was about all we knew for sure. I had no right to assume that he came to see me, but I made up my mind to see that he would after this.

He did come again, the very next afternoon. He came this time on what I like to remember as though it were from a fairy tale, "charging like a knight on his great white stallion." Only his horse was not white. That was good. One white horse, Cora, was enough in my life. He rode a dark bay mare. He rode down the lane along one tire-track trail while Walter rode on his horse along the other. They were buddies and often rode all Sunday afternoon; then they rode again to church that night into town. In the mornings, Arthur used his new car; but at night, he liked to hear the clip-clop of the hoofs of the horse on the newly cemented streets in town.

We really had a hey-day that Sunday. Of course, it would have been all right to have had all these friends come even if our parents were at home, for they approved of company. Seems, though, we must have had the whole community there. At least, it seemed that way next day. If Mama had been at home, the dishes would have all been washed and put in the china closet after church that night .Olga and Pearl had dates, however, and the twins and I hit the beds early. We were too tired to give dishes a second thought.

Just as I was done with the milk and cream separator work the next day and Fanny was doing the washing, Arthur came to the house. This time he walked over from his fields where he had left his team in the care of some men who were pulling up large blood-weeds along the Ronshausen lane. I did not see him until I turned when I heard Fanny say, "Mornin', Mr. Arthur. Is you all looking fo' Mr. Ebel?"

He stayed a short time, talking again of the weather and then

73

wanting to know if we had seen one of his hound dogs. How many more times in the next few years he came looking for his hounds, only God knows.

The next day as I was walking back from town, I heard a horn tooting a long way behind me just after I left the city limits. I was thrilled, for in the last few weeks Mr. Halm had stopped to pick me up several times. My, he had a nice car, and now I thought he was coming again. And so soon after I started the long trek. How lucky! How lucky was right, for it was not old Mr. Halm, my grandpa's age, but Arthur.

Why was I so sure he would stop to pick me up? He took me all the way home this time, and when I invited him in, he said we could sit on the porch for a while. That suited me fine, for I had yet to learn not to be afraid of every young man. I was just as anxious as any girl to catch a fellow, but I was puzzled as to what I'd do with one if I caught him.

He asked to take me to the youth rally that weekend, and I said I could not go for I was not yet fifteen, the age one was allowed to join the group in which he belonged. And the silly boy said, "My goodness, I sure thought you were now seventeen. I can remember when you were born, and I was glad when my mother said you all had another girl."

Queer how people can live within a mile of each other, go to church and prayer services together so often, and then see each other "once upon a time" as if they never before had met. While his mother was yet living, we visited often at their house. Perhaps, though, we never saw Arthur, for they tell that he hid for hours and hours under the log-barn to keep from playing with girls. Could be!

Now, all of a sudden, he came on the scene, just like magic. With a new car, a good-looking Stetson with an eight-inch brim, high top shoes in the new oxblood color, and breeches as tight as the best that Hoskins Brothers could find, he was a "killer" (the kids say these days).

The folks came home, and the call came one noon to ask for permission to go with him to the Thanksgiving youth rally. I did not get to go. I had told Papa and Mama when they returned that I had been invited, but I had better sense than to tell them who had invited me and just when and where.

When he 'phoned, Mama told him that of course I could not go with him. She said *Pearl* was staying in town that evening, but that he should come by to pick up *Olga;* and she had made a

74

large enough cake for them to take that his step-mother need not trouble herself to make one. Mama! I could have screamed. What did she mean by that? *I* was just then making the cake, and I had a good notion to leave out the baking powder so it would be a flop. How dare she say we were making a big cake for them to take when it was my date-to-be?

She wound up saying I was to stay over at the Buckholtz' that night with the little ones while "his age" went to the rally and the old folks finished the milking. They always milked until about midnight.

Heavens, I was not going to their house at night! I never told a soul about the scratch on my hand and neither Walter nor I ever had words of love, fears and such again. I did not go to the party, and I was too sick to go take care of any children. By night, I had a fever, and Olga had to have Papa take her to the church rally. Goody! Arthur didn't come!

More and more now, I would visit with our hired hands as I would walk by their place going to the pasture to look for some cow that had dropped a new calf. Or I would have to go ask the mother of the hired family to come and help us with the work. Mama was much better spiritually since her trip, but she did have so much trouble with backaches. Papa, too found the work harder and harder as the children became less and less able to help with the chores.

The twins were now taking their Catechism and Olga was beginning to think of graduation plans. We surely hoped graduation day would not be as it was two years ago when on the Saturday before Baccalaureate Sunday, the storm had come and killed more than two hundred young turkeys. Pearl had graduated that year. Graduation expenses with other things had made it very hard for us to have such a loss in May. Not only were the young dead turkeys scattered all over the barn-yard, but the houses were ruined; more than one of the pig-stalls were blown over; and piggies were drowned by the dozens.

Pearl had needed money for extras for graduation things such as a beautiful white organdy dress. In those days, only colleges used the caps and gowns for their commencement exercises. Any-way, as far as we knew, the schools all had their girls dressed in white for the big programs to which the whole community went (unless it rained). This was the case for Pearl's day. Papa had to take her in the buggy and he had to hook two horses to the buggy.

75

Not that her dress was that big, but the mud after the night's storm was knee-deep all the way to the public road.

It seemed my fifteenth birthday would never arrive. I had made myself a promise: I would catch that Adlof boy for keeps, and I would make sure he admitted it.

If so many other girls had not openly told me they were after him . . . their Mamas were in favor of their plots . . . maybe I would not have been so bent on my intentions. I did not want to be left out of everything; already I felt left out by being out of public school.

It was a Sunday morning in late spring when Miss Meta Nagel, our Sunday School class teacher, asked us to take turns at reading the lesson text that this complex came to the surface.

Several girls had read a verse each. As it came my turn, one of the girls cut in to declare that I should be excused from reading. She said in tones that rang through the one-room church where all classes were assembled in small groups, "Viola doesn't go to school anymore so she, maybe, can not read those big words, Miss Meta."

I almost bawled. How dared she? Did she not know that I not only read many hours each night, but I also wrote stories, pages and pages of longhand? Why, I had even gotten so good at riding old Filly that I could ride backwards and write on her rump while astride watching the cows. Filly walked back and forth between the patch of grazing the cows were to stay in and the field they were to stay out for later grazing.

The lesson must have been about judging others, for Miss Meta defended me promptly by telling the class that we should not attempt to judge others; especially did she drill into us the folly of judging people by groups. Each of us was to be responsible for our separate actions. I can still see Miss Meta in my memory today.

She now lives in Houston, and I'll bet she still dresses like a fashion model each Sunday and goes to church. She was a seamstress as well as a bookkeeper for a downtown business house. Each Sunday she would bring to us some real-life experience. I recall one time she told us of a little boy pressing his nose against the showcase so hard and so long that it began to turn blue. All he wanted was the last Sunday's funny papers to take home for his mother.

"It takes so little to make some people happy," Miss Meta said. That day when she defended me as being able to read, she used only time and words; but, oh, how happy it left me. I have been aware ever since of the value of a few kind words spoken in defense of some person or cause. I pray daily for the courage to speak up when the opportunity presents itself. I owe Miss Meta a life-time of witnessing.

On another occasion during those same days, it came to my attention that one often errs when he uses such expressions as "those Niggers are all lazy" . . . we knew better as we had many about our neighborhood who worked hard. Or "Mexicans all steal; better lock your barn if you have one working for you" . . . could anything be more unjust? Or in the case of many of us who had German heritage: "You can't expect anything better from a flat-headed Dutchman."

Miss Meta was and still is right — as right as day follows night — that God created man, each one, (not in the plural) in His own image and breathed the breath of life into each . . . "into him," not into "them," the lesson teaches.

Would that I had also learned at that early age to tackle *days* one at a time, rather than in the far distant plural future. Life in those days took on such a huge dimension — still does many times — that it seemed and seems impossible to make the grade. Now, after stumbling time and again, I have learned how to tithe my time better. The first requirement is to take time a day at a time, one by one.

Early in the week, usually on Sunday mornings, I take a pencil and make myself a week's schedule. Is that contradicting what I have just said — a day at a time? It is not. By setting all known tasks on certain days, I can wipe them from my mind and remember only one thing: read my list each afternoon. On days when everything clicks just right, I often find as I read the list that I have time left over. These are the times I can afford to do as I please — do some extra reading, plant some flower seeds, take a bouquet to a friend or help someone who seems to be behind in his work.

That's how I can manage to keep going despite a heart ailment, frequent illnesses and many hours spent out-of-doors on the farm. As in the days when Miss Meta was my teacher, when Elvira Neumann and I were close pals, when sunset meant time to milk cows, when rainy days meant extra chores in the barn and in the house, my life continues to be happy. Happy because it is so full of work to be done every day. There are tasks that someone is expecting me to have completed.

"Give us this day our daily bread." Bread to me means the total substance necessary for life worthy of a Christian: work to do, strength to do it, patience and courage, love and inspiration. These must be on our daily diets or we shall be undernourished.

Fish Must Be Caught

We often went over to the river on the Otto Ehrig farm where the two families would fish, swim, and eat all day. Their children ranged from my age down to a baby still on the lap these days. Usually we went only during the hot summer months, about three times a year. This spring for some reason we went early. It was just April.

Mr. Ehrig frankly announced at the picnic spread on the huge wagon-sheet and white tablecloth that it was high time some of of August and Emma's girls looked good at his nice big boys. True enough, they were as handsome as any boys could be. Yet had I not made up my mind otherwise? After lunch Mr. Ehrig flopped back onto the sand and announced that he would first nap even though he *knew* fish must be caught that day.

He was so positive about it. There must have been something planned like a fish-fry at the church or at the Woodmen's Lodge for which they needed good, freshly-dressed river catfish. Perhaps the fish at Gonzales are still the best. I wouldn't really know for the only part of his booster-talk that stuck with me was "fish must be caught."

I made up my mind to do just that; early the next day, I would! So on April 29 when the milking was done, the others were off to school, and Mama was safely seated in the kitchen with a bushel basket of green beans to snap, I went "fishing." For bait, I used my older sister's new pink checked gingham dress that had a complete circle for its skirt. I knew from ironing the dress how pretty it would look on my skinny frame.

I was taking an awful risk; not only would Mama have Papa tan my hide with his razor-strop if she saw me stop to "fish for a date" with that Adlof "scamp" (Mama called him that since the night he didn't come for Olga and the cake), but I was putting on the very dress Olga forgot to take along that morning to wear for a tea at school. Brother! It's a wonder I ever made it back alive. I was so excited that I couldn't get the whole mile to the fence row by the time Beck and Judy pulled the cane-seed drill there.

I ran into the house at Ronshausen's and pretended I was

79

just coming to see her. You couldn't keep a secret from her. Mrs. Alma, we often called her Aunt Alma, looked right at me, handed me a cup of strong black coffee, and demanded that I wait for "him" to make another round in the field and then be there "just at the right minute." She even went with me to the fence and helped me get through without tearing my borrowed lure.

It was perfect fishing weather, cloudy and still, and the fish I caught was a gem. I was the only one, though, that knew I had caught this gem. The "fish" didn't know he was hooked until a long time after this.

"Where are you going?" he asked, just as if he hadn't seen me walk right by there many times before when I would be allowed to go to Reid Ward to visit or to coach the girl's basketball. They were little girls and they only played for the fun of it.

"I'm not looking for hounds, that's for sure. I was told to come over and remind you not to miss the Shivaree tonight for the Pagels."

He said he knew about it and intended to go. But I just could not get him to ask to take me. Fearful that Papa might be coming home and see me in Olga's good dress, I was in a hurry to get back home. I had not learned fisherman's patience. As I was about to leave he said, "What do you have your hair pinned up on your head like that for? Looks like an old woman. Take it down like it belongs."

Oh! That made me so mad. After all the trouble I had taken to look old enough to be asked to go with him. I hurried home; to save the risk of tearing Olga's dress, I gathered the full skirt up in my arms and ran the long way around by the open lane and public road. I was just a-flying along when the rural mail carrier came to the box. He laughed and laughed at me.

"Who's growing up? Honey, let that skirt loose. You are going to crush all that starch job that way."

Troubles, troubles! Safely back in the house through one of the front doors on the porch, I managed to get the dress pressed and hung up before Mama finished with the beans. Then we strung beans together. She noticed my flushed face. I get as red as a beet when I hurry about anything.

I guess I made up some sort of excuse. (The standard one of not getting an answer from some farm magazine about some story I had sent them usually served for any upset I had.) Mama agreed with me about being a good writer. Actually, Mama and I were my only real fans.

80

At noon the telephone rang to tell us that Olga was heart-broken because she had forgotten to take the pink dress along. This was Monday; and this spring, she, Pearl and the twins were staying in an apartment in town until school was out early in June, She said the tea was postponed anyway until that night because of some conflict in the school schedule. Would Mama, please, have Papa bring the dress in by that time?

Bring the dress to town? Drive all the way back to town, six miles round trip, just so one of his daughters could wear a certain dress! Mama knew Papa would say, "And what is wrong with her other dresses? Indeed not!"

Papa had taken the "tribe" and enough produce to keep them through the week to town that morning. After all, Mama explained, that was the idea of their having that apartment in town. (They had been forever wanting the car to go back at night, and they all had such different schedules.) Mama was afraid of Papa in some ways. Perhaps she knew it was only by wise use of money that we had as many things as we did. I know sometimes she thought he was a real "knoster." That may not be a word but we used it to denote a miser.

Oh joy! It was a good day after all. The telephone rang again during the noon hour. This time Papa answered it. Mama had told him of Olga's call, and she thought this was Olga again. I guess Papa thought it too. Never one to overlook an opportunity, either to serve or to let someone do a kind thing for us, he swallowed this particular call hook, line and sinker.

I was so excited. I knew from Papa's half of the conversation that I was to go to the party at Pagel's that night with Arthur. Immediately Mama threw a wall-eyed fit! I was not to go; I was too young to be alone with a man on a country road at night! Gosh! I had not even thought of that angle. Thank goodness for all the information Mamas give their daughters when they shout out," Don't you dare do so and such!"

But Papa had said, "Arthur, could you please come by six-thirty? We need to send something to the children in town that they want by seven and you would sure save me a trip." Oh, joy! It was now already one and in just five and a half hours, I would be on my way. Like Mr. Ehrig said, "Fish must be caught."

Of course, a cake had to be baked. Mama would not dream of letting one of her girls walk onto the scene of a church party without a cake in hand. Mama was mad, though, and nothing short of a hurricane would move her to make the cake.

Papa knew this. He went out to the wood-pile to cut some kindling and came in and poked up the fire so the oven would heat. He swore he was going to buy us a kerosene range if it was the last thing he ever did. He hated to make fires. In the kitchen we had pots and pots of green beans in jars processing with some sort of acid which he had brought from the drug store.

Papa said, "Bake one of those raisin cakes. Maybe you can write "Pagel" on it in raisins. Get you some cream out of the milk-house icebox for the icing." We called all cake toppings "icing" whether they were fudge, egg-white or butter-scotch.

It turned out to be a real nice cake. It made much more of a hit with my neighbor boy date than did my hair knotted on top of my head that morning or my sister's borrowed dress. I was very careful to wear my own dress that night, and I let my hair hang on my back, tied back only with a blue ribbon to match the embroidery on my tan pongee dress. Pearl had made the dress for me for Easter. It is among my souvenirs.

Mama reminded me that this was just a neighborly good turn. I was not to talk about anything that went on at home. We were to go directly to the apartment to leave the dress which she had carefully packed in a large box; were to go to the "Katzenyammer" (that's another name we called house-warming parties for newly-weds) and to be at home by ten. She did not mean maybe!

I did start out with those intentions. I did sit there just as if I were riding home from my music lesson with, perhaps, good old neighbor Halm. But it was a windy evening; and, my, how silk pongee can blow in an open touring car. We were hardly to our mail-box when that naughty neighbor giggled and said, "Having trouble with the wind? Move over to the middle of the seat where it won't blow so much!"

"Which seat, the back seat?" I asked. For the moment I was a scared little fourteen-year old again who did not get much schooling.

He assured me he did not mean for me to get in the back seat. I soon found out what he meant, really. So I decided it best just to put the dress box on my lap. That way my bony knees would not show and I would look so much more grown-up. Mama had carefully set the cake box on the seat between us. Soon we were in town, and everyone knew it for blocks around! It was the fad to pull some button on the car "dash-board" which would open the cut-out muffler, and the noise it made! My, oh my!

People today think teenagers are "hot-rodders." They only go faster; they could not think faster. That would be impossible.

We had a wonderful time at the party. We played ring games, and then we had the cake feast. The long table on the lawn held all manner of cakes. The couple was sorta' in the family of Adlofs as the groom was a brother of Arthur's youngest sister's husband. She and her husband fixed several pitchers of iced lemonade for the refreshments.

Suddenly, it was ten o'clock. Dear me! I insisted we must get home. Anyway, most everyone was getting ready to leave. It was not our custom to stay much later. Most of us had to work in the fields or elsewhere every day, and by ten we were ready to make friends with the feather-beds.

Scrambling into the car in my worry about what Mama would say and Papa might do for my coming home late, I became very careless. The wind blew. The dress fluttered. All of a sudden, in a bright flash of lightning, I saw my legs were uncovered at least an inch over my knees. Gracious, woe be to me if Mama had seen it!

"Are you afraid it will rain?" I asked my date.

"No, I am more afraid it will not. I hope that it does so that cane I planted today will come up and grow. I surely need a big hay crop. I'm buying another team of mules this fall. But, honey, (I almost had heart failure) I *am* afraid for it to rain on you."

"Why, I have been wet before in many rains. I even helped get those little pigs in that time we had the storm and . . .," I started to explain.

"Yes, but sugar melts in the rain, and you are pure sugar."

I knew I had caught a fish . . . a real fish! Even the sound boxing I got on the side of my head as I went through the bathroom hall at home did not faze my enthusiasm. I was as happy as a lark, full of lemonade and cake, and I had no intentions of sleeping that night anyway. I had thinking to do . . . no time to waste sleeping, crying, or even explaining that I had no watch and did not know it was a quarter after ten before we left the party.

Summer came and crops were bountiful. Work, work, work — we never lacked for work. Yet we had lots of fun along with our chores. Either we would be at the Buckholtz' on Sunday afternoons, or they would be at our house. Later many other friends would be there: my sisters' boy friends, other neighbors, and even lots of the "Americana," like Grandmother said. We would spend some afternoons in town with our friends after church, but mostly only one at the time could do this so there would still be a full enough crew for the evening's milking.

The town kids thought it was a real lark to come to our house. They would scamper around in the barn and up the silo to help throw down the ensilage and hunt eggs with us like they thought it was all some sort of an everyday Easter hunt. Sure, it was all fun for them. Things we do not have to do usually are more fun than work.

We country kids got many secret thrills out of their accidents, though. It was probably not very nice of us to laugh, but who could help but roar with glee when the bull chased that woppy fat Nixon boy? Or how could you keep from snickering when Stella tried to milk the bull? (At least, she told George he had forgotten to put that "cow" in the clip-row in the stall.) George, always full of spark, advised her to go out in the lot and run in "that" cow for him. Good thing Olga was there!

Then there was the time when our cousin from Dallas was visiting, and she had never seen chicks hatch. Why she wouldn't leave the barn until the old cluck had actually pecked that girl's knees until the blood ran.

Imagine! Children who didn't know all these important things!

Growing up on a farm makes up for all the hard work one has to do. It is like Papa used to tell us about a friend he knew in his early days in Lavaca County: the man had more than his share of misfortune. Papa went one day among many such visits to console his friend. The friend, in turn, taught Papa this great and simple lesson, "How would we know to recognize sunshine if we had never had cloudy days?"

How would we?

Years, Tears and Careers

After Olga graduated, she found a good position in town as a bookkeeper and moved there. Papa was so proud for he had often said, "Now that is the business woman of this family."

I have never wished to challenge that statement. Today, just for the heck of it I still have a silver dollar dated 1924 with the head of the statue of Liberty on one side and the American Eagle on the other. It is as bright as the day it was given to me by Papa. I handle it often as it is in the bottom of my letter-box on my typing table.

He was all dressed and waiting for Mama to get ready to go to Olga's commencement when he gave me the dollar. It served its purpose for I have forgotten why I did not get to go along. I have saved the dollar all these years. Olga, no doubt, would have invested it.

We were proud of her and the other sisters who were doing fine. But we did miss her as it took another good helper out of the "cowpen" force. Mama was not getting any younger and stronger. Papa had to help more than ever, and so again it was decided I might as well stay out of school.

This time, it was not my idea nor fault. I had intended to sacrifice only one full year. Even though I still hated climbing stairs, I did hope to return to school. I knew that most of the classes in high school to which I had now advanced by home study were in the first floor rooms — just about a dozen steps higher than the basement and entrance doors.

I cried and cried, but nothing could be arranged except for me to stay at home and help. That is, until one day the Morelands came seeking a place to live and work. At last, though now it was already November, I could go back to school again.

Mama was glad for me, too. And Olga was glad. She brought some material for me to have a new dress to start in when she came home to spend the weekend. It is the only time in my life that I can recall Mama sewing on the sewing machine on Sunday. And Papa did not scold about it being done on Sunday.

I dearly loved all my teachers. High school grades then were eighth, ninth, tenth and eleventh. Today, our high school has twelve grades. My favorite teacher was a Mrs. Hemphill.

She was very thorough yet very understanding with us. We would go from room to room for our class periods. The newness of these many changes was too much for my nerves, and by Christmas I was sick in bed again. I do not know what was my trouble.

Mrs. Hemphill had sent me to the principal's office one day to get a box of chalk, and there I just konked out, dead as a doorknob.

At first, the principal thought it was from an injury, for only a few days before I had gotten in the way of a fast-moving baseball. It had laid me out, too. I had been taken into the little "recovery room" in the girls' basement and stayed there until time to go home at four. (School in those days started at nine in the mornings and ended at four in the afternoons with a full hour for noon recess — the best hour of the day.)

But evidently the injury did not cause the flop-out for shortly I was back in circulation again.

This Moreland family who had come to live on our place were truly fine workers. They had more workers in their family, in fact, than Papa could afford to pay; so their eldest son Freddie needing to look elsewhere for work, found it with Arthur. Arthur had bought an extra team and needed another plowman. I soon developed a grapevine system through the plowman's mother to keep posted on how "my" Arthur was getting along. I waited and watched for an opportunity to see him all by myself once again.

Early in December on a Saturday, Papa gave us three younger children each a dollar to go Christmas shopping. Now we made a list. It had something on it for every member of the family: Papa, Mama, the two sisters away, Pearl who was teaching school, Olga the business lady, the twins, my father's mother, my Sunday School teachers and, of course, a couple of close friends. Imagine trying to buy all those gifts for one dollar. Imagine even more: going into a jewelry store to ask what they had to offer in the way of bargains . . . with only three dollars between the three of us!

Or maybe I went into Jahnke's Jewelry Store just because I saw a certain shining bay mare hitched to the post in the square by the fire-station, across the street from the stores.

"Goodness, Arthur! You buying that for somebody for Christmas?"

"Sure am!" was about all he answered. I wondered how puzzling a person could be. Last spring he had the nerve to tell me I was his honey and that I was made of sugar! Here, in the store, he hardly knew who I was.

86

Just for meanness, I told him if I were going to spend that much money, I'd at least buy something useful — like maybe one of those new "vanities." That is what we called compacts holding powder and rouge.

I was very depressed trying to buy all my gifts with so little money. Yet it had its advantages. That way, we did get to spend hours looking. We went from Duke and Ayres to the racket-store on main street comparing prices of their tin pie-plates, cotton handkerchiefs, and such items as picture postcards. These we finally bought, and among us we had enough money left to buy a package of tissue paper and a spool of colored Christmas twine.

But depression turned to exhilaration the afternoon of Christmas Day! I was now fifteen and a half and belonged to the Epworth League at the German Methodist Church. We had given our Christmas program early that year as other conference plans were underway for December 25. So this afternoon, the whole gang was in our play-yard. And Arthur was not missing.

He had ridden his horse over so we could enjoy taking turns at riding, he confessed. We knew he came to show off the beautiful mare. Waiting my turn, I leaned against the sunny side of the carhouse. Before you could say "Jack Robinson," he came over to my side and slipped a package into my overcoat pocket.

I was thrilled speechless (for once). Unwrapping it without everyone seeing me took some doing. Gracious! It was the very vanity I had pointed out in the jewelry store. "I can't take this. Mama would have a spell," I confessed quietly.

"I did not buy it for your Mama."

"I know that, but what will Mama say when she sees it? She will make me give it back to you. It isn't proper for me to take it," I said, while all the time I knew I would keep it — no matter what!

He suggested letting him keep it for me. I thought that a good idea, and he slipped it into his inner vest pocket. I thought, of course, I would get to see it often as surely now I was his steady girl. But I was wrong again. Very few times in the next months did I go with him or on any other dates. When I did go, there would always be a sister along. Once when there was no sister available to accompany me, Mama told my little brother to go. He refused. And that was that. When George said he would not do a thing, seldom did anyone persuade him to do otherwise.

During the Christmas holidays, Miss Lula (Arthur's sister) came home for a visit. She was now a graduate nurse from the

Santa Rosa Hospital School of Nursing in San Antonio. She brought a uniform along so we could all see her in it. Mrs. Adlof invited us over for coffee on one of the days. Now that was just what I wanted to be — a nurse! She did look so beautiful.

I pondered the idea for many days to come. I did not get back to school the next semester and the next best thing we could do was order a correspondence course. When I mentioned wanting to be a nurse, Papa said that took a strong person, not one who got the tummy-ache every time something unusual happened. Mama suggested I just study the lessons in the school books we had at home from the older ones. We bought text books in those days.

So a choice of a career rocked along until sometime that fall. It was September again and a new minister had come to visit "just to see Papa and find out what our church was like." We liked him very much and looked forward to annual conference, hoping he and his wife would be sent to Gonzales and Stieren Ranch, the country charge connected with our church pastorage. They did come, the Rev. and Mrs. O. C. Raeke, and they had no children. At first we missed the preacher's children so much that we were not sure we liked the Raekes after all. Soon we changed our minds.

Here was a couple one could talk all his troubles over with and even get some real honest-to-goodness answers to questions. I recall my first visit with them while I was staying an afternoon with my Grandma and aunts. We were setting out all manner of plants in their garden plots, made up of tiny beds with little foot-paths just wide enough for one to walk down single file.

The chubby little pastor and his even chubbier little wife came down one of these little paths where my aunts and I were working. The first thing that I recall the preacher's talking about was how amazed he was at all the things that could grow in such close quarters. My crippled aunt explained that because of their shading each other and protecting each other from wind, her plants did much better standing that close.

They visited quite a while. I adored them both, right from the start and even that very afternoon I asked them to advise me what to do with my life. I, too, wanted some type of career. They did not laugh at me like everyone else did when I told of first wanting to be a preacher, then hoping to be a teacher, and now wanting to be a nurse just like Miss Lula Adlof. But the kindly little minister reached down and took one of the cabbage plants we were setting out and said, "Plant this one and mark it. If you take good care of it, it will probably make a nice big cabbage

88

head; but I believe you will find there won't be another head in this whole garden just exactly like this one."

I asked Aunt Lou later what the new preacher meant about the one plant being like no other. To me, cabbage heads row after row all looked like cabbage heads (and potential sauer-kraut.) Not to my dear little crippled aunt, they didn't. She knew that everyone must make a career for himself.

"You mean we don't pattern after someone else? If not, then why is it that so many farmers have farmer sons and store keepers have store keeping sons and . . . "

"We had better get done with the plants. Now you do as the pastor told you. You set out that one!"

I made some sort of excuse the next day to get to walk to the country school when all the morning work was done. The truth was that I just had to tell Arthur about the new preacher. I liked being the messenger for the folks around our neighborhood. I'd hurry with my work on days that I felt well and take a walk here and there to tell some neighbor about something. I used the excuse mostly, however, to walk toward the school where I would perchance find Arthur at the end of a field row.

We came to know each other quite well in this way. On days when I was ill, he usually came looking for stray hounds. I think Papa was wise to our little tricks, for one morning at breakfast he said, "I wish you all would look out there! There really *is* a a stray hound in the barnyard. I did not think there ever was such a thing." The way he looked at me and laughed, I had a feeling he "smelled a rat." That's what we said for "found us out."

He must not have minded, for he went away from the table to see about watering the dog at the gate. And as he returned he was singing. He was singing, "Du, du liegst mir im herzen," (you, you are always in my heart.) When Papa sang that I felt secure and happy.

The new minister had approved the idea of the women raising money at the county fair and had wanted them to continue to have their benefit dinners for the church funds. Yet he was the first one I ever heard tell about the possibility of us someday selling or taking down our buildings and worshipping with the so-called "English" church. At first some of us thought he must have no notion at all what a difference there was between the Dutchmen and the Americans.

We soon learned better. Rev. and Mrs. Raeke came from the Texas hill country near Fredericksburg, and they knew as much

89

about such matters as could be known. He was so interested in making friends for the church that soon even some of those who once ridiculed us during the war now began coming to our services. A few of the young men and women even dated these "foreign" creatures.

It was a blow to my plans when this tall farmer I claimed for my very own started dating girls with such names as Smith, Slick and even Brown. This was too much to keep all to myself. I just had to talk with someone. So to Mrs. Raeke I went. They were both at home, and what else could I do but tell them both, right then and there, all my worries? I just knew they would advise my parents of some school to send me to or of some place I could work, something like nuns do. I was now almost sixteen and I still had no steady fellow.

Life now certainly appeared to be a dark and gloomy affair. If I had only had a chance to finish high school, to teach, or even just work in the candy kitchen and look pretty there by the pink taffy, I could see a way out for me. The preacher told me I would probably make a good wife and mother and that was the world's greatest career. I decided then maybe he did know about my greatest desire; I told him I'd be back someday with a man for him to marry me to. Today I blush to think of my brazen announcement.

When Christmas came, my campaign was well underway. I had found many new ways to get to see my lover. Freddie Moreland carried little notes back and forth for both of us. I recall one that was a dilly. Arthur wrote that "come heaven or hell fire, he was going to come over for a date once a week from now on." He reminded me of the many times he had told me how pretty I was and a bunch of stuff like that. There was a poem, "As sure as rats run over the rafter, you are the gal I am after," and on and on. It must have taken him the whole time while the mules ate their noon feed to write me.

At the very end of the page, in sweated penciling, he added: "It is drizzling now, and so I may not get to see you tonight yet."

But he started coming each week and not only to ask about stray hounds. He came in the car or on the horse and was dressed up fit to go to a dance. We would sit in the parlor and talk; or sometimes while I played the piano, he and Papa would exchange farming ideas and plans.

For Christmas he brought me two packages. The larger one he handed me with the whole family looking on as I had been

90

allowed to invite him to the family gathering in the afternoon. It was a mirror, comb and brush set. Very pretty!

I was really happy with the gift, most especially since Mama was sweet about it. She made the remark about the girls had always wished for a mirror on each dresser so they wouldn't have to borrow back and forth.

Being one who was always either way up in the clouds or down in the ditch emotionally, I probably prissed around looking at my hair in every mirror in the house. The one we all liked the best was the little oblong mirror hung on the back porch where Papa shaved. I went out to see how I looked by using two mirrors there, and Arthur followed me.

Right there on our back porch, he gave me another package. It was a gorgeous white gold wrist watch — a real, genuine Elgin from Jahnke's.

The Raekes were there, too. I showed the watch to Rev. Raeke first, and he complimented me saying that I was making real progress. He winked at me. Mama blushed as she happened to see his wink. Later, she scolded about it. She was afraid there might be something very sinfully wrong with a preacher who did not know that winking is flirting.

"It does not say anything about that in the ten commandments," I argued.

When the folks were over-tired, anything could and usually did happen to set off a real lively argument . . . about this, that and some other things. Now Papa reminded us that it was his mother's firm belief that it meant bad luck for the next year if a family argued at Christmas. That is how we came to the custom of being asked every Christmas if we were content with what gifts we had gotten.

This year, although Papa had asked it as routinely as ever on Christmas Eve, he asked it again. He shouted the question to us from his bed after all lamps were blown. It was I who answered first, "It is a start anyway!"

No one listened; or anyway, there were no other answers or comments.

When A Girl Is Sixteen At Last

Is there anything as slow in arriving as a girl's sixteenth birthday? There was an endless amount of work to be done, and plans were humming for the best and the biggest county fair Gonzales had ever had. Mama and Papa looked forward to this with enthusiasm as they were certain many of their entries would take blue ribbons. Extra care was taken when doing the spring and summer canning and preserving so that the best looking Mason jars would be set back on the pantry shelf; protected even farther with a paper bag or newspaper wrapping. The best heads of grain, ears of corn, bolls of cotton, pumpkins, pie-melons and what-not-all were carefully prepared for the fall show.

In Live Oak County these years as I assist with county fairs, it is with a feeling of tribute to my parents' interest and pride in showing that with which the Lord had so bountifully blessed us. A county fair is not true to its name, I feel, if there are no shining rows of canned goods from the kitchens of the farms and towns. If there is no display of produce . . . no plates of pecans and peanuts, no corn-ears made even more beautiful by rubbing them gently . . . no homemade syrup or jars of honey, it just is not a county fair for me.

I am sixteen again, each year, if I am asked to help with the county fair.

With all the work, there were still chances to get little snatches of visits to the Reid Ward School, and always, I looked for just the right day when I would be seeing my lover along the lane. Never was I more thrilled than when on an unusually tiring day I stopped to rest under the big oak tree in the corner of the road down in the first valley. To my delight I saw a heart carved on the trunk of the old tree. In the heart my initials and "A.E.A." were carved. Did I need to ask who did that?

I did ask anyway. Just because I wanted to hear him say he did. At first he teased me saying I must have done it. This made me cry. I had a feeling he was catching on to how desperately I was "chasing" him. I knew in my heart that it was not considered right to be so eager that a boy could notice. Then he admitted that he had worked far into the night with his coon-hunting head-light to get it done by this particular day — Valentine's Day.

My brother and I became very close pals. When he and Celia would come home from school in the evenings, she usually had to help in the house or in the milk-house with chores that Mama could not get done alone. Bud and I would do the milking along with Papa, and ofttimes a hired man would have to help.

We made up sort of a clique in teasing poor little twin-sister. She hated to wash dishes with a dark brown hatred, and we always accused her of "getting sick hiccups right after meals." She did have this ailment, and now we are old enough to know that it was not any more laziness than was my diarrhea.

She also had to wear glasses earlier in life than any of us; the big, perfectly round horn-rims made her look like an owl as she peered out from under the thick bangs of her hair, cut in the then popular Dutch bob. As we passed things at the table, George and I would say to Celia, "Like to have a worm?"

I recall our parents forbidding us to call that style of hair "Dutch." And what they did to us when they heard us tease Celia — well, you wouldn't believe it anyway.

The twins are three years younger than I, and though any of the rest of the family could tease and pick on one of them as much as we could get by with, we never tackled them as a team. They truly stuck together when it came to a show-down. Mama used to tell us that she now believed the old-wifery about twins feeling pains at the same time even though they were miles apart.

George even tried for a long time to imitate Celia's hiccups.

The twins were very popular at church, too. When summer began to draw near, we started practicing for the program we would give at the annual Sunday School picnic. That was the event of the year. The adults would set the date in a special conference; and committees would get ready for an event that could only have been out-done if the president of the United States had come to town.

This year it was decided to have the picnic in the park on the San Marcos River about a mile from town. This was now a well-developed park with swings in the trees, both rope swings for individuals and lawn swings that seated two or three persons. Electric lights were swung from tree to tree, and there was a nice concession building. For our picnics, though, we would have our own soda water and ice-cream stands.

Our parents would give us enough money to spend that day

93

to wreck any budget and stomach. After all, it was for the church, and it "only happened once a year." We invited hundreds of friends to this picnic, and each year a few joined our church. I suppose they were too full to worry about belonging to the "Dutchmen." Even several of our American friends had joined in former years.

The world was such a wonderful place to be those beautiful early summer days. For months we came back to the church on Sunday afternoons after regular services to practice the program for the picnic.

I remember many heated contests that arose among the oldsters as they sought to set the date each year. Seems many of them wanted to be sure the date was not in conflict with the Monthalia Methodist Sunday School picnic or with political rallies.

There was a certain Mr. Lang in the congregation who thought we should pick our date first . . . and it should always be July 4, unless that came on Sunday.

"I make the motion the picnic be on July 4," his voice would boom out; and then from the strain of shouting and from a throat ailment, he would almost strangle with coughing. Sometimes I think they all voted with him because he was so well liked and the cough sounded so pathetic.

This year the date was set for later. Somehow Mr. Lang either was absent the Sunday morning it was set, or he had by this time decided folks were having too much fun playing dominoes at the Monthalia picnic to keep on missing it. He lived on dominoes as did many other retired persons in Gonzales. It was their way of keeping happy. All of us learned our additions by playing dominoes, but most of us only played them at home (except at the picnic and at our parties.)

We were at church Sunday afternoon, July 3, practicing our program when we heard the telephone ring in the parsonage. Someone ran to answer, and before I could find out just what was so exciting, there was screaming and crying going on everywhere. Someone had drowned in the river down at Wolf's. My heart almost jumped out of my throat. I cried with the others as we clung to each other in huddles. Soon someone said, "Wonder where Arthur was . . . he is such a good swimmer . . . he should have been able to save Walter."

Elvira phoned her brothers, they came in their long, beautiful car, and we crowded in and rushed down to the river. When we got to the Wolf farm entrance, folks were coming out. We turned back. It was terrible. We had played with the Buckholtz kids all our lives; Walter just could not be dead.

Why just yesterday afternoon, I had talked with him in town. He and Arthur had gone together to the photographer to have their pictures made. It was the first time either had ever been photographed. I wanted a picture of Arthur; and when he told Walter about his appointment, he dressed up and went along. I happened to see them on the sidewalk just as they were trying to sneak back to the car without anyone's noticing they had their Sunday suits on (on Saturday afternoon.)

As always, no matter what happened, on a dairy farm somebody had to milk the cows. We all cried. We cried so we could hardly keep the cows from kicking us. Cows are very smart. Just try milking one when you are angry or tense. Papa cried aloud. We could hear him as he shoveled the chopped ensilage in the long feed troughs to which the cows' heads were fastened with sliding clips.

Mama cried so we had to put her to bed. In all the confusion, somehow we made it to church and Epworth League that night, although at the youth meeting all we did was talk of the accident and cry some more. After church I went with Arthur to see the body. Then we went for a ride on the Harwood Road, the road we both lived on but seldom had ventured far on together. Now that Papa and Mama had given their consent for me to marry Arthur, we felt somewhat freer to enjoy regular dates.

Our engagement had happened on my sixteenth birthday. After the revival service in church that night, we had been with another couple and one of my sisters in the park. While swinging in a pair of the swings that faced each other, someone had suggested that we go to the concession for pops. Arthur had tugged at me to linger back; and it was then, he gave me a ring. He had asked me many months before this, time and again, to be his true and loving wife (so poetic like) and I had always said that I must wait until my birthday. Really I had meant my eighteenth birthday but had hoped perhaps my parents could be persuaded to see it our way.

Though consent had been given, it was not for two years yet that I would be allowed to marry. Papa had said it would be all right with him, but Mama had stated that she would not think of a "child" marrying. I must wait until I was of age, for she would certainly not sign a marriage certificate.

So it was that on this Sunday night with parental consent and

95

a ring on my hand, we decided to park by the side of the road to talk and to cry about our dear friend, Walter. Arthur went over the happenings again and again in detail and just could not forgive himself for not getting there in time to save Walter. Arthur and others were swimming and boating in the same party in the San Marcos River.

It was late when we went home, but the family was still all at Buckholtz'. Arthur told me later . . . and I saw . . . that he had hung his brand new one-piece swimming suit in the carhouse where it hung till it rotted off the nail. Swimming was over for him, he vowed.

He told me of hanging the suit the next afternoon, after the funeral. Then he wanted to know why in all the world in this heat of the summer was I wearing a long sleeved dress with a high collar. I refused to answer. Several days later when he came to see me, it was Papa himself who told of whipping me on that Monday morning with a thin rope we always used to "pull off the calves." Papa apologized to Arthur. Why to him? We never knew. For days after such an outburst of rage, Papa would be so quiet and sad. I knew even way back then that he was sick and was working too, too hard. And though at that time I was angry and hurt, it made me love him even more dearly. I, too, would be very quiet for a change and completely lost my desire for food or friends.

When we did begin to go back to the park again, there was the same old lady working in the concession who had been there for ages. Anyway, she was supposed to be working, but she was so lazy that the young folks nicknamed her Lady-lead-legs. The boys snickered about her . . . as she would groan just to answer our questions.

One day while we were picking up rocks in the field to fill mud-holes in the lane to the public road, George and Freddie were talking about the park and the way kids swiped things 'cause she was too lazy to get up and wait on them. She would just sit and swing and let the customers help themselves and bring her the nickels. Perhaps she invented the self-serve method we honor today.

"I bet'cha her bottom sho' be glad when she passes on," Freddie ventured.

"I hope we are there when she does so we can swipe that pillow she sits on because it has her money bag sewed tight to the

96

side of it," George yelled back so he could be heard over the pounding noise of rocks being gathered into old paint buckets.

Picking up rocks by the bucketsful or scrapping cotton until every last lock was in the sacks . . . stomping down the ensilage as it came pouring in from the overhead pipe . . . shoveling manure . . . cutting seed heads for chicken feed with butcher knives . . . holding young bull calves while Papa did the surgery . . . fishing in the creek with a bent pin . . . life on the farm is great. Great! Just great . . . if you don't have a hankering for a lead-legs life with a built-in money bag on your swing-seat cushion.

September came again as it was bound to do. Back to school the twins went and on with the work went Mama, Papa and I without their help. I walked to the ward school that day "just to be there to write a story for the Gonzales Inquirer," I said at the breakfast table. By now, all the family doubted my reason. They were well aware of the chats with Arthur as his fields could all be seen from our home and by many of the other neighbors.

Though it was a custom for neighbors to visit at their several fence lines, it was not the usual thing for a young girl to do. Mama did not approve. Papa did not seem to mind this part of our courtship; but he did tell me time and again the fellow is supposed to do the courting.

"Sure, I know that, Papa," I snapped back and added, "The men are also supposed to do all the field work. But in Texas anything goes, Uncle Frank told you."

It is not — nor was it often I complained about having too much work. Spending days, weeks and even months at the time in idleness caused by illness will cure one of the wish for more leisure. Work is not only the soul's salvation but it kept us out of many arguments and troubles. In fact, a heavy assignment of work was the usual prescription for complaining about something that did not suit us.

For instance, "I just am not hungry and I don't like turnips" would bring on "maybe you could spade up Mama's rose garden this day."

With Wedding Plans Humming

September meant getting the last of the cotton scrapped. It also, this year, meant an end to my music lessons as there was so much to do to get ready to be married. In all my spare-time and on rainy days, I would embroider or make some other little things for my trunk. Town girls had cedar-chests. I was glad to have Tanta's old trunk. I loved it for it had meant a nice place to sit when we were visiting in her room.

George was thrilled over the prospect of a big brother. Each time he had saved a few cents by buying less lunch at school, he would give them to me. I bought some lovely wash-cloths, a few of the shiny pie-plates like we gave Mama for Christmas, some stamped pillowcases and even one real heavy bath towel with his money-gifts.

My sisters were nice about sending me things like that for the next Christmas. But somehow, it was George's gifts — he being a boy — that touched me so. Mama had Papa bring home a bag of the freshly ginned cotton, and together that winter we made a heavy comforter with white and blue striped outing flannel covering. I felt like I was as important as the gal in the song we all sang, "When my sugar walks down the street, All the birds go tweet, tweet, tweet." (Jack Mills, Inc.)

Late in the summer when I was seventeen and had just one more year to wait for the wonderful wedding day . . . we had decided upon my eighteenth birthday unless that came on Friday . . . I took very sick again. When the Rev. Raeke and Mrs. came to see me, I told them I had decided to break the engagement. It just would not be fair to marry a big, strong man who would need help in the fields and me be puny so often. Nothing they said changed my mind.

To add to my decision was the news from my well-meaning friends that Arthur was dating a couple of other girls from our Sunday School class. When he came to visit me after I could sit in the parlor again, I confronted him with this and he did not deny that he had taken them to their homes. But he would not hear of our breaking up. I was not to work in the fields, anyway; and if I were puny a lot, then I needed someone who really loved me to take care of me.

For three months, I would not accept a date though I was well again and back to the usual grind. It was now September again and though I had been out of school three years, I was going back. Papa and I had talked it over one afternoon while we were cleaning the corn-crib getting ready to put in the new crop of ears. He agreed I should give it a try, and he asked me why Arthur had quit coming. I lied to him, telling Papa that Arthur had too many things to do these days.

Papa threw back his head and roared with laughter, "An Adlof have too much work to miss going to see the girls! Who do you think I am?"

"You are Ah Ha Able," (that's how you pronounce A. H. Ebel in German) I said to my Papa, who slapped me even while he was laughing. It just made him furious for one of us to pronounce his name that way, and I had forgotten on the spur of the moment.

That was the answer I needed. That afternoon as I walked down the cow lane to get old Stormy, the one that always lagged behind the others because she was so sway-backed she didn't know if she were coming or going, I stopped to talk to Freddie. He told Arthur the next day at work that I had said to come to the party we were going to give for Pauline on her birthday. Pauline was to be home September sixth.

He came, she came, many other friends came and so did Aunt Frieda. By the time she finished asking me all the things she "truly needed to know so she and Lou could get something together," I was as good as marching down the aisle.

It was just as well I changed my plans, for nothing else would ever have made me happy. Besides, before the week was over my invalid Aunt Selma, wife of Papa's deceased brother, came to our house to live. Poor dear was so sick. But she was good company when she had her better hours. I would sit up with her until very late at night to keep her company, and many times I got some hand-sewing done that way. I made myself a beautiful wool dress with a high-standing priest collar. It did not take much cloth as I weighed only ninety pounds and styles were for the knees to poke out when one walked.

Aunt Selma's life had not been a bed of roses either. She was a person who loved nice things, and they had a beautiful white home on the hill overlooking a lake with huge oak trees surrounding it. We had spent many Sundays over there before my uncle died and before Elvira, their only daughter, married. Later in her loneliness Aunt Selma had remarried, the boys had left home and the beautiful house burned to the ground one day while she was at her sister's who was also ill.

Yet she was cheerful and encouraged me to marry. "Love him, love him," she would say to me so very often.

"Just what do you mean?"

Then she told me to love my man, not only secretly in my heart but to let him know that I loved him. She criticized the custom of keeping one's feelings to oneself. She said to tell him you love . . . tell him now and tell him often while you can. She told me of how she had wished lately so often that she had said right out loud to her first love how it was with her. It was a simple and yet a valuable lesson. It was worth all the trouble of keeping her for the whole winter

I decided to try her advice, and on the next date I spouted over and over how much I love "you" and brother! The trouble I almost got us into. . . . Don't ever, ever try that line on a cold winter night in the parlor with just a tiny kerosene lamp burning. At least, that's all the fire there was supposed to have been in the room.

I had a copy of some cute sheet-music about some song saying, "By-by black bird, make my bed and light the light, I'll be home late tonight," and by time I soloed it over twice . . . Aunt Selma needed me to bring her a glass of water.

Even if one thinks a certain day will never come, it does. So November twentieth came; and I became Mrs. A. E. Adlof, something no one else had ever done. At last I had a career started all my own.

The afternoon before, Arthur went for our license at the courthouse. I was well past eighteen and needed no one to sign for me. We had waited this much past my birthday to give his parents time to move to their new home in town. We were to live on in the old home-place, which had been bought by the Simeons who owned the Modern Bakery.

Arthur had forgotten to check for sure with the preacher, and so we chased around until past midnight doing this and that. One thing we still had to do was go to Aunt Selma's chicken-house and catch us a dozen hens. She insisted on our having them for our wedding present. Arthur couldn't see why we had to get them that very night. After all, we were not even going to eat breakfast together the next day and didn't need eggs for that or for supper.

To top it all, her caretaker came after us with a long shotgun and flashlight. It's a wonder we didn't get shot stealing chickens the night before our wedding.

I was too excited to sleep even when I did get to bed and so I got up as usual when I heard Papa clanking away from the milk-house with the buckets. I felt so sorry for him I almost backed out. Now he would not have anyone to help him in the daytime when George and Celia would be at school. They were seniors this year and had so many things to go to and so many home-work assignments.

Papa was so interested in everything that morning. He made sure we found Brother Raeke, made sure Arthur bought the license (there were no blood tests to make in those days as now) and that I had not forgotten to pack plenty of warm clothing.

"There is going to be a norther, and maybe you all better not go to San Antonio."

"But Papa, we have to. Lula is looking for us, and besides I have never been to San Antonio; and you know good and well when the plowing starts we won't get to go, and besides his sows are supposed to start having their . . . "

Papa interrupted. He knew well and good that I understood about being a farmer's wife. Papa decided he would go along to see the "knot tied." Then we hurried through the milking, and for the first time in my life Papa let the milk stand instead of rushing it right through the cream separator machine. I was too excited to eat breakfast and promptly at eight o'clock — yes, in the morning — Arthur came.

Gee! He did look so nice; and, goody, he did buy some ox-fords. I so wanted him to, for the young men just were not wearing laced high shoes this season. Even though I looked him over real well, I did not see the price tag left on the back of his sleeve.

Brother Raeke spied it in the parsonage, where we went to be married. "Mister, you have a price tag this morning!" he teased. "Great day in the morning, the man must have sold all his cotton . . . ninety dollars for a suit of clothes!"

"I have two pairs of the pants," Arthur said . . . right there in front of God and the wedding witnesses . . . and then he turned as red as fire coals.

Now with two rings on my hand; a husband who had two pairs of pants to his brand-new suit, a new suitcase, a good car, all his tools and four mules and even some other livestock; I was way up yonder, like old Aaron always said.

101

By the time we got to Seguin at forty miles per hour — after all, we must hurry as fast as the car would go for Lula was expecting us early in the afternoon — I was very hungry. Still too bashful to say I needed to find the ladies' lounge, I headed for the door marked the way only to find it had a nickel-latch-lock.

There I almost died with fright. I had heard of such locks, but I thought maybe that was way off in some place like New York or Berlin, where utilities were high. In Seguin, for heaven's sake, where there always had been water enough to pull anybody's commode string or chain or latch. What in all the world would I do now? I had a new purse but it had not a penny in it, much less a nickel. There was nothing I could do but ask for a nickel.

It took all the way to San Antonio to get over this embarassment. To be right truthful, I still haven't gotten over having to ask for money. When we got to Lula's, she informed us that she had found us a room in the St. Anthony Hotel next to the Travis Park. As if the Seguin trouble weren't enough, when the bellboy took us to our room it had a double bed by the window and a baby crib by the other wall.

Lula went up with us to make sure the room was nice as she had reserved it and we were to be her guests. When she spied the crib, she was very indignant and demanded that the baby bed be removed. Arthur must have felt sorry for the boy, knowing how Lula could scold, and so he quickly spoke up.

"Now you don't need to do that. I can just use it to lay my hat on . . . and you put yours there, too, huh?" he said turning to me and Lula.

The day had started after a sleepless night, and the day ended with us watching a stage show with Lula still our hostess. She had also taken us to every part of the Brackenridge Park that afternoon, and I was tired enough to drop dead by time we got to bed.

This year on our thirty-second wedding anniversary, in the same hotel, we ordered our meal sent up; and we had a great time laughing about our honeymoon. I asked the bell-boy if he knew what a meal like that would have cost us sent up in 1926. He should know. He has worked there almost that long. He also said folks just did not do such things "in them days." The room, he said, was reasonable then, too.

We wouldn't know about "then," for Lula was our hostess. We left early Sunday afternoon, the next day after our wedding, for home. It was drizzling and sleeting a little. In a touring car with the celluloid-windowed, buttoned-on side curtains flapping, we made it back to Gonzales alive. But as fast as we could get into them, we put on our longhandled underwear and went out to feed the animals. Even they were so glad to see us that one sow had pigs, and the cat brought her new kittens out from under the barn for us to approve.

The Real Wedding Trip Begins

Of course, I did not realize it then, but now, years later, I know the wedding trip began on that Sunday after our wedding vows. The day before with rushing to the ceremony after the last minute decision by my mother to attend (Papa had said he was going, and she could just stay at home if she did not want to go) . . . spending the whole afternoon in the park where red-bottomed apes added to my already over-ripely embarrassed mind . . . consoling a brand new husband whose new oxfords had pumped up and down on his heels until great big water blisters arose . . . finding him in bed in his BVDs . . . wearing a silk nightie . . . could not have been truly a honeymoon.

But turning east on the highway the next day to go to our first home started the honeymoonish feeling. It was cold as only a Texas blizzard can be after a day of over 90 degree temperature. We snuggled up close; but still by the time we got to the Oak Forest gas station, we were about frozen. There the attendant noticed some heavy gunny sacks in the back of the car and suggested we wrap our feet in them — at least *my* feet, as Arthur needed his to drive. (The curtains and the mud-chains were kept in such bags until needed.)

We stopped in town in Gonzales to see how Papa and Stevie were getting along. Stevie was my nick-name for Arthur's step-mother. They all called her Step-mother, but I disliked the term very much. They were glad to know we were home and seemed very pleased that we thought to stop there first. Stevie fixed hot tea and served some of her delicious cake. So, now — I thought — we do have some wedding cake. She also gave me a small velvet rose to pin on my coat . . . so now, I thought, I do have wedding flowers.

It was just after that that we rushed out to the big two-story house where we were to spend our first years, changed to our work clothes, and fed the animals. Then we went to spend the night with my folks as we had no heaters set up in our home.

"My goodness, I can't tell any difference in you all . . . look just the same as you always did," George said while we were all gathered around the fire that night. We all laughed at him, for after all it had been only two days since he had seen us.

The next morning I over-slept cow-milking time. But Arthur did not. He had slipped out, dressed and gone to the barn to help Papa and George. When I woke up, he was kissing me and telling me to come to breakfast. Mama had the breakfast ready and some of the family were anxious to get on with their school and work. Papa read the scripture that morning. I only remember one verse of it: "With God all things are possible."

I had worried about many things. I had wondered how we would ever have money to buy furniture and also plant the crops next spring. Arthur and I had discussed finances, and he had told me we were not to buy anything on credit. My anxiety was for naught as the day proved. First Papa told us that he and Mama had purchased a dining table, six chairs and a matching buffet, a double bed, mattress, and a small dresser Saturday. The Klein Furniture Store would deliver it today, he said.

Stevie phoned to ask us to bring some little pictures she had forgotten to move to town when she and Papa Adlof left the farm two weeks ago. When we went by to do that, he gave us a nice gift of cash . . . enough to pay for the fifty dollar ice-box and a wood heater for the huge dining room. It seemed nutty to buy an ice-box and a heater on the same day, but we would need both — this being Texas.

Then we went hand in hand, until we got on the sidewalk where A (his new nickname) was too bashful to do that, into the F. C. Nagel grocery store. There were already a number of the people from our church shopping, and all had to make some wise-crack about our being absent from the services yesterday. Here after stacking up more "store-boughten groceries" than I had ever before seen purchased in one time, I was told to sign the check.

The Farmer's National Bank was down at the corner, and we went there next to register my signature. They gave us a beautiful calendar — even though the year was most nigh spent, this being November 22. I should not have worried so, I told myself, as I sat in the car later and waited a bit while A went into the bakery and into Kluge's butcher-shop.

Why, I did not even have to cook our dinner that day. We sat on the big heavy kitchen table that Papa and Stevie had left back for us and ate: warm bakery rolls, honey and sausage. Never did any couple have a better feast for their first home dinner together.

Later in the afternoon, the furniture arrived. We went upstairs and brought down A's quilts and clothing. He said it seemed odd to come out of the attic bedroom where he and his older brothers had slept for the past twenty years until, one by one, they had moved on to their own homes. That afternoon Brother Raeke phoned to tell us the young people were coming the next night to give us a Kattzenyammer party. And later Miss Ora called to invite me to come on Friday afternoon to a little surprise party at the school.

The best gift of the whole day, though, arrived when night came and as I sat on A's lap in the big rocker Grandma Sturm and my two aunts had sent out, he said we would keep our daily devotions. "Your daddy 'read' this morning and so we can skip tonight, but tomorrow morning we will read right after breakfast just as he did this morning." I cried. I guess for joy; maybe a little for sympathy, too, for I did feel so sorry for Mama and Papa with all that work to do. I knew I had been a good helper. My aunt had been taken to other relatives as Mama would not be able to care for her, but yet it would be so lonely for them.

"Don't cry about it. You can drive down there every day and see about them. And besides, do as I have done all my life: go upstairs and look out of that north window. You can see everything from there. I knew when your Papa was in the field, when you all washed, when you scrubbed windows on the south, east and west — why, I have kept my eye on you ever since I could reach up to the window sill."

What a wonderful feeling . . . to know that someone really wanted me . . . to know that he meant it when he had so often told me while in close embrace that we were born for one another. This must be what the songs meant when they spoke of heaven on earth.

My heart most nigh jumped out of my throat a few more times that week of our wedding trip — a trip that still brings new surprises, new thrills and new hurdles around every corner of the road. The party the young people gave — even though some had a couple of babies palleted down in the spare rooms (where we had no furniture at all) — was a lovely thing for them to do for us. They brought hand-made dresser scarfs, cup-towels, pillow slips, china bowls, a black pottery tea pot in which I now grow Ivy, and all manner of kitchen tools; even one real smart-aleck brought a dozen diapers.

At the school party, the children (Miss Ora did not tell them she had tipped me off) brought me jars of pickles, ripe persimmons, pecans, peanuts, syrup, honey, and a small puppy of the alley breed. And one girl brought me a Sears catalogue. She said she was afraid I, being a new wife would not have one in time to order my husband a Christmas present. How very thoughtful!

Miss Ora was a wise woman. She knew very well that if she told me this was to be a party, I'd have sense enough to bring the children some refreshments. I did not want to risk getting stuck with the car, and so I had walked the mile to the school, a mile directly west from my new home. I also carried a few extra cookies and stopped on the turning row to give them to Arthur, who was working in the back field.

"It sure is sweet of you to bring me some lunch every afternoon. It reminds me of when Lula was still at home and of even longer ago when I was a very small boy and some days when Mama was feeling good, she would come out late in the evenings. Poor Mama, she had asthma so bad . . . she did not get to walk into the fields very often."

"That is sad, I think, also," I said. "For to walk into the fields for me is the best part of the day. I feel closer to God here than any place. It was here in this field that I found you and it . . ." I was going to say that I hoped we would always stay here, but he interrupted to tell me that very soon we would be planning our new home out in his new land. The place he had bought a year ago was in Live Oak County.

"You will love it there. It has many live oaks like that tree down there with our initials on it. Grass is knee high blowing in the gulf breezes each evening; deer and quail are everywhere. I shall take you to see the place as soon as spring comes."

"Now," I reminded, "I must hurry on to Miss Ora's or she will be worried."

After he snitched a couple of more cookies out of the bag meant for the school party, he held the barbed wires apart so I could crawl through the fence. While I had my back-side handy, he popped me right hard and said, "You need to eat more cookies yourself."

Another bright and shining memory of the first year of our marriage trip through life was our first Christmas. I had bought some cotton flannel outing and gone during the afternoons twice to my sister-in-law's, who lived at the south of our back field. Charlie, Arthur's brother, had some nice long sleeved night shirts

107

. . . on the clothes line I saw them. So I decided I'd make one for A's Christmas present.

On the Sunday before Christmas, George, A and I went to Smith Creek to get our Christmas trees. We decided on two beautiful Red-Haws. They were loaded with red berries. Of course, we cut the largest one we could cram into the back seat from each side, never once thinking about the amount of trims a tree that size took. At home we had made and saved trims for all of Mama's and Papa's years, but this was our first.

We wound up hanging almost a whole box of apples on the tree and two dollars worth of candy kisses. Now in those days, two dollars worth of candy kisses wrapped in multi-colored papers filled a large dish-pan. I tied strings until I thought I would never finish. It was all so exciting.

The last afternoon before Christmas, George came over for a while. He looked awful. He had the whooping cough and spent most of the time hanging over the edge of the back porch where our chicken hens enjoyed his chopped nuts, candy and apples more than he did. In fact, today as I looked at George in the throes of cancer, I have to think again of how bad he looked that Christmas when he was a senior in high school.

Arthur had a nice package for him. He gave him a purse and a pocket-knife which he had selected all by himself. I gave George a white shirt — looking ahead to graduation dates. He had such a good time helping us with our tree and was extremely cheerful, even though he must have felt terrible. Today, he still teases, "I look like I'm coming unglued . . . yep, feel sorta like that Christmas when I had the whooping cough and didn't wait for you to peel my apple. Remember?"

Another and perhaps an equally exciting event was a day in our first September together. By now, we had somehow consoled ourselves over the death of Papa Adlof in March. We had gone to their home on his birthday, all of us — even Max and Lonie had come from Houston, and Lula was at home from San Antonio. I had baked a beautiful cake and had encircled it with fern fronds and some of the wild lavender Verbenas which were his favorite flowers. He had been so happy over the whole party idea. He retired later than usual and never woke up again. Two days later, he died in a long struggle — perhaps from a cerebral hemorrhage.

But life goes on . . . and as Papa always said, "His mansion was ready for him to go live in."

Now it was September and time for the usual rush and push

108

to help with the county fair. Time for remembering that last year, when I was left at home one day to bake twelve pies for the food stand our church had at the fair, it was too much of a temptation for Arthur. The pies were the temptation, I like to tease him, Anyway, he had come over after making sure from his north-window lookout that Papa and Mama had left in the car. We had baked pies, milked cows and separated the milk, taken care of my aunt, and smooched to heart's content.

"Guess you better make some pies for the church stand this year, too."

"And how many and what kind for you?' I asked that September morning.

"Pies? Lemon! Kisses? Hot! Do I have to help you make them?"

I answered I could manage the lemon pies since I did not have to milk cows and look after a sick aunt, but the kissing would be an impossibility alone. I was hurt deeply when he gave me a quick peck, the first time ever of such, and hurried off to the field saying I should make nice, full pies . . . not to spare on the ingredients . . . and we'd go to the fair that night. There was still cotton in the fields and it was bringing 19c per pound of lint.

The pies turned out fine and so did the smooching after we got home from chunking cats, riding ferris wheels, seeing horse races, and looking at six large buildings of exhibits ranging from farm produce to school children's art work. Soon afterwards, we knew for sure just how well the smooching had paid off.

This made it the September to remember with great joy for it gave us our first baby . . . Ruth, who was born the next June while we were living on still another rented farm. By this time, we were again told we would have to vacate in fall. Arthur had fixed all the lot fences and we had put the barnyard and everything in neat order on this farm just to be told the owner's son had decided to farm instead of completing his college training. It made me think of Papa's decision long before when he came into a new county to seek a permanent home for his family.

So it was that our first two years were mostly on the move — from home to marriage to pregnancy to another farm and then to our own place down in southwest Texas. As quickly as we could get the crops harvested and the baby would be big enough to move to the wilds, we would be off.

"Off" is exactly the word most of the relatives used when they spoke of our departure. Those who had never gone to see the place used it the oftener. Those who had gone looked forward to our moving so they could come to see us . . . could come to hunt our birds and deer . . . could spend weekends in the really and truly "country." Sometimes, in the later years when droughts came, we even spoke of how "off" and how "touched" we must have been to come to Three Rivers. But just let a good soaking rain come again and you couldn't drag either of us away.

Going Out On Our Own

Maybe Arthur missed his Papa so much and felt that now that he had to make all his decisions alone — his Papa thought Arthur had always done that anyway — maybe it was simply the adventurous spirit, but move we would, no matter what the folks, friends and foes thought. With the trip to make in advance to build us a house to move into, the new baby to care for and the crops to gather, the honeymooning spirit sometimes burned at a low flame for the next few months.

One day there was a yardman named Luther Price sent to help me take up some Easter lily bulbs and other things we were to take along to Three Rivers. In packing, I had found a portion of a package of some fireworks Olga had left at our house during some holiday, perhaps the Fourth of July. We had a three foot picket fence around some flower-beds, and I decided to light one of those sonofaguns and lay it down quickly behind Luther — just to see what he would do.

What he did was jump flat-footed right out of his big heavy shoes, which perhaps were not tied in the first place, over and out of the picketed bed. The blood-curdling yell he let out scared me half to death. In fact, when he lay flat on the ground yelling, "Lawd have mercy, Miz Adlof, what the hell was dat?", I panicked. I meant to just go over to tell him it was all just a joke. Instead I forgot about the bulbs and stepped on the pile, slipped down, and almost cracked my skull as I fell head-long right down beside old Luther.

I screamed for pain. He helped me to the porch and then he tore out across the field to get Arthur. After all the commotion was over, Luther said, as he looked down on the baby crib where my beautiful child was asleep, "Honey chile, your Mama done almost dug herself a grave today. She done scared old Luther and herse'f most nigh to death."

Like fire spreads, the story got going; and by the time it had made its first week's rounds, Mama was furious with my husband. She thought it was most negligent that he leave me at the house in the first place with that colored man in the yard. Mama! Who

111

had gone to New Orleans and who went every Ladies' Aid Day without ever a thought about my being alone? But then I saw it her way. Mama had always felt nothing wrong could happen at *her* house. Bless her heart!

She came with Papa on Sunday, and it took her only a minute to get Arthur told. But he appreciated her view-point and consoled her by promising it would not happen again. He said that was the one big worry about moving to Three Rivers. He felt like crying —and I suspected they would have been big black tears—when he thought that none of his hired hands would move with us.

If only one of Hannah's daughters would agree to go to help with the moving, chores, caring for the baby and helping with the garden. I had talked with Hannah in the field one day. In fact, as we were talking, her youngest grandson came up to get in on the rest and conversation.

"Nome, we jes' can't go off out there in them rattlesnakes; and besides there ain't none of our people out that way . . ."

"What you doing over here, Mose? Now I done tole you time and again I'ze going to whop you if'n you done quit every time I does, and now I'ze done through lying" she said all in one breath. She reached down and pulled up a thick cotton stalk and as she began to lash the youngster, she repeated,"I done lied as often as I'ze gwine to. I'ze done said I'ze gwine to beat you, and I is now gwine to do that, so hep me Lawd to tell the truth."

I begged and pulled at Hannah to quit hitting the boy until she turned and gave me a glance. That was enough to send me flying across the rows to the cotton-wagon where I had left Ruthie with Arthur who was weighing the sacks.

Max wrote to beg us not to move to that God forsaken part of Texas. He was planning to go into a business for himself, and he could give his brother a job. If things got bad, Arthur could always be there to help out with such things as yardman or even drive one of his trucks. He wanted us to promise to come that very afternoon when the letter arrived to talk the matter over with him.

I thought he must have lost all his marbles not to remember that on the farm one has crops to gather, cows to milk, and butter to make; and now we had a tiny baby. Arthur just laughed when he read the letter. He put it in his dresser drawer and said, "Let time answer it. He knows better."

One encouragement came from Brother and Sister Raeke. The conversation was again on our moving when one Wednesday evening in early July we had cottage prayer meeting. Afterwards, Rev. Raeke christened our baby—Viola Ruth—and then we had a little tea-party to celebrate. The Raekes had served as pastor of a new community near Three Rivers named Ray Point and a rural church at Fashing in neighboring Atascosa County. They loved it down there and assured us we would also like it in that area.

So it was in September that our very first home was constructed. In the very last days of the month, Arthur and his two older brothers, who owned adjoining tracts of land near Suniland, set out with tools and a drawing we had made. It took many hours in those days to make the trip, which yesterday (to check some dates for this manuscript) I zipped off in less than two hours . . . just a hundred miles. Odd, it was that same distance always!

I spent some of the time while they were gone with my parents so they could have a nice visit with the baby. One of the weekends, Lula came to visit us. She was uneasy about our new endeavor. She came on Friday to help me bake and prepare a nice homecoming for A. Lula often, in more or less anger, implied or even accused me of not cooking "good enough" for Arthur. She did not like him to be thin. He was (and is) proud of his slenderness.

As we were busy gathering fresh vegetables that morning, she almost stepped on a huge rattlesnake under a squash bush. I ran to the corner of the garden for a hoe and found the snake under the next bush. With one lick, I cut the snake's head off and broke the hoe handle in two.

"Good gracious, you don't have to move to Three Rivers to get snake bit," she exclaimed. "You can get bit right here. I haven't seen such a big snake in Gonzales since we were little children."

I did not tell her that I had. I did not tell her that I had never killed one on the first wham before, either—nor that I had ever broken a hoe handle in one lick. I did not tell her later, either, that it was the first time I had shot a rooster for supper with Arthur's pistol. He had left the pistol for my protection and I had taken a notion to target practice while he was away.

I had only the one shell left in the gun; and I knew that if I missed that rooster, I would have to go to town for fresh beef. (Those were the days before our wonderful home deep freezers.)

When Arthur came home, there was so much to tell and so many questions to ask; yet Lula got priority. And what did she tell first but this, "You don't need to be afraid to take Viola to the wilderness. The snakes and the birds better be afraid. My

113

goodness, she can shoot and chop like any woodsman. Papa would have enjoyed seeing her do that."

The open life and hard work had agreed with all three of the brothers. They had enjoyed their adventure and were ever so proud of the four room house they had built. It has only taken us thirty-two years and about a dozen remodelings and additions to make it serve us well. First, they had decided to build it closer to the public road — just as though a crooked, ungraded dirt road could be called a public thoroughfare. Then they had decided it would save land if the house were not so far from the barn and lots; and worst of all, to make it nice and cool, they had changed two doors so that the breeze did not have any trouble getting straight through the house.

These changes only came to light when I arrived . . . when the first norther arrived . . . when the first road was finally graded a few years later. In the gulf-coast country, one does not need to make a straight path through the house for wind. There's always plenty of breeze, and it is strong enough to make a few detours on its own. That delightful cool wind that comes up about eleven each day, in normal weather, makes it impossible for folks to be happy elsewhere.

Arthur often does things the difficult way—planning, perhaps, to save money and to get it done just exactly like he wants it done. This time, to save money, he decided to move his tools and teams by land instead of hiring an additional rail car. Fodder for the mules and our milk cows, and the cows themselves were shipped by rail to Suniland. But two weeks before that, he and a nephew, Elmer Froehner, left with a wagon and the two teams of mules.

The wagon was loaded with small tools and supplies for their trip. It took them three days and nights. On the weekend one of the brothers went to get them in our car. They tell of all their "adventures," but A usually winds up saying it was a waste of time and energy. But it is a great memory to the nephew who tells it with pride as he would really be too young otherwise to tell truthfully of having crossed five counties by wagon.

The day to move arrived. By now Arthur had Loui Vanek and his wife hired to come with us. They had a boy named August who was just a little older than our six-months' old baby. We all rode down together in our car, the same car we had gone to San Antonio in on our wedding day. We came by way of San Antonio this time as it had rained near Nixon and there was no pavement

114

on much of that way. This way, we had pavement all the way to Whitsett. There, we sunk to the axle.

Papa cried when we moved. Mama had fixed us a nice dinner, and she busied herself with the dishes after she bundled up the baby for me. As we drove away, I saw her rub the dampness away from a window in the dining room to look at us leaving. She had not said goodbye, and I had thought she was coming along out to the car with Papa. Now I was packed in like a sardine and so Papa said, "Leave Mama alone. She will be writing you. Have a safe trip and, and . . . " and he walked away very quickly.

I turned to look at Arthur's old home-place—our first home together—as we passed on toward town, thought of the cat that brought out her kittens for us to see that day we returned from our wedding trip. Just then the car stopped, and there was Joe Gonzales at the road with a package.

Joe, the dear Mexican man with his little red-haired girl who had lost her mother when she was born, had worked off and on for us. Now he brought a gift for our baby to take along. He so wished he and little Annie could have moved with us. The package had a lovely little dress with the price-tag still attached. Joe could not read but he knew we would see that he had spent three days' wages to buy the baby a gift.

"I wish Joe and Annie could come, too. But I guess we will be doing good to pay Loui and Annie," I consoled myself. I had been to the Three Rivers place once for a few days' camping trip while the men built fences. I was not exactly dumb about the work that awaited us.

Though it was drizzling rain when we left Gonzales where we stopped to take on Loui, Annie and August and their "much a plunder" as she called it, everything spiritually was so bright and gay. In fact, we forgot to bring a lantern. As if we thought it could never get dark tonight. We bought one in Whitsett from a grocery store. The owner was so glad that some more people were moving into his trade area that he filled the lantern bowl with kerosene and gave us a box of matches.

"He would make a good Chamber of Commerce president," I told the others in the car.

"Or a Methodist bishop," Arthur quipped.

"How come you all are Methodists?" Loui wanted to know.

We both hesitated, not knowing exactly how to put it in words. Arthur answered him, "We were born Methodist and haven't had cause to change."

115

The sun was shining and Loui remarked as we continued down the road a few miles, "Well, so this is Sunny land (Suniland)! And, by golly, there is a car on the side rails. Betcha that's our things."

We stopped to check with the station agent, Mrs. Margaret McNeese. She told us the way to get to the house of the persons who had written to invite us to stay with them. Arthur had the envelope in his pocket with the return address—Mrs. A. H. Muenzler. Mrs. Muenzler had written that we would be welcome to stay over-night with them and also a Mrs. Weichman and her son and daughter would like to have us visit them. Now in those days there were no Welcome Wagons, nor do places as small as Whitsett, Suniland and Ray Point have Chambers of Commerce. They did not need them. The people make it their personal business to see that new-comers are welcomed. I recall that Mrs. McNeese already had a houseful of guests; that she was amazed that we did not know the Schweikerts, since most everybody that came through the country stayed with them; and that we knew people way over there in Ray Point. Why, that was almost ten miles from Suniland!

Heavens! Ten more miles of this mud, and it was now already getting dark. We pushed on. Most of the way, we were able to drive without too much "pushing" on the part of the men as I drove through the big mud holes. That's how I began to get my training at being a crack driver, forwards and backwards, in mud. There were no fenced roads—now it is a Farm-to-Market Highway —so in bad spells folks would just "cut a new track around some more bushes on some more tall grass."

We let the Vaneks out at our place as they insisted. We had a small two-room house built for them in our back yard and they were content with it right away. Loui was disappointed, though, that the train car had arrived and would have to be unloaded the next day as he meant to get in Thanksgiving Day fishing at Suniland in the Atascosa River. He was a fine fisherman, keeping us in fresh fish while we were neighbors at Gonzales and soon did the same in our new home.

We went on to the Weichmans. We had been told that Muenzlers had a large family of young children; and since Mrs. Weichman only had two, Arthur said she could probably use the extra guests easier. Besides, Mrs. Muenzler had written that each family would send a team and wagon to help us move our goods from the depot. We reached the place about midnight and our decision was good, for the lovely widow was waiting up for us. She had set a

116

lighted lantern at the gate of their farm with a cardboard sign saying, "Weichman's home." It had been a day—and a half! I slept so soundly in spite of sharing the bed with husband and baby that I did not wake up until the sun was shining in the room. At first I was frightened, but then I quickly thought Arthur was perhaps bottling the baby as he often did for me the last few weeks if I overslept.

But it was Mrs. Weichman who was bottling my baby. A and her son, Hans, had left very early after she had given them a good hot breakfast. They hoped to reach Suniland in time to get the car unloaded that week. After all, it would take many, many trips for the wagons to go back and forth the five miles to our "farm" (Who could call that brushland a farm?)

It was Thanksgiving Day. Soon the dear lady had a hen baked, four lovely pumpkin pies made, bowls and bowls of garden fresh vegetable dishes cooked, and a table fit for a king set in her cozy kitchen. Annie and I crawled behind the table on the wooden bench and feasted while Mrs. Weichman packed pans and pans of food for us to take to the men.

Annie was the daughter. She was about six, I recall, but could play the piano like nobody's business. Mr. Weichman was a very accomplished musician and had spent all he could spare to provide a fine piano for his children. He also left them a large collection of music, mostly classical works.

Mrs. Weichman had a car, but she feared she might get stuck so she brought us and the pans of food in the buggy. Annie cuddled and sang to little Ruthie all the way, saying time and again that she was going to have "me a whole nest full." They had a chicken farm and to little Annie babies came by nestsful. Bless her!

It was a beautiful Thanksgiving evening. As they drove away and I was left alone at our new home, I came out to sit on the front steps to look at the sunset. I have always loved sunsets. The men had set up the baby bed and I had brought my little one out here to breast-feed her as it was bedtime for her. As I looked into the sunset, I began to sing one of my favorite hymns:

"Day is dying in the west
Heaven is touching earth with rest
Wait and worship while the night
Sets her evening lamps alight
Through all the sky.
Holy, holy, holy—Lord God of hosts
Heaven and earth are praising Thee."

117

I sang it over and over and over until the baby had emptied both breasts and was fast asleep. Then with a chuckle, I thought about the lamps we would need in the house. This was a standing joke with us. At first when it happened so often that night came and I had forgotten to fill the lamps with oil, trim the wicks and clean the chimneys, A did not scold. But you know how with time things either grow to be an irritant or a joke, this one fortunately turned out to be a joke. But this night, there were no lamps unpacked, and I wondered if there was any oil in the big can which was also in the train car.

So with the baby in the bed and darkness coming on, I went out again on the porch to listen for the sound of mules, men and wagons. Bauers, Lueschers, Freidles and goodness who else all? These soon came, four loads of them—our one and three of our new friends, some using their Model T trucks.

"And we thought we could go out on our own," I mused. There is no such thing as a person's living entirely unto himself. I vowed I would always remember to be a good neighbor. Have I been?

Company's Coming

To me, it seems, Thanksgiving and Christmas should be one holiday. For after all, the greatest gift man has to be thankful for is the birth of Christ. Spiritually one can not truly observe Christmas without being also thankful. (In a pagan vein, one would suppose it a good idea to get all the house-cleaning, baking and company over in one long drag, too.)

Company is a wonderful thing and now that we are better equipped to care for company, it seems to have become fashionable not to visit in homes as we did back in the 1920's and early 30's. We went to town every Saturday unless it poured down rain, and Arthur was always generous with buying food supplies. Yet it took some planning to be sure to have all one would need for the week . . . no extra running to the store for a loaf of bread or a box of detergent.

The pantry could get mighty bare if more than one drove of kith or kin pulled in unexpectedly during the week. Sometimes they forgot to bring along anything at all, but often (maybe for the lack of it the first time) relatives brought a package of fresh meat. This pound or two of hamburger, we called it simply ground beef then, would turn out to be a meat loaf to feed a dozen hungry men. 'Course, they never spied the rolled oats left from breakfast, the fresh carrots ground up in my sausage mill, the pint of thick cream and the stale corn bread mixed into the meat among other fillers.

That's why I just never got around to writing all the copies of the meat loaf recipes the men wanted to take along home to their wives. They would have thought our cupboard surely was bare. Well!

Of course, if we had known they were coming we could have done like the song says on the radio today, "I'da baked a cake." But the mail was picked up in the Three Rivers postoffice ten miles away on the same trip for the groceries on Saturday. So mail was not much help in letting one know who was coming and when. Except for my folk's first visit.

About a week after we moved, Mama wrote to tell us they

were coming to see us for Christmas. They would come on the twenty-sixth and Pauline could come with them. We counted the days.

Annie was a wonderful cook. She had shipped some of her home canned things down as we had also done. Among these were several large bags of pecans which she and I would shell in the afternoons while our babies napped. Then we baked pies and all manner of cakes and cookies together. I had a new stove and she had a small camp-style stove without an oven that winter. We also baked our bread loaves together.

But, of course, we had not started a garden by Christmas, and so we almost shouted for joy when Papa unloaded two or three large boxes of fresh "plunder from Aunt Lou and Aunt Frieda's garden."It was the best Christmas he could have brought. And bless him: for me he brought a picture album, for Ruthie he and Mama bought a small rocking chair, and for Arthur Mama had knitted two pairs of heavy, pure wool work socks.

We truly had a wonderful Christmas. Annie, Loui and little August ate dinner with us and were invited to eat again at supper. But Annie said, "No thanks. Once is enough to kill us once."

"That's all the times we need to kill you, Annie," Loui chimed in and with disgust added, "unless we have to hit your mouth another lick or two with a post to kill that."

We all thought it was a rich joke, and so Loui decided to let it be one and laughed and laughed. Papa enjoyed that joke over and over for many years to come. Each time Mama would tell something that Uncle Windy, one of her brothers said, Papa would use this old joke about having to hit one's mouth another lick or two after the head was dead.

We not only had company often but we sometimes enjoyed a Sunday visit with other families in the neighborhood. A very young bride with whom I felt I had much in common since her first child was a girl just a little older than ours, her husband was a farmer, and she loved music as much as did I, was and is our neighbor, Lena Koemel Schweikert.

She soon came to be known as the best cook in the territory, and folks have flocked to her kitchen door even more than they used to when her husband's sister and mother were hosts to the "whole area" and every land agent's clients.

My mother also had a half-sister and family living near Oakville with whom we often spent Sunday afternoons . . . unless they came to our house first. Aunt Annie was not the world's finickiest homemaker; and we often thought her husband, whom we called Rattlesnake Bill, wanted a change of scene on Sundays. She was a marvelous cook, though, and my husband was just as anxious to get to their house. It was for us a very sad summer—a few years later—when they both died. We will come to that.

We attended the church services in the Ray Point Methodist Church as often as we could. Services were on a circuit basis and so were not held each Sunday; and if it happened to be muddy, then perhaps it would be several weeks between our opportunities to attend. This often brought up the temptation not to give the accumulated offering when we did go. There always seemed to be so many other things we needed the money for much worse. Somehow, we managed to keep the faith. And when the crops have failed and we have had to borrow money to plant another year, we have always also borrowed to pay the Lord's part.

The Lord was good to us. The first year though we had very little field land of our own cleared, we made a wonderful cotton crop. There were very few insects in those days. I guess it took a while for them to learn that folk had moved into a new area. Arthur worked his brothers' acreage on shares. He was hell-bent on getting ahead.

At noon while the mules rested, he would take up the grubbing hoe and spade and help get the yard and garden land cleared. Bit by bit he soon had several acres nice around the house and barn. He built hog pens and a lot for the milk cows. We set out some native shrubs, built a large sand-pile for the baby, and even had several kinds of vegetables and flowers the very first spring.

When it came time for cotton picking, some of the young men from Monthalia wanted to come for a few weeks. First, Emilie's two sons, Elmer and Erwin, came. Later, a cousin, Robert Pape, and one of the Ehrig boys, Alvin, joined them. They were good workers, both in the field and at the table.

They still enjoy recalling that time together. Robert claims he drank a gallon of iced-chocolate milk for supper each evening. It was really something for the books to get up early enough to feed five hungry men in time for them to start picking cotton (we did not pull the burrs then). Then there was lunch and supper for them! When a rainy day hit, they had a ball.

Loui must have looked forward to a rainy day and set the "stuff" brewing. Always ready for some real fun, he had a batch ready when the day came that they could not work. The men

121

gathered together on the porch for resting and talking. They laughed until the house seemed to shake.

When Arthur came into the house, the boys went to Loui's to "just taste" some of old Loui's brew. That evening, trying to help with the chores, Robert picked up the first basket of ear corn and started marching round and round with it — as if he were marching in a parade.

Not to be outdone, the others picked up corn and bundles of corn-tops. They really meant to feed the corn to the pigs and the fodder to the cows. After a few rounds, while singing at the tops of their voices, Robert couldn't tell pigs from cows and over the fence into the cow pen he dumped the whole bushel basket of ear corn.

Too drunk to know any better, the other boys fed the surprised pigs the dry fodder. The cattle and pigs—by now just as excited —squealed and bellowed in just about the same key as the cotton pickers on a lark. The lark was the first ever for them, and if their mothers and dads ever learned of it, it was not our telling.

Loui was scared green by then. "That's one bunch of Methodists I don't want to play any tricks on anymore. They really go loco when they get a little swig, don't they, Arthur?"

Of course, I always contended they were more putting on and acting silly than drunk. But Erwin, the youngest, said he even had a "modern headache—one like he never had before in all his life."

Robert said the thing he hated about it most was that I refused to fix their usual chocolate milk that night. The reason I did not fix it was that the cows, both the Holstein and the Red Poll, kicked the buckets "plum across the cow-pen." There was only enough milk left for the next day's cream.

Arthur got the biggest bang of all out of the whole ordeal. He was in a ring-side seat, up on a ladder cleaning our windows. Loui had up until then put this by him. Until the corn went over the fence into the cow pen, he thought they were just putting on an act.

Annie and Loui soon found friends to their liking to visit who lived on the rivers. There are three at the town—the Atascosa, the Frio, and, merged together, they become the Nueces River which flows to the gulf at Corpus Christi. Naturally, Loui would find his friends where he could fish. Often in the super-markets today, their friends and I stop to recall the fine fish Loui caught for all of us.

Some of our company in those days was frightening. There

122

were the soldiers who said they were from San Antonio and they had permission from Mr. Eckhardt to hunt on our place. I was at home alone with the baby that day. I tried to explain to them that this was surely not true as we owned this farm. One of the men asked for a drink of water, and I sent him to the cistern at the back where a dipper hung on a wire.

He was insulted. He told me he was wearing a uniform for my sake and I could, at least, give him a drink of water. My conscience was softer than my wisdom, and I was just opening the latch on the screen door to ask them in for coffee when Mr. Eckhardt rode up from his pasture across the road on his beautiful bay horse.

"There is Mr. Eckhardt. Go ask him about hunting," I said. They drove away, but they did not stop to speak to Mr. Eckhardt. I went out to explain to him what they had said, and he said he had never seen them. He also said they should not have been in those uniforms at this time.

Not many days after that, a land agent came to ask permission to take some pictures. He said he wanted to use them to advertise the fine soil and the wonderful crops we grew here. I could see no harm in that so I said he could. But I knew he was a crook when I saw him standing by a corn stalk in the garden holding an ear in each hand. Those were ears he took out of his pockets to hold by the two there were already on the stalk. He also laid two huge watermelons down in the garden and was just fixing to stand over them as if he were plucking one when I noticed his error.

"Wait, that is a pumpkin vine," I called out to the two men.

They huddled together for a few minutes talking and then put the two melons on our porch; one of the men took out his pocket knife and cut them both. He sat down beside them with his legs swinging; the other man snapped the picture. They got into their car, said not a word, left the cut melons and drove away.

I rescued the melons. When the others came from the fields, we had a feast. Annie had been hoeing in the fields and I had kept little August. We let him eat all he wanted. He got very sick the next day, and I was so afraid. It was a long way to town when a baby was sick and the doctor, the only one, might just as well be in the opposite direction forty miles.

Luckily, I knew a lot about care for a case of diarrhea, for I had attacks of it all my life. Annie was so confident in what I would do for her son that she went to work in the fields as usual

123

the next day. She was a wonderful cotton chopper. Besides, Annie said the exercise was necessary for her as she was carrying another baby. This one, she vowed, would not be named for the month in which "it" came, but for the doctor. She hoped for a girl but wondered how Charles would sound for a girl "after while when she goes to school."

Charlie sounds fine, as it turned out. He is a grown man now and often visits with his parents who now live in El Campo. It was hard to give them up but like Papa . . . and later like Arthur . . . a man must seek a place of his own for his family.

Other company that often came was Uncle William and his sons. Uncle William was my husband's mother's brother. He owned a fourth of a section of land next to our farm. He also owned large farms at Robstown. He owned their home place at Monthalia in Gonzales County. There he and Aunt Mary reared a large family of cousins for Arthur to enjoy. I don't imagine that was their purpose in having them, but it was a side blessing. Arthur spends many evenings recalling the days when he, the Hornungs, and the Pape cousins who lived nearby got a chance to visit.

Like it was, the mail was in the postoffice while the company was at the door. Many fine dove and fat quail died for the "cause." Often, in the years when company was constant, I went into the fields or woods for a short time to bring in the meat. I never got a shot at a deer. It aggravates me. To console me, my silly man says I smell too much like sugar and they can smell me coming.

Other company was the preachers. We always enjoyed having them, for most of them either knew our parents personally or had heard of them. It gave us a moral boost to hear the kind things they could truthfully say about our families. Many of them wondered how it was that two of my sisters decided to be deaconesses. I did not know either, but one day Arthur hit on a clever answer. "There are so many of them, they had to double up on the choice of occupations unless they wanted to stay on the farm and milk cows."

The preachers did not exactly take to that answer. It seemed to imply that some preachers (and deaconesses) may be working at their posts as though they were jobs instead of "callings."

The company we probably enjoyed the most was old Luther and some of the others who had worked for us "back home;" they decided to come down and pick cotton a few days for "Mr. Arthur." For them, A killed the best hen in the flock and made an extra trip to town that Sunday afternoon for ice to make ice-cream. Picking started the next day, and what a crop we made!

We were ever so lucky in our new location until the second January, when Arthur took the flu and later "yellow jaundice" as it was then referred to by most folks. We had to go to San Antonio to put him in the Santa Rosa Hospital. The baby and I stayed with sister Lula.

It was a long walk from her apartment on Brooklyn Avenue to the hospital with a twenty pound baby, purse and diaper bag. But Lula walked to work and so there wasn't anything said about my taking a street car.

One day at the end of the week, it just got too much for me, and I inquired of a policeman as to the cost of riding a street car. I told him I had never ridden one and was embarrased, not knowing how to pay and how to get off. The kindly fellow told me exactly how to do it, and that day I saved a nickel from my lunch money and the baby and I rode home in style.

How excited and rushed we had gotten to get Arthur to the hospital in San Antonio! He had even suggested that Loui tie him into the back seat with a strong cord, just in case he should actually go mad on the way.

For heaven's sake, how could anyone be so stupid? But we had never once doubted that Loui had understood the doctor when he said "it sounds like hepatitis." It was a long time afterwards when we returned to Three Rivers to question Dr. Williamson that we learned what he had said.

Loui had told us "hydrophobia." It wasn't impossible, we had reasoned, as A worked with cattle and we had several dogs, cats and even a pet coon. Some people had told us that deer often have hydrophobia. We were scared green. So scared in fact that I was allowed to drive the car all the way into the hospital emergency driveway.

It was like heaven on earth to get Daddy (we all called him that now) well and home again a month later. With sheer will-power of which God has granted him an ample supply, he pulled his work plans together and started a crop again.

Should There Be Secrets

In late April, we were both over the shock—we were as happy as on our first date—and we started another "crop" all our own again. I hoped for a son from the very first, but Arthur insisted it would be much nicer to have a girl. "Besides, it is cheaper: they can share each other's room, toys and clothes," he reasoned. Times were not too easy for us, and he was determined to get ahead while he was yet young and strong.

"If it is a girl, then the next time we will order a boy," was his way of planning. He got his first wish, but for the boy he had to wait fourteen more years — a son-in-law, the next-best way to have a boy.

In our case, it was not our choice . . . it was just that with the complications of this pregnancy no other babies were ever ordered. Much of the remainder of the year was spent between bed-sheets, and I fairly earned a "degree" in planning my work. Keeping a lively two year old content and a household going without hired help is what I made my major that year.

I learned to write, iron, hand-sew, read, eat and feed a baby while staying relaxed in the bed. I am proud of this accomplishment when I see my "degree"—a second daughter, born on February 6. Both girls were born on the sixth of the month. Mama could not come to stay with me. Therefore, many times during the worst days, the doctor would have me stay at a nursing home — Mrs. Paul's in town. Sometimes, when all her beds were taken, I stayed at the Montgomery's—the mayor and his wife, no less. This was their first year in Three Rivers, and even then their apartment was home to many in need.

Now they have a large rock home; and when I attend a bridal shower there or just stop for a chat, I always remember their kindness to me. In later years, their son and daughter became our daughters' best friends and schoolmates during high school days in town.

Time just doesn't wait for anyone. Arthur was elected school trustee and he immediately set about studying what could be done to improve the entire school system. A library was installed, catalogued and widely used by children and grown-ups.

We had a telephone line built out from Three Rivers, and the whole community had access to the phone in a small room of the school building. By "we" I mean the school and community as a whole. Everyone joined the Parent-Teacher Association, attended the school functions and made many lasting friendships.

This year a friend from Gonzales had come to be one of our teachers. As we still did not need our spare bedroom, except for the many over-night guests, we decided to let her board with us. We could use the five dollars per week; and besides, she was more or less "family." At least, we hoped the courtship with Bill Hornung would come to marriage. We hoped right.

She was so sweet to our children. I helped her make her wedding dress; and little, roly-poly Ruthie was a flower girl in the wedding. Many interesting things had happened that year. Among them was snow on March 31st . . . of all things. And Arthur out there cultivating his corn! Two days later, he started replanting the whole crop.

The teacher — and later cousin-in-law — was our first baby's namesake, Ruth Sievers. This day when the snow came and there was no school because of the weather, we talked of many things. She confided in me that it was about to break her heart that Bill had refused to be a farmer.

"Today you would know better, I'd think — with corn in the fields six inches high and this blizzard comes along."

"I don't care. Farming may be a gamble, but so is all of life. No matter what one chooses to do, there is risk in it. My father said once in a sermon that when one prays for rain for his fields, he must remember that rains will also bring the weeds. You know, the best roses have the thickest thorns."

"All right then, take Bill for what he is and not for what you wish he were. After all, everyone cannot be a farmer. Some have to be policemen. You are a teacher and I am just a homemaker . . . see?"

It just seemed impossible that any storm clouds could gather on our horizons that year. I enjoyed our boarder Ruth so very much. During the spring she and Bill were married. While we were visiting my folks after the wedding, which was held in the Monthalia Methodist Church, Ruth and Bill spent the night in our spare bedroom — After all, the rent was paid.

The next year we would have to have new teachers. The summer was hot and trying. It was dry, and we ran out of cistern water. My brother spent a few weeks with us, and later another young man came to work to weigh the cotton and do other chores for us. Those were the days before contractors came and made a trade for a whole field or farm and, as now, brought in their own hands and trucks.

We had an old second-hand Model T Ford truck that got as hot as a fire-cracker when it chugged along to the cotton gin. But it was as faithful as the sunrise and sunset and served us for several years. Steam would fume out of the over-flow pipes and dance the radiator cap up and down when we would stop at the gin or come back to the field for another load.

With the new baby—Carolyn Marie—so tiny and Ruth so spunky that one could hardly keep up with her, I would not get to see much of A during the long weeks of harvest. Except each evening just after we had supper, he would take us along to the gin. Imagine the thrill of going to town five times a week! While we waited our turn at the sucker-stands to have our cotton ginned, he would walk several blocks to a little cafe and bring us some treats. The babies were put to sleep on the porch of the Schulz gin; and sometimes, when it got as late as midnight, we would also snooze sitting against the wall beside them.

Those were the days—days to remember with joy. Would that one had the ability to forget all days that were not filled with joy. Like a thunder storm, some came looming up late that summer.

Maybe it was all meant to serve as a test for the durability of our love for one another. Hannah would say, "Nome, it ain't that at tall. It is jes that the devil done made hissef at home in somebody's soul and heart and mind and spirit." The question is then in whose soul and heart and mind and spirit was the devil lodging so comfortably that the end result almost drove us to a loss of goals.

Max had come to see us briefly one Sunday. He and his wife had reached town late on a Saturday and decided to stay in a hotel there. We knew they were to come. He had telephoned a few days before to the school, and we had called him back to see what he wanted to tell us. We had fixed a nice supper — cake, ice-cream and everything—It was not really trouble, for it was Saturday and we had shopped that day. We waited and waited.

Next morning they came about ten, just as we were leaving to go to church. We had a friend spend the night with us, and we were going to the Lutheran Church with her. It irritated Arthur that Max came late . . . now that we were ready to leave. But Arthur was nice to him anyway and we enjoyed their visit, up

128

to the point of his conversation when he insisted we leave the farm that year.

"After all you don't think you can raise decent women out here in this God forsaken country, do you? How in the name of common sense will they ever amount to anything? We will all be ashamed of them, being raised out here like real country hicks and . . . "

"You just mind your own business and I don't want to hear another word about it," Arthur raised his voice and his eyes which, on such occasions, can look right through a fellow.

I just can't stand for anyone to be insulted in my home so I tried to smooth things over. A misunderstood and thought I was agreeing with his opponent. A battle-royal followed with Arthur getting in the last word in defense of both their parents and mine as being farmers.

"I am proud of our folks and don't you ever forget it. The sooner you get over the idea that you are a self-made man, the happier you and all of us will be. There is no such thing; and if it had not been for Papa's hard work and Mother's patience with us all, where would you and I be today?"

I went into the house where our friend, Noonie, was waiting to be taken back to town. It was now noon and so we first fixed a bit of lunch. Even then, Arthur and Max were still standing at his car talking. At last, he came in but excused himself from eating. Poor fellow, I thought. He always has trouble with head-aches' being worse on Sundays than while at work. This would be a horrible afternoon.

Noonie (now Mrs. Olan Cavitt of Sinton) sensed the strain and, bless her heart, did all she could to ease it for the day. She was one person we both enjoyed talking with and could benefit from even today visiting more often for a chat. (People should really keep up old friendships more than just the annual letters at Christmas.)

Even Noonie could not help entirely with strengthening me for the battle of forgiveness I had in the next few weeks. It seemed nothing was good enough or pleased Arthur now like it did before his brother's two hour sermon on why we should leave the farm.

It was my firm conviction, like Papa used to say, that a wife owed it to her husband to "save" wherever she could. Papa had an old German expression about a woman's being able to throw more out of a small window than her husband can shovel in through a wide door.

One day I was pouring the coffee for our dinner when A noticed I had a large patch on the shoulder of my dress. The patch I had set very carefully; but, naturally, it was newer-looking in color and did show.

"What are you doing with that old rag on?" he asked.

"What old rag? I have had this dress for years, and now you notice it. I'll have you know this is the very same dress you thought was so pretty when I first wore it to the school program."

"I'll not have you wearing such stuff . . . with those big patches on it. Besides, it doesn't look like you even ironed it."

Words flew by then. I had ironed the dress but not really too carefully. Heating flat-irons on a kerosene cook-stove was a terrific chore. By the time I got all the other things ironed, I would give my dresses a lick and a promise to do better next time.

It was the first time in all the days of our being together he had ever said I was not dressed properly. It cut me as if a knife had been inserted in my chest and twisted. So this was what country-life was doing for me, I thought. Even Arthur thought I looked like a tramp . . . In my mind, it grew larger and larger. Instead of taking it for a clue to go to the store and buy some new clothes, I was hurt.

As sure as a person attaches pity to himself, it grows like a tumor; and before one is aware of its presence, it has become a malignancy. So self-pity almost destroyed me for a while.

Several long letters continued to try to persuade us to leave the farm and move to Houston. Each time, the letters were quickly read and put aside to be answered, "when it rains and I have time."

Finally, I talked to Noonie about my hurt. She laughed at me. As we were laughing, at least she was and I was trying to, Pansy Elliott joined us on the pallet where we had spread a picnic lunch down at the Kittie West townsite.

"Tell Pansy. She will never believe it . . . a gal with a husband who likes pretty everyday dresses, and the gal thinks she is helping by 'saving' the price of them."

Pansy said she knew about it. She said she had noticed that I wore prettier things at home this year than I even wore to town. "But gosh, I thought you were just afraid we were flirting with A," she said and then we all laughed.

That night after I told him about confiding in the girls. it all turned into a simple little joke. And forgiveness was as easy as taking a drink of water. The next day as we said the morning

130

prayer, I had a wonderful feeling when I came to the words, " . . . forgive us our trespasses as we forgive those who trespass against us."

"I feel good this morning," I admitted as I kissed A when he left for the field.

"Good! That's a lovely housecoat. I like pink and white checks on you as well as on the kids." Our life grew stronger with just such a small statement as that.

"Maybe I shall find I am wrong, but where else would I be happy but on the land?", I dared to ask again that day.

Septembers Bring New Neighbors

Each fall new families would move into our school district. It really was not surprising as the Fant School was the only one in the county that owned a bus and hired a chauffeur to go around each day to get the children and take them home again in the afternoons. This was as unheard of as was the idea of teaching Mexican and Anglo children in the same rooms.

One family moved in with the knowledge of the bus service but did not know of or approve of those "beans" going to school with their children. The father came to introduce himself one day and to introduce his problem.

As A was telling it to me that night at supper after the children were asleep, he said, "I told that guy just to be real sure his kids were clean. I told him the teachers would see that all the children were clean and that the teachers we had didn't care what the color of the pencil just so the child spelled the words correctly and got the answers to his problems right. The pencils all write black, and the chalk all writes white no matter what color the hand that holds them."

I was so proud of that statement that I wrote it into my diary. I added, "He knows more about missionary work than do I, and I read and study the missionary literature every week."

Another family that came, the Kelms, were a real joy to us, especially to Arthur, as the Kelms are fine farmers. They are also true Christian neighbors and friends . . . make me think of our very own parents. Mrs. Kelm, we soon started calling her Mama Kelm, has gone to many tenant homes to help with baby deliveries or help care for the sick. Pappy, Mr. Kelm, has had his hands on most everyone's well pipes when the wells gave troubles — anytime — summer or cold winter days.

On to our farm we moved a family who were as lovely neighbors as any we have ever had — the Velasquez family. They had more grown children than we had year-round work for, and so they did not all get to stay with us but a few years. Some of the older boys were excellent musicians and soon found employment with a dance band in Beeville. The girls often helped me with my work and never would they take pay. In turn, I would set their hair or let them make clothes on our sewing machine.

Each September as school was about to open, new teachers — or perhaps the same ones with new additions to their families — would come back to the teacherage. And always there would be the big September P-T-A. school party welcoming the new folks and giving all of us an opportunity to see each other after long and busy summers.

It wasn't anything new for me to be present on the first day of school; but the year that our first daughter started, even Daddy took the morning off to go along. And then he made a special trip to George West to report to the county school superintendent, to get instructions and supplies. It was a big day for all of us! Is there any greater joy than to see happy children?

This year we did not have to board any teachers. The couple who taught and who lived in the teacherage were willing to board the one other teacher. So we had room for parties in our house, and the first neighborhood friendship-quilt party was held there. In all my excitement to get ready, I got too keyed up — I guess — and I missed the party, spending the next few days in town under the doctor's care. The ladies were so sweet though. They came and finished my quilt, left the house in apple-pie order, and filled the cookie jar full.

One year after school started — I'm not sure whether it was the same year — we decided to plant native shrubbery around the campus. We picked a school holiday to do that. Imagine going to school anyway, even on a holiday. You must understand that to rural people their school was their total community life. Everyone brought his picnic lunch; and after we had gone to the nearby woods and brought in the Cenizo and laurel plants, we ate together. There was an early norther, and it was quite nippy.

We built a fire in the big pot-bellied heater in the building. Everyone gathered round to sing and chatter. The men huddled off in one corner at first to talk farming; but soon Mr. Matthews got them to sing, too. Matthews, a good singer, had a way about him that could just about get anybody singing, no matter how reluctant the singer was when first the circle was formed.

One of the girls in the group was missing for a few minutes; and when she came in, it seemed she sang like a bird, high and shrill, like she had never been heard to sing before. Matthews asked her, "What's with you?"

She held up her left hand and showed us a beautiful ring.

Then everyone sang more happily, for when there was joy in the community everyone shared it. When there was sorrow, everyone was concerned. At least, I always felt the people were closely knit and interested in each other.

One night as we sat discussing first one thing and then another — this was the way for us in the evenings after supper, for we had no radio and television was just then being read and talked about —the subject came up of how much neighbors mean to us. I pointed out the vast difference in all our neighbors and A insisted that was what made them so fine. Talents lacking in one family were found in another. All put together we made one large happy community.

When school consolidation came — and it was good in many ways — it would and later did bring to an abrupt end this community. Burdened with the terribly low prices for crops, many men began to wonder where and how to manage for their families. Cotton had dropped in a few years from 19c to six cents per lint pound and livestock raising was not looked on as a quick way to get rich either.

In our own little family, illness had come to camp. First, it was surgery again for me, and that meant another trip to Gonzales (to leave the babies with my folks) and a couple of trips to San Antonio. Now, we hop in the Chrysler and zip up Highway 281 to San Antonio to shop for shoes or maybe just to attend a play or the opera. Not so in days of six cent cotton and second-hand Whippet cars.

George had married a young widow who had a daughter just older than Carolyn. This was the cousins' first visit together, and they became real pals. My girls looked forward after that to summers at Papa and Mama's, where George and Beatrice and Betty Jo lived on the farm. We called Beatrice Pat, but Mama never did. Pat helped care for the two extra babies. Together, she and Mama were life-savers for us several times.

Before Nookie (Daddy's nickname for Carolyn) was three, she had to have her tonsils removed. She breathed like a freight train. Dr. Dan Russell, the EENT specialist in San Antonio, thought it best to also remove Ruth's tonsils and adenoids. So back to Santa Rosa Hospital we went.

I can still feel the ache in my heart as Arthur and I sat on a small walnut love-seat in the ante-hall near the doors of the operating rooms waiting for the circulating nurse to give us the good news. Arthur cried like a baby when he saw the nurses and interns roll Ruthie into the operating room. By the time they

134

took Carolyn in, he was too sick to even raise his face to watch. All went fine, and by night he and Lula went home; and I stayed with the children.

Our girls love to sing. In fact, they started singing as soon as they started talking, and to us it seems they came talking — especially Carolyn. That year a very popular song was, "It Ain't Gonna Rain No Mo'" (Wendell Woods Hall—exclusive Victor artist).

It has twenty-four verses, and I knew them all. I sang them and sang them to the girls. I would try changing over to songs I liked such as "Marcheta" (Victor L. Schertzinger) or the very popular "Smiles" by J. Will Callahan and Lee S. Roberts, but each time I did Carolyn would set up a howl. Ruth was very quiet and good the whole day and night.

The next morning, Ruth was as stiff as a stick and couldn't even whisper; Carolyn asked for fried chicken and managed to swallow some. The doctor said she had limbered up by yelling each time I changed tunes.

For years after that when we were in the hospital again, the supervising Sister on the third floor would greet me with, "Well, did you ever finish singing 'Ain't Gonna Rain No Mo?" Then she would laugh and tease us about that tonsilectomy when "your Mother almost sang her own tonsils out for you children."

Luckily, the Velasquez family returned to Three Rivers, and one of the married men came back to work on our farm that spring. His wife was a wonderful neighbor to me. I could talk to her when I was worried, and she usually came up with some very sound thoughts.

One day as I was helping her give her infant an enema, she said she often wondered why people made such a difference about colors. She was, of course, speaking of racial prejudice, but we neither one used such terminology. In Houston where her baby was born, she told me, they had been asked to use a ward room until her doctor insisted on a private room.

"The doctor is a Mexican, too. But they didn't notice that he was a different color. What do you say about that, Blanca Muchacha?"

The whole family called me that even though I had often asked them not to. They said they liked it and that because I was so pale and my hair so blond, it just suited me to be called "white girl." I guess I did look more like a girl than a woman as I walked across the fields with my long blond hair blowing in the breeze.

Thank God for the answer he put into my mouth to her that day. I told her she should not think or speak so often of the difference herself, for truly it did not matter. I advised her to see that her babies got an education and to take them to church where everyone was welcome. In my heart, I knew this later statement was not entirely true. Not in our church anyway. For if the brown skinned citizens felt welcome there, surely they would come.

I felt a sudden happiness in my reasoning; and as it was the day — March 10 — for writing to Miss Ora on her birthday, I started to write all about that. I was interrupted for some reason and then later went to the mail-box (we now had rural free delivery three times a week). We had a letter from Mama, and she wrote of Miss Ora's death. Mama always wrote about everyone who "passed away." I never finished my letter, but I kept it to remind myself that it was my responsibility to show kindness to my neighbor, not to judge him.

A farmer's wife has much time on her hands to think. While walking to the fields with an afternoon jug of coffee (toddling feet to guide slowly along), doing a large washing on a rub-board, churning cream or mending the ever-present torn work clothes, surely one does not want to keep his mind on the task at hand. It became a pleasure to anticipate to have a large ironing to do or a real big stack of mending and sewing. Even today, those are the best hours of the week — the hours for thinking and dreaming and scheming.

Lena and I found we liked thinking together. Many times, Paul would bring her and the girls over for the day. Other times, I would drive over with my two. And the playing and teasing the four girls could do would fill a book in itself.

It is not hard to practice loving one's neighbor as one's self. The test for me is loving myself. I often drive myself as if I were a team of mules, trying to do the utterly impossible. I have written four complete manuscripts only to tear them up, fearing in my heart that I have no right to expect anyone to read them just because I wrote them.

The kindly old Doctor Williamson gave me some sound advice one day when again I was very sick. He had gotten me to admit that I was worried about things I could do nothing to change.

"You must learn as I have learned that problems have to be faced and taken up and weighed. If there is something worrying you which you can do something about, get at it and do that. If there is something you have no solution for and cannot do anything about, leave it to the man upstairs. There are others who also can do things."

There are others who also can do things. It opened a new field for me. I must learn to organize better and learn to work with people. Instead of trying to do the work of the P-T A that year, I learned that I could be a good president even though I had to miss many of the meetings because of illness. It was a real joy to have the officers gather around my bed and plan the school closing program. Neighbors worked shoulder to shoulder in the Home Demonstration Club and the 4-H Clubs as well as in the Parent-Teacher Association.

I had to learn to not be the wheel nor even to try being the hub cap that kept the wheel on the axle. I learned to be one of the spokes. With other spokes firmly staying in place, neither the hub, the cap nor the rim can get out of place. It was the start of years of joyous community and civic work. Many times again, I have re-learned, "It's the many little cogs that turn the big drive wheel."

It was the spring of 1934, when we were planning the school closing program and picnic afterwards at Suniland, that Rufus (Ruth's nickname at school) came home with an odd story.

Ruth was really too young to go to school, but Betty Schweikert had wanted Ruth to start with her; and as there was room for her in the first grade, no one objected. Ruth could recite the twenty-third "Psolemn" (the way she said it) very nicely. Mrs. McNeese suggested she say it for the program.

The mothers thought, in fact, it would be nice if the whole class said the Psalm in unison. This brought on an odd report a few days later from Rufus. There was a little boy in the class, new people that year, who said to the teacher and classmates that his Papa would not allow him to use the word "shepherd."

"We lost our home on account of the wool prices, and Papa gets mad every time Mama talks about when we used to have lots of sheep in West Texas. Papa was a wonderful herder, but he won't like my saying Jesus is one of those guys."

"For heaven's sake, are you telling the truth?"

"Yes, she is," Betty defended Rufus. "Mr. Matthews said the girls could say the Psalm and the boys could sing "Ain't Gonna' Rain No Mo' — the first twelve verses would be enough."

What a combination! What a day for understanding neighbors. It was a good thing Dr. Williamson had told me "hands off of other people's problems" that very morning.

137

Daughter Starts A Diary

It was not surprising that Rufus started writing a diary at a very early age for folks often remarked, "you two are just like two peas in a pod."

Rufus was helping me shell fresh English peas one morning. It had been a very good year for the garden; and, you know, when peas have plenty of water and plant food, they often crowd into the shells so tightly that they are misshapen.

"Look at this pod full of old wrinkly ones. I hope that's not what people think me and you look like!"

"You and I!" I corrected her.

"You and I don't look like no peas in no pods like this."

I let the correcting go and had a good laugh about it as we continued to notice the many shapes of the peas we shelled. After a while, my little daughter decided there were really no two peas exactly alike. She felt better, I could tell from the expression on her face. I thought the subject closed.

To my surprise, at noon when she passed the peas to her Daddy, she told him all about learning there are no two peas exactly alike.

"Some are more wrinkled over this way," she jumped off her chair to demonstrate by twisting her bottom and, "some this way," she pushed out her chest and, "some are . . . "

"That's enough. Get up here now and eat your lunch."

"It's important, Daddy. I and Mama don't look like no old wrinkly peas. And we don't look like those all round and fat cooked."

Daddy explained to her that it was just an expression people used and did not really mean anything. She was glad and made no bones about telling us that she was glad 'cause she sure did not want to be skinny like her Mama, whose feet were too big. The only thing she wanted to do just exactly like Mama was, "marry you, Daddy."

"Oh, you can't do that. Patsy Montgomery has already asked me to marry her, remember?", he teased. Patsy is Carolyn's age and every time she and her brother Bobby visited, she would cuddle

138

up on Arthur's lap and ask him to marry her. She liked everything about him, she said. She mostly liked the chewing gum he always kept in his shirt pocket for the children.

Another major surgery for me brought me to the position of feeling like I was a burden to Arthur. We were having it rough, as was everyone. The depression was not only in the nation's economy: it was very real in my thinking. I found it hard to keep up my chin. There was a young student nurse at the hospital who had the time to chat with me one day after her duty hours.

"Why are you so sad?"

I tried to deny that I was sad. I tried not to admit that I was homesick, that I could hardly wait until Sunday when Arthur would be coming to see me, when Papa and Olga would be bringing the children for a visit. But she seemed to sense that I was holding back.

So she told me of her family—the one she had had, that is, before a train ran into their car in another state as they were seeking work. She said of the seven children, mother and father, all in a Ford car, she alone was left. She was then a senior in high school but had quit because there was no money left for shoes, a graduation dress and such things. She knew the name of the San Antonio doctor who had delivered her parents' last baby; and when she could not think of anyone else to tell the police that she knew, she gave them his address. The next thing she knew, she was told to go to San Antonio on a train; the doctor and his wife met her there, and the next week she was back in school during the day-time and working in the hospital evenings and Sundays.

"My goodness!" was about all I could say.

"I have decided since I am now all that is left of my family, I will have to be nine times as busy as if we were all living. What about you? Do you like to stay busy, too?"

"Do I! That is what is the matter with me. I miss my work even more than I miss my family," I confessed as I then first realized about what I was so depressed.

She enjoyed hearing about our life on the farm and my many community interests. I thought I was telling her something very novel, she showed such fascination. When I had finished, she calmly said she understood, for she and her family had once lived at Lytle; and they had gone to a place near Oakville to pick cotton.

"My goodness! We live right there in that area; maybe you all even picked cotton for us."

"Small world!" she said. It was the first time I had ever heard the expression. It is a small world indeed. Yet, there are many immense hearts in this so-called small world. The very next morning, she came rushing into my room with a Kress envelope in which she brought me a stamped doily and some pink and green thread along with an embroidery hoop and needle.

"I forgot to get a thimble so I borrowed one from my roommate," she said as she left in a hurry to get to Mass and then to her duties.

The little doily still had "10c" stamped on it, but it was worth more than ten dollars to me, the receiver, and to the little student nurse, the giver. Several times in the next few days she would pop in for a moment to see how I was progressing. It was hard at first to hold my hands up to do the stitching from my absolute supine position. But in a few days, I was elevated a little higher and then even higher and the tingling left my hands.

I finished the little doily the day before I was to leave. I showed it to the Sister, who volunteered to have it pressed for me. When she brought it back the next morning, she also brought a yard of lace edging and told me it would be nice if I would put that on "today."

It was the medicine I needed — work to be done and work that someone expected me to get finished. I finished it and lettered it very neatly in the center, "To a loving nurse." When I left the hospital, I had the doily sent to the nurses' station.

"How will they know who to give it to? You have not put a name on the bag," Arthur commented as I asked him to deliver it down the hall.

"They will know. Everyone has been in here to see the doily. I have never made anything that so many people were interested in in all my life."

"It was not altogether the doily," the supervisor said as they wheeled my chair to the elevator. "It isn't every day that we have patients like you who try to be cheerful and who do so want to get well."

Then she teased my husband by saying that if everyone had such a will to get well enough to get out of the hospital, they would go broke. Lula was there to see us off and, as usual, to put a ten dollar bill in Arthur's shirt pocket with the admonition," Now you get yourselves some good things to eat with that." Dear Lula! She just could not see how we managed with crops so cheap and expenses so terrific.

Ruth and Carolyn were easy children to manage, thank God!

They were both book-worms, Carolyn trying to read when she was only three and Ruth doing a marvelous job of teaching her. As we would be driving along, they would read road signs. Often Mama would come and stay a few days with us and then we would take her home or to the bus station in town. She was thrilled that the girls liked to read, for she was a devoted book-worm, too. My fondest picture I have of my Mama is one of her reading a book.

When Carolyn was four, she could read fourth grade readers. One afternoon (this we should never have allowed) she was asked to be on a program in the school in town. Mrs. Drozd asked her to read. She handed her a sixth grade Civics book she had never seen. Carolyn read the whole page. It was not the thing to do as it perhaps started a streak of jealousy Carolyn had to face later in high school.

The days of spelling between us to keep the children from knowing what we were saying were over, alas! Even today, we say "c-r-e" instead of "ice-cream;" for when Carolyn was so tiny that she could not remember the whole spelling, she knew exactly what we meant when we asked each other if we had time and money to get some "i-c-e-c-r-e-a-m." We learned that one afternoon when it was very warm. She came to us and suggested we drive to town to get some "ICE" to make some "CRE."

Papa had written that we should get the piano from home so the girls could learn to play. There wasn't anyone there to enjoy it, he thought. I objected because I knew Mama often played to herself and sang her favorite "Trust and Obey." Also, when we visited we played the piano. But Papa insisted, and so Arthur got the Froehner boys to haul it for us on the truck. Erwin, Arthur's nephew, was now married to one of our school teachers and living a mile from us.

Came the fall of 1936. Papa wrote to us more often that year than ever before — telling once about getting the piano; sending us original canceled stamped letters commemorating the Gonzales Centennial; telling of the possibility of his losing the place he and three partners had purchased a few years before at Los Angeles, Texas; and mentioning several times how lonely he and Mama were.

It was also the winter the doctors put Carolyn to bed. She was very scrawny and ran a temperature when up and trying to keep up with the other children. She had begged to start school, and we had let her; but in about a month, nothing would do but bed-rest. I think that was why Papa wrote so often and why he felt so blue about us.

141

Not one to be depressed though was Carolyn, now called "Monkey" by all the neighbors. Everyone was nice about coming to see her. She had captured the heart of old Doctor Williamson long ago. She used to slip away from Arthur in church (we now attended the First Methodist Church in Three Rivers) and go way up front to sit in the end of the pew by the doctor. The doctor modestly said he suspected she did that so she could pet his big shaggy dog that always came along and lay under the bench. I was then in the choir and Arthur sat with the children.

We found out better. It was the doctor she adored. In her very childish handwriting in the front of a hand-me-down second grade reader which she used for a text book to teach her dolls, she wrote: Dr. Carolyn Marie Adlof. She would line up the dolls, the stuffed Oswold toy and her big piggy bank at the foot of the bed and pretend they were her pupils.

One day when she was unusually sick and the doctor had to come and lance a gland that had swelled in the side of her neck, she took the book and showed him the inscription. She could not talk that day, the swelling was so tight.

Neither could the doctor talk, his throat and eyes filled so with emotion. After a long watch over her during which he caught a nice nap out in the quiet and peaceful country, he told her to be a good doctor. She promised him she would. She kept her word.

At Christmas, we went home to stay for two weeks with my folks. Ruth visited some in town with her cousin of the same age, Warren, who is the younger son of Arthur's sister Ella and her husband Ernest Pagel. Betty went along and the three enjoyed Warren's new skates until Ruth fell down and used a bad word. Aunt Ella made them put up the skates and play dominoes.

When Arthur came for us at the end of our stay, he told the girls that Lubber, their dog, was missing. It made going home a sad occasion. They asked over and over all the way, "How many miles now, Daddy?"

Quickly when we got home, the nine year old ran around the house to look for Lubber. Peering under the back porch, she yelled back with glee, "Here he is, Daddy. Here he is. Lubber, he had some pups!"

This Christmas, 1937, Mr. Matthews gave all the fifth graders diaries. To read a child's diary is a real experience. Many days, the entry is in my hand-writing for if Ruth would forget, she would probably phone me at recess and say, "Mother, please write yesterday down." We had a telephone now as did several other families along the line.

"We are practicing for county meet. We went home this afternoon with Betty and Marie. Marie bumped into her aunt and broke a bucket of eggs. Erwin and Daddy butchered two hogs today. No school today, it rained and the bus could not go. There are spinach cutters all over the field."

"Mother won her bet. We did sell more spinach than Daddy said it would be and so Mama gets the over-money for a radio and couch. We played "radio" this afternoon just like we hear them doing. Bobby was the singer, and I was the piano. Mother had a wise tooth chopped out and it got reflected bad and she can't open her mouth."

"Doctor came to see Tootsie (Carolyn) but he just barely looked at me. I had to vomick the most though."

"Today is Daddy's birthday but we are in Gonzales. I think Tootsie is going to die like Lubber did."

" (Feb. 6) Carolyn is six today and Betty Paul, Eloise George, Marie, Betty Marie and Gladys came after school with their mothers to give her a surprise party. Duane Stearns is mad because he has a birthday tomorrow and never has had a party."

"I am getting big and poor Tootsie weighs 40 pounds now. We like Amos and Andy on our new radio. Mother started teaching piano lessons today."

" (March 1) Aunt Mary and Uncle William Hornung brought Mr. and Mrs. Letterman from Oklahoma to see us today. They had spent the night with Milton and Lois, their children, who live behind us."

"Uncle Letterman gave me and Tootsie each a dollar bill. We have six each now. He said Grandpa Adlof paid Uncle Letterman's way to America from Germany about a hundred years ago, I think."

" (March 8) Betty and I won the county meet contests. I won by saying 'Somebody's Mother' without missing a word. Hurrah! Our teachers got married today. I will have to say Mrs. Matthews now instead of Miss Johnson, Daddy said."

"Mother let Tootsie read the eighth chapter of Matthew for Missionary meeting today and Daddy was real proud. You could tell!"

" (March 20) I could not practice my music today because the radio kept me crying for 400 children were killed in London, Texas, in an explosion. I wish we did not have a radio to tell us so many bad news."

"April 18 — We went to church this morning; had dinner at

143

Milton and Lois and we all went to the school this afternoon for a baseball game. Pulled a tooth yesterday in town and put it under my pillow and found only nine pennies under it this morning. No wonder Daddy says it is hard times. We used to get ten cents."

"April 23 — We saw the Battle of Flowers parade in San Antonio today. We went on the school bus and Daddy carried Tootsie so she could go along."

"May 1—Mother looked so pretty in a new hat she made. Mrs. Gray said I made a star in memory work on the Ten Commandments today. Daddy helps Mother with the housework now 'cause we don't have a crop in the field. It is too dry. Last year, Daddy helped her after he had his index taken out. It was so rainish last year we caught an alligator in the cow-pen and we are lots of miles away from the rivers."

"May 7—Hoorah! I won a dollar on a radio contest from Dairyland. We heard it while Mother and some other ladies were making our new red and white rhythm band caps and capes. I sat on the floor and pedaled the machine for mother part of the time 'cause she cannot do that yet. We have to hurry because our band is going to tourist Three Rivers next week. We are going to play for the Rotary Club in the Modern Cafe, for the Missionary Society and for the high school."

"May 13—This morning when Daddy was praying, it began to rain. It poured three inches. Mother always told Daddy he better get down on his knees and pray. Daddy said God can't have wet weather all over the world on the same time and we just have to wait our turn."

"May 15—I heard Mr. Matthews tell the other teachers that lots of people think Mr. Adlof is crazy because he started planting cotton today in the the almost mud."

"June 1—We went to Gonzales with Papa and Mama today. Daddy stayed home to tend to the work. He took Papa to Los Angeles yesterday. It rained again last night. Daddy's cotton sure is pretty."

June 6 (This is really good for a laugh.) Ruth wrote in her diary, "Well, Daddy did not forget my birthday after all. I sure was afraid he would 'cause he is getting so old now." (He was 35) "I am nine. Mama baked a pretty cake. Daddy sent me a dollar and Papa gave me a half-dollar. We went to see my Grandpa Menking and he sure is monstrous old. "Gee! Grandma can sure talk that German."

"June 14—Daddy came for us and we all went to Landa Park

144

in New Braunfels where Aunt Peanut-butter got on the train and went back to Cincinnati. Aunt Celia came home with us. She said it is not nice to say 'Nigger-Day,' but Uncle George said that's what the niggers call it, too. Anyway, it is going to be Sunday. It is also going to be Father's Day. Daddy said looks like everybody claims a certain day now."

June 27—In her diary that day Ruth wrote, "Simsens had a baby today. I just asked Mother how babies are made, and she told me all about the whole world. Aunt Ella is coming to see us with her two boys, and Daddy was grouchy because he thought mother was turning the whole house over cleaning it."

July 10—A few sentences recorded that day reminds me of the way we used to share meat. It was called the Butchering Club. Each family took turns at slaughtering a large calf and cutting it to pieces according to a list. In time, one received the whole calf back. The children always enjoyed riding the rounds when it was Arthur's time to butcher. This time I drove the car around, and Ruthie felt real grown-up for getting to lug the big sacks to the doors. I wonder now how she ever managed to carry them.

She tells also an interesting account of hearing Mr. and Mrs. DeGosserie of Beeville speak about their work in the mission fields of Africa. Mr. DeGosserie showed a ten foot long snake skin, and on the way home Ruthie declared she had decided not to be a missionary to Africa. Later she said maybe she would like to be one after all, for then she could just fish her a baby girl out of some river rather than do all the stuff I had told her about last week.

"What sort of stuff?" Carolyn wanted to know.

"About having babies! You are too young to know."

"Ah, that! I don't want you to tell me anyway, Smarty. I am going to bring the babies like Doctor Williamson does, and when I want to know anything, he will tell me."

Probably that is the reason the second daughter has never asked me to explain things like the first daughter did.

On July 26, we all went to Grandpa Menking's to celebrate their golden wedding anniversary. There were actually many relatives there that I had never seen. Long tables were set out under the palms and huge shade trees in the back yard, and you just never saw so much food. The photographer took a picture of the four generations: Grandpa, his daughter Emma (who is my mother), me, and Ruthie.

We were so proud of our girls as they sang a duet for the

145

ceremony. I had made them very pretty dresses out of organdy, and we got them some new white slippers and socks.

The next day Arthur's family had their reunion at Woods Lake on the river. We had lots of fun talking, eating and wading in the shallow water with all our youngsters.

The girls were glad, however, to get back home to play with Dorothy Valesquez. The whole Valesquez family had returned to stay with Louis for the summer. Arthur asked me to let the girls learn some popular sheet music and Ruth really went for the idea. She played "When I Grow too Old to Dream" and "There's an old Spinning Wheel in the Parlor" until I could almost hear it in my sleep.

Whatever was the matter with me that summer, I sure don't recall and wouldn't believe I was sick so often if it were not for the diary. Ruth tells of learning to cook and how proud she was of helping me. She tells me of wishing she had something wrong with her sometimes, too, like Tootsie "who can't stand to dust the chairs or even sweep the play-house." She tells of the many little pleasures Arthur provided for us "just so Mother can get out a little on Sundays."

One Sunday we went to Lake Corpus Christi to see boat races. Another Sunday we ate supper down by the tank; and one Sunday we took a nice long walk. Many other Sundays, the diary says — and how well I remember — we stayed in town after morning church services and had dinner at Ray's Cafe. Ray Bomar always came up to our table and talked to the girls. A hot, precarious summer was often relieved by happy family jaunts together.

Then it was again September and time for a new start. We had made some cotton after all! Now Arthur was plowing land for spinach another time, if rains came. If rains come! That is a Live Oak County theme song!

Carolyn weighed less than forty pounds and still could not go to school. Perhaps worrying over her was my illness. But it seems we made as light of such things as possible for we still had many jolly times together. On September 17, our children were again invited to appear on the Three Rivers High School amateur show. It was sponsored by their P-T A and always drew a large attendance.

Betty Paul and Ruthie really did their stuff with a piano duet I had taught them. Carolyn read a page out of a sixth grade Civics book again. Mr. Matthews drew two encores after his first solo, "Shorten' Bread."

Returning home that night, we remarked as to the pleasant change townsfolk's attitude toward country children had undergone since we were youngsters. "Maybe," Arthur remarked, "it is because after all Three Rivers is just a country town dependent on the country folk for their trade. Maybe that's why we like it so well here in Live Oak County — everybody is necessary and cooperates toward building the whole area."

We celebrated that September by buying the children the best winter clothes they had ever had. When I finished the bookkeeping at the end of September, we had forty-six bales of cotton which we had never expected to get from planting as late as May 17. Shirley Temple styles were then the thing for little girls, and we made a special trip to San Antonio just to shop.

"Seems we never get to San Antonio unless it is an emergency for one of us; so this time we are going to just have a good time," Arthur declared one Sunday afternoon.

He brought me a pencil and tablet and said to list what we had to have. That was his undoing, for after two years of just making do, just remodeling old clothes — buying nothing new except shoes — what a temptation this list was to me! The girls were to get Shirley Temple felt off-the-face hats; Ruthie's should be blue and Carolyn's red. There would be matching taffeta to buy for their winter dresses and what not all!

I did not list a thing for myself, for I had a closet stuffed full of dresses I had never worn. They were from my sisters and from Lula. (All were good clothes but all hung on me like a scarecrow in those days.)

"You may just as well make up your mind that we are going to buy you some new clothes, too, or we aren't going," A said when he read the list.

"Not unless you buy yourself a new suit, too."

So the whole family got new duds. My purchase was enough wine colored wool flannel to make a three-piece suit with silk crepe lining to match. The blouse was of the silk, that is, it was after many weeks of sewing. I had it all ready, and I was very proud of my work. The girls' taffeta dresses were beautiful, too. Millionaires could not have looked any finer, I thought when we were all dressed for church.

To be real honest about it, we would all have been happier without the new clothes. Many farmers in the area were not as reckless in gambling on the weather and did not plant their crops in May . . . did not gather and could not buy new clothes. "Clothes

147

don't make the person" may be a wise saying, but clothes someone else has sometimes do.

It was all so foolish and need never have happened. Of course, most of our friends and neighbors were very happy for us, but does one ever notice the good majority? Oh, no! It's the minority like a bit of sand in an otherwise good shoe that rubs a fellow sore.

The pastor, a temporary parson in our church for a few summer weeks, remarked that the girls' dresses were too much like those movie stars wore. At first, I took that for a compliment. Then he asked Arthur if we thought it was good to take our children to so many movies.

"So many? We usually stay in on Sundays once a month to see a matinee, and those are usually Shirley Temple pictures. How many do your kids see?"

Arthur was never one to let a preacher push him around. He has the highest respect for the "cloth" but not always for the form that wears it. He thinks preachers' children are no better nor worse than laymen's children, and preachers should start at home to practice their sermons. Many times his bluntness with pastors has brought anger to me, for in our home we were never allowed to speak out to the clergy.

(Not that we didn't talk about preachers' kids at our home. There were always a tribe of them; and our home was, more or less, the center of hospitality since we, too, were a large family. Many of the things our parents would have washed out our mouths for saying we learned from these pals who came and went as the conference assignments were read each fall.)

The next day our big $200 bull turned up his four hooves and died — just like that. Angry over the loss, I just poured fire on a smoldering flame when — without thinking — I said, "You should not have sassed the preacher."

Brother Foster came to see us that afternoon. The young pastor holding the fort for him a few weeks that summer had told him about the "run-in" concerning movies on Sunday. Brother Foster was going to conference that week and wanted Arthur to go as a delegate. He couldn't as I was not able to take care of the chores.

We had planned to go to Gonzales to the fair but Ruthie protested — as much as she likes going — she had not missed a day at school and wanted her second year certificate of perfect attendance. She had missed some days but those were days when the bus could not run. That's the way it was in our school. If the bus could not make the country roads, then everyone stayed home and the classes stayed together real nicely. Neat trick until the State of Texas passed an entirely different set of rules — referred to as ADA (average daily attendance)!

The daughter's childish diary continued to describe that year: On November 10, she recorded that the school got a new flag and flag pole. On November 11, she wrote, "It was to be a holiday today but we've missed so much school already anyway (gosh, where did she get all that Deutsch?) that we had classes and then we raised our new flag and said the Pledge we all have to learn. Bobby Montgomery visited school and he played the violin for us. I think I love him. I am sure I love his violin music. Betty does, too."

Ruth also wrote about getting ready for Thanksgiving. She spoke of all the friends making up a box to send to the Reavis family as Mr. Reavis had broken his arm and could not work and Mrs. Reavis was bed-fast, too. She wrote of being heart broken because a pal, Mary Cook, who was quite an artist, was moving away. Wonder where Mary is now?

On our eleventh wedding anniversary, she wrote about friends coming to play 42; about the men claiming it had only rained seven inches in 1937 and how they just could not understand how Arthur made that cotton; how turkeys were selling for 15c per pound and some of the men thought it would be a good idea to have a community turkey dinner at school so all our field hands could have a Thanksgiving, too.

And what do you know, it rained that very night. Not much, the diary says, but too much for the people to travel the roads. It rained some more before Christmas and then several farmers planted spinach for a cash crop and some planted oats for cattle grazing.

That week our friends in town had a ten pound son and when we went to see him, Ruthie told Mrs. Clark that they sure did everything just right to make "such a big pretty boy."

After looking at the baby for a long time, however, she asked Mr. Clark, "But how can you be so sure he is a boy?" And I thought I had explained all very plainly! Oh, woe!

Mr. Clark is six feet and six inches tall and when that much man blushes a deep purplish-red, well, that's when you wish you had explained it over and over until you were sure your daughter understood.

149

It made conversational material for the Clarks for weeks to come. It was no worse, of course, than the "baby story" Ruthie had told Mrs. J. F. Gray (her Sunday School teacher) a long time before that day.

Seems Mrs. Gray was reading her class the story of God making man out of dust and breathing the breath of life into him when Ruthie interrupted to tell Mrs. Gray that we were going to have "lots of babies, then."

"What do you mean?"

"I mean if God can make people out of dust, you should have seen under Mother's bed this morning!"

Mrs. Gray explained that it was a certain time and a certain dust that God used and then could hardly wait to tell us what the child had said. Realizing she had implied I was a poor house-keeper, Mrs. Gray then apologized. She need not have for it has given us years of merriment to recall the whole incident.

On December 6, the Matthews girl, Mary Virginia, was born and by this time I had made sure both my daughters knew enough not to ask embarrassing questions. Besides, Ruth was now in 4-H Club and Miss Eugie Baker, the home demonstration agent, kept the girls almost too busy to think. She was a wonderful asset to our community and all of Live Oak County in her club work with women and girls.

Carolyn was gaining a bit of weight and was keeping ahead of her class by studying at home. We were now allowed to take her along to town, to the mail-box each time and even most Sundays to church. She did not cough and the doctors said she was com-pletely "arrested" from tuberculosis, which is what they finally pegged her trouble.

It set in raining that month and it was by push and heave that folks got to the school on Dec. 20 for the Christmas tree and program. We had not had classes in two weeks; everything was green as it usually is in spring; people were over-joyed to see mud once more, . . . men rode horse-back to town to get groceries; and sometimes, they spent the night at our house when their horses just got too tired to go on.

It was exactly what I needed to make me feel well — some-body to help along life's way. I even forgot that a few women had suggested I need not have spent all forty-six bales of cotton on new clothes. I had not really spent much money; it just was not the right time to doll up!

It was a fine Christmas. Olga brought Papa and Mama down.

150

Mr. Kelm pulled the car out of a mud-hole near their place, and the rest of the visit the weather was fine. Papa was pleased that we had continued the custom he and Mama had of giving the tenants and hired hands a box of fruit and candy. Arthur went it one better this year. The Velasquez' wanted a record player so they could practice by it. They all played by ear so we sold ours to them for $5. After all, we had the radio.

Ruth closed her first year of diary writing with some remarks about growing up. "I am already getting bumpy looking like some of my old friends, but Mother said that was just like she did, too. I sure hope I don't get sickly like Mother and Mama. Even Papa looks sick now. But Daddy doesn't and that's what really counts 'cause he has to work for us. Carolyn eats good now 'cause Papa always says, "Eat, Pete!" I am glad he doesn't call me Pete . . . that is a mule's name. I'm not a mule."

The Next Six Septembers Scoot

By this time, Arthur had farmed with a tractor for a few years. Each week, along about Thursday, he became violently nauseated. We watched his diet closely and still after about four days of sitting on the tractor, he would be sick. Little Carolyn came up with the solution when quite by accident she said on a Wednesday evening after supper, "Now Daddy don't you crank that factor."

She hated the nights that he left again after supper and chores. For this was the time of day when he usually spent with the children, especially with her since she had been put to bed for the year.

She sounded so pathetic that he stayed at home that night. Before he would turn the lights on and plow until about midnight — all that after plowing ten to twelve hours by daylight. The next day, he skipped being sick, and we decided it was a combination of gasoline fumes and over-work. So he limited himself to running the tractor less; and, too, he stuck tall pieces of gutter-pipe on the exhausts to lead the fumes far over his and the hiredman's head.

The next few years were so packed full, and yet they scooted by so quickly that it seems impossible so much could happen in so short a period of time.

Septembers still seemed to be the months of most changes, most good days and most ill days. September in Texas is said to be the time "when most anything can happen and usually does" . . . the time for storms to come in from the gulf; the time for prices to flip-flop on farm produce; the time for school to start; the time to check incomes and pay mortgages.

In September 1938, Papa died of cancer. He had had surgery in June; and though he had never said he knew he was doomed to go, he knew that. He suffered terribly, finally getting so thin his knees and elbows refused to stay in joint. We went often to be with him, sometimes staying two weeks at a time. Pauline, Pearl and Lydia came. Later Pearl's husband, Harold Gordon Warwood, also visited during his vacation time.

Papa had worlds of friends: Negro, Mexican, Irish, German, Polish . . . Americans all! His mother was now ninety-six and Papa felt she did not need to know of his "plague." Only twice did he let us get her to visit him. After he got so thin and pale, Arthur did not like our girls to see him. Arthur always sheltered the children from sadness as much as possible. When Papa died, they were not taken to the funeral though now they were quite big kids. Papa died with a song on his lips; he even sang a whole verse that morning when the hypo had given him some relief from his excruciating pains. We had been at home, but we came back when they called us that day, September 14. When we came into his room just at daylight, he knew why we were there. He smiled and said, "Where's Pete? Where's Ruffy? Always you write, 'Love, Ola and Family' . . . now Papa wants to say I do love you and all your family, and forgive Papa for every time he beat you!"

"I never remember your beating me," I lied to Papa, for I now realized how he must have battled all his life to keep a temper like he had (and I have) under control. I turned to him again after turning away for a moment to gulp. Then I asked Papa to save a mansion for us, too. Papa loved to sing about "mansions in the sky." Now he tried once more to sing it . . . a German song.

Mama went to live with my sisters in town. George and Pat and Betty Jo moved into the big house. Life had to go on . . . each sunrise lights a new day and it is up to us to make the most of it. Lydia came home with us for a few days and then returned by train to Ohio.

Papa had looked forward to going to the Unification Conference of the three major Methodist branches. He had asked me to go. Just as if I thought it possible, I had promised . . . why, did I ever do that? Did I not know it would be impossible? But when the time came in 1939 for the conference, I went. In the meantime, I had been back to San Antonio and back in surgery. I had stayed in bed over a month.

Mama had come to stay with us, but in a few weeks Celia phoned to tell Mama that Olga was very ill. In all her excitement, Mama even quit worrying about Hitler's invasion into Danzig. Hitler was screaming up a storm these days in September 1939 over every radio network. Nothing would do but Arthur had to take Mama home.

It was a battle to get back to normal activities this time. I had excellent care under the surgeons and Lula by day, Miss

Bessie Sims and Miss Josephine Shay the other graduate nurses, by night. It's no Sunday School picnic to have three hernias repaired, a large mole dug out of a hip and an ovary removed. I had set my house in order, I hoped.

Yet after a month in bed with a restless urge to get going, it took all the love and kindness of my many friends to keep me from "rocking the boat," like old Hannah used to say. The day Mama had to return to Gonzales, Mrs. B. L. Brown brought me a new book, Lloyd Douglas' novel, "Forgive Us Our Trespasses." It was like throwing a rope to a drowning person.

Then Lydia sent me a bedspread to candlewick from Berea, Ohio, where she now taught in college. Mrs. Schweikert kept the girls many hours while Rachel Matthews and others came to visit and cheer me.

Preacher and Mrs. Foster even drove over from Floresville to visit. It was heartwarming just to see them, and they were happy that I could ride into town the last Sunday in September for church services. We had lunch at the Clarks. I was embarrassed at the number of home-made rolls Arthur ate. But Helen was pleased. She knew he had missed home-made bread.

Coach and Mrs. Weldon Bynum brought me good news that Ruth had said in school she was going to college to study journalism and music.

Jacinta Castaneda, a neighbor girl, luckily came looking for work, and for the first time ever, I had a full-time maid. She was wonderful and was pleased as punch with her good wages — $3 for the week. It gave me the spare-time to do some writing, to sell a good many magazine subscriptions, and to help with the county council P-T A in our school. I was now writing news for the San Antonio Express and taking subs for them.

I first felt wasteful having hired help, but Helen set me straight on that with, "After all, Jacinta needs the money worse than you do."

Celia (we called her Teeler) married Charles G. Riggins on October 14 but we could not go that far. It was nearing conference time and the church was making a special appeal for funds to complete the budget. Our pastor had completely ignored us the past year, not even coming to call during the long, shaky and dark days. We felt a bit mean toward him for that until I read the book Mrs. Brown had brought.

We set aside $20 to pay the first Sunday I could go back. Then came the word of Celia's wedding, and Arthur said I would have

154

to choose between spending the money for the trip or for the church budget. We did not get to go. After all, the money had already been "set aside" for the church.

I had saved another $20 out of magazine subscription commissions and made a very careful list. On it I had busfare to San Antonio — round trip — $1.50, street car fares to Lula's and back to church 45c, wedding gift for Teeler and Charlie, a black slip I needed to wear with a new Alpaca dress I had made, something to bring back for the girls and Arthur, meals and offerings which I knew would be taken in every session. And there just must be a corsage for Lula for Sunday.

Even I who can stretch money until the eyes of the faces of the bills are slanted, hid this list and revised it and hid it again several days over that September and October.

Finally, I could hide it no longer. It was just two days before October 19 when the uniting services were the night program. It was the conference Papa planned to attend in which the West Texas Conference South, the Protestant Methodist Church and the Methodist Episcopal Church would become the Southwest Texas Conference of the Methodist Church.

"All things are possible with God," Rachel Matthews told me when I told her how badly I wished to attend the unification services.

"With God and our help," Bill added as he went on to say that the girls would be cared for after school at their home in the teacherage in the evenings until Arthur came from the field. The Clarks, the Schweikerts, Froehners and Hornungs — everybody seemed anxious for me to go.

"You must be daffy! You can't stand that sort of trip alone," Arthur objected. But even as he said it, he said to go ahead and pack and he would take me to the bus the next morning. He warned that Lula would be furious . . . me in the hospital so often and then take a bus ride!

I did go, and it will always be a treasured memory. The service was held in the beautiful Travis Park Methodist Church, right in the heart of San Antonio. I stayed over-night with Lula. She came to the church services that night to meet me; and to my amazement, she was glad I had decided to come.

Later, we attended another conference together and we both became charter members of the Wesleyan Service Guild, an organization for employed women to enrich their spiritual growth. I chuckle as I think how much that fit both our needs . . . for

155

surely life at best was complex. Life with constant interruptions can easily become confusing, and life as a private nurse is no bed of roses. You should hear some of the complaints patients give their nurses!

Lula used to get a real bang out of telling us about her many experiences with the patients. Lately, she does not talk about her work at all. Most of her conversation these last years are about their brother Max . . . and how terribly life has treated him.

True! Life has given him its cruelest blow. He lost Carlyle, his only child . . . his and Lonie's. He was born the September before our first child.

Arthur and I had gone to Houston to see him when he was just a few months old. He was a nice looking baby and we saw him many times afterwards at family gatherings; and once they had brought him to our house on a visit.

On a Sunday afternoon in June, 1941, as he and his father were returning to Houston from Gonzales, they saw a wounded dog. Wishing to see about the dog sprawled out on the highway, Carlyle persuaded his Dad to turn around and go back. While Max was getting a Boy Scout hatchet out of the car with which he meant to put the wounded animal out of its misery, Carlyle stepped into the path of a speeding car. The blow burst off a part of the boy's head and he died a few hours later.

Ruth was thirteen and Carolyn was just going on ten. We were in Vacation Bible School that morning when Mr. L. O. Hartman, the depot agent, brought us the telegram. The news was tragic for everyone; it meant of course, the end of dreams for Max and Lonie.

That September, the three rivers went on a rampage all at one and the same time, coming into Three Rivers six inches deep in Key's Drug Store. The flood could not seem to get up quite high enough to cross the street there (really it is Highway 281) to get into the Witt's Drug Store and the bank and other business establishments.

The government had, many years before during the depression, built about fifty nice houses for low-income families to rent. In those depression years, even the banker's son came in that bracket for all incomes were low. The Nueces River got into most of these houses and into some two or three feet deep.

People and other politicians began to talk about conserving all that flood water. Corpus Christi interests thought about stacking it up, and it seemed to them that right here in Three Rivers was the place to do that. A long range legal battle started, and just this year the Wesley Seale Dam at the original Lake Corpus Christi in lower Live Oak County is under construction. Seventeen years of water and words have gone under the bridges and over the lands and court records.

School consolidation storms were also brewing. Most rural schools had sent their high school students to town for many years now. Most folks had to provide their own transportation; but many like us, with roads that a mule cannot get through when it rains hard, had to board our high school students in town.

Ruth was staying with Miss Gladys Cunningham, a piano teacher who lives in the first house that was built in Three Rivers when the town was founded in 1913 by Charles R. Tips. It is a lovely home; and Miss Gladys and her father, publisher and editor of the Three Rivers News, were good to our little girl.

Ruth soon found her way into most of her class' activities. She had a knack for getting into the band and anything else that needs a lot of up-and-go spirit. It was a trying time, though, for parents who wondered if a fourten year old should board away from home.

The first day of September 1942 found us with every fence and clothesline hanging full of clothing, bedding and hand-crocheted rugs. It was the day after a hurricane that had brought fifteen inches of rain, twisted our homes and ruined our crops. The storm came up on a Saturday morning, really sneaky like . . . a bit of north wind now and a bit of west wind then. At noon, we listened to the radio. But even the radio did not warn us to take every precaution (as if one can against such a furious demon as a Texas gulf storm).

Arthur was rather provoked with me as I fretted more over losing a large box of news-clippings and photographs than over the bales of cotton.

"You can always plant another patch of cotton, but I will never be able to get back some of those things. The story of Papa's funeral — of how there were four ministers who asked to witness what a good friend he was — the picture of the Negro preacher who said the benediction — the story of Grandma Sturm's death in January 1940 — and my goodness, what a mess all this soaked box is," I lamented.

"Mother, after this let's keep the beans and rice in boxes and your clippings in these big glass jars," Ruth suggested. She hates beans and rice. Arthur agreed fully about the beans, but the rice, never! Rice cooked with cream and sugar, topped with butter and cinnamon and some more sugar could even make him forget a storm for a while.

Even gulf storms left our family with some good jokes to tell over and over through the years. About midnight on the Saturday, when I thought surely any minute the house would blow down, I insisted we all get up and dress in warm clothing. Arthur was sound asleep. "After all," he said, "I cannot stop the storm, and there will be lots of mopping up to do tomorrow." What an attitude! Always making sure he would be ready for the work of the next dawn!

When he stepped out onto the floor, his weight broke huge pieces out of the linoleum as the water had gushed under through the doors and under the floor coverings.

"I've had my bath, thank you!" he laughed. In a few minutes, a brilliant flash of lightning showed him the whole front yard where two huge Mesquite trees were already uprooted. He did not laugh again until near day-light when it was just too, too funny — how many times Carolyn bumped her head.

We had taken some food and bedding and, clinging together as best we could, made it to the brooder house — a new long building with a concrete floor and oil heated brooders. Arthur had already put a board across the center of it and had moved fifty new-born pigs into one half before we went to bed that night. Rushing to get into the shelter, we had not thought about the pigs. Now, where should we sit — or lie down — in the half with the pigs or with the chicks?

At first, we sat down beside the pigs. Our clothes were wet and soon the pigs woke up; of all the squealing and grunting! It was a hilarious sight. They thought we were their mothers, no doubt, and piglets are hungry every time they wake up enough to think.

"Get away from us. We're not sows!"

"Well, Daddy, we look like sows. I am so wet and nasty. I wish we would have brought some dry clothes. But how would we have gotten here with anything dry?"

So we moved over with the chicks. At least, they didn't grunt and push their noses against us. There was a window on the pig-side through which we could see our house. We hated to move over here where we could not see each time the skies lighted up. One flash right after another of lightning made "day" out of the night. Carolyn decided to stand in the feed basket by the window and watch. That was her way of keeping the pigs away. But she could not make us hear her constant reports of the things she saw because the rain was pounding so hard on the sheet-iron roof.

So she would come back and forth to where the three of us were huddled together, covered over with pecking chicks. Each trip across the building, she would bump her head on a vent-pipe across the center of the low ceiling. Each time we would yell at the top of our lungs, "Look out for that pipe."

But she could not hear us; and luckily, we could not hear her though we could see she would cry out each time. After a few moments of sympathy from us in the chicken corner, she would take out across the building again to the window and bash her head again. Could anyone be so engrossed on one thing that he could truly knock himself out at the same time? We laugh and laugh about it every time a storm comes up these days. But luckily, we have never had a storm again as bad as that . . . or she may have completely bashed off her noggin.

The next day or so, Aunt Annie Hornung came to visit us. She was very sick. We persuaded her son and daughter to leave her with us as they, too, had so much damage to repair. Their windmill had even blown down. The children were already at such a loss as their father, the one we jokingly called Rattlesnake Bill because he had moved to this rattlesnake country years ago, had died so suddenly that June.

Annie stayed. We had bought three bushels of peaches to can and besides that I had a terrible boil on my hip. (Seems one never had a grain of sense in those days.) But then, one did not have deep-freezers, and canning seemed an economical thing to do. It was the last time I ever competed with commercial canneries. Annie tried to help with the peeling but was just too sick. In about a week, Freddie came for her; and in a couple of days he called from town to tell me she was in the Gipson hospital.

A few days later, after major surgery, one Sunday noon she died. I had gone to stay with her. She was much too sick to do much talking. She did ask me if I thought she would die. Oh, why did she have to ask me? I did not wish to lie to her. Since she had asked what I thought, I answered, "Why Aunt Annie, I have not even *thought* this morning . . . I was in such a rush to get here to see you."

"You see that Eunice gets a nice wedding?" she asked of me
"I'll help you."

"You see that Freddie doesn't try to farm all by himself down here?"

"I will talk with him about it . . . maybe he can come to stay with us until you are home."

"Home" was the word she caught — "Home." She repeated it a few times, turned her head upward and gasped — leaving me with promises I should never have made. As it turned out, I did help to see that Eunice and Frank Jostes, a school teacher at near-by Fashing, had a nice wedding. I did talk to Fredwill about leaving the farm. It was to his paternal grandfather, Louis Horn-ung, in Lexington that he went. It was a fine decision for both children, time has proven.

Miss Emma Hornung, their aunt, had come from Robstown just a few minutes before Annie died. Later, George and Olga brought Mama. The next day, after the funeral, Mama stayed; and the following day we went over there to help the children and their Hornung uncles and aunts.

We were packing away many things out of dresser drawers and closets when I found an envelope with "Boops Adlof" written on it. In it was a negative of a picture taken of Arthur thirty-two years before. Later, I sent the picture to the Fox Company in San Antonio and it made a perfect print. It was such a joy to find. I had no pictures of my husband when he was a child. Mama was restless to get back home and we were glad, for we knew I had to have a hemorrhoid operation very soon. I did not want her to have to wait on me so I did not tell her. I just stuck it out until she decided to go home Monday morning. Then we took Ruth to school in town for the week again, put Mama on the bus to go home, and left Carolyn at the country school.

By noon I was back out of surgery and, of all places, in the same room in which Aunt Annie had died last Sunday. It did not seem to depress me. The first day I was too dopey to care, and the second day after one of those damnable "rearend parties" one doesn't care about dying. In fact, one wishes he might. Coming back from a Sitz bath down the hall in the bathroom, I plunked out on the floor.

Emily Schattel, the nurse, had gone to answer the telephone. This was the event that brought to me a new friend, Martha. She is Mrs. C. E. Walker and is now my neighbor, just up the hill to the east in Three Rivers. That day, as was her custom, she came to see who might need her help in the hospital. She picked me up off the hall floor and off of the list of those who wished to die.

With her cheerful banter about bathing before "Sad-day" and her chatter about my cute girls her girls had learned to know at

160

Sunday School, I was soon fine. After all, my girls are my career. I knew they would be the only way I would ever produce anything to this world.

Dr. Gipson apologized for letting me take a hot bath that day. He thought perhaps it would make me feel better. "It did help your bottom but played hell with your top, eh?" he teased. He knew of my extreme low blood pressure, but like other doctors before him, he just couldn't believe how quickly I could konk out when the blood all left my head.

"My brother says I couldn't possibly have blood enough for my head and my big feet and so when the blood runs down to my feet when I stand up, it naturally drains every drop out of my head to fill my big feet."

"They sure are big feet," was all he commented as he laughed until his belly shook.

Why do doctors always get such a bang out of laughing in the room of their surgical patients? As sure as you are stitched up from here to there or are packed as tight as they can get it, the doctor comes in for a real good laugh.

I vowed I would never speak to him again. But then . . . how silly? It was funny how I tried to tell him about fainting and he only saw my big feet. The next visit he explained that I had solved a puzzle for him.

The puzzle: What were those two big shadows on the operating wall that Monday noon? Now, he knew. They were the shadows of my raised feet on the ends of my very skinny legs. I should have shot him.

It wouldn't have been so funny if he had not told it just when I had a roomful of company: Mrs. Jack Montgomery, Mrs. Williamson, Mrs. Biddle and Mrs. Gipson were there to enjoy his joke.

September got in its last lick to disturb me that year by Ruth's starting to date — a boy named Lee Roy Haak, on the 30th. She had asked her Daddy if it would be all right, and he did not object. I was perturbed about it as I had heard from other women that Ruth was beating her pal's time. Emma Reynolds was such a sweet girl and so nice to Ruth. I spoke to her about it when she came to tell me she was going and she said, "Oh, we fixed that. She is going with Jack Davis. Jack and I agreed that would be fine."

"I thought you was going with Jack."

"Sure, but a girl has to look around. After all, I am already way past fourteen. Gracious, Mother!"

161

We bought one bull for $200 that October and paid only $250 for a good house which yielded over 5,000 square feet of good lumber. If we were going to repair the storm damages, we might as well add on to the house, which up to now was still the original 26 by 26 feet square. It was a pain in the neck to entertain relatives and friends that came by the carsful in such cramped quarters.

Odd things: the bull was not to our liking as we found we still preferred horned Herefords, and we never have had as much company since we have a large house. It could be that we were so busy with building that folks mostly stayed away that winter; and after that for several years, rationing controlled pantries and travel. Many customs began to make drastic changes in the middle forties.

It was nice though to have a few families come, even in the commotion of remodeling. One day, all unexpected, Arthur's sister Emilie and one of her sons, Erwin, (the one who had lived in our community) and his wife and baby came. Emilie always had such a lovely house and she just had to come see about us. She was really pleased with what we were able to build, considering new materials could not be had. Nails were very scarce. Perhaps, if the storm had not come, we would not have been allowed to buy any nails.

They came the same day that Ruth was all excited over making honor-roll; for a reward, we had bought her a lovely hand mirror and the reddest lip-stick she had ever had. Carolyn had also made five A's and Daddy had given her a dollar for each one. Emilie thought a quarter would have been sufficient; but when they left, she gave Carolyn another dollar.

"You don't practice what you preach, Mama," Erwin laughed. Then, he gave Carolyn a quarter "so you will have a quarter to spend 'cause if you are like Mama and your Daddy, you will want to save the dollars."

We took a load of cotton seed to Gonzales, pulling a trailer behind our car, in which, besides ourselves, was Miss Roby — Ruth's band teacher. We ate our lunch at Hewell's in Nixon and spent the night at George and Pat's. The next day, Sunday, Olga took us sight-seeing all around the town in her car; by mid-night we were back home — trailer and all. George loaned us some tools which Papa had left.

And of all things to bring home — the mumps! Arthur swelled up like a toad. By this time we had the roof off of the house, and though there wasn't a cloud in the sky all day, that night a norther

162

blew in with a drenching rain. Arthur helped us get into the car to stay dry. He spent the night in the clothes closet. The closet has an upper-section and this was full of blankets which kept him dry. Again, the washlines were loaded for days with things to dry until we got the roof back on and furniture moved back in place.

As I was lamenting about it, the radio was telling about bombings. I felt so ashamed when Arthur said, "Be glad it was rain and not bombs!"

"And that you and I just have mumps and not cancer like Papa had." Carolyn put Arthur to shame, too.

It really was a touchdown. It was November 6 and we saw Ruth's new ball-playing boyfriend make three touchdowns. He not only wiggled and raced his way under and around the tall boys from Hot Wells High School, he made a touchdown in our family.

It was good to be well enough this fall to again take an active part in the school and the church. Our Wesleyan Service Guild was a real challenge to me. A teacher in the Three Rivers School, Miss Bert Hardison, who came to us from the Waco Home was my new inspiration.

One of the high points of my life occurred November 15 when Miss Ruby Curd and Miss Mae Huegler were baptised in our church. I had so hoped they would come to our congregation's roll as they were both so much inspiration to me. They were young beauticians, just back from college.

Eunice and Frank were married on the 26th of November, and Ruthie played their wedding music. The wedding was in the Fashing Methodist Church, and I especially enjoyed fixing the flowers as I had never had the opportunity before — having had no formal wedding nor had either of my sisters.

It was also the month to add another Hornung to our family. Milton and Lois got their second adopted child — Gail Marie — a wee, bitsy little girl. The first, Grady Mack, was now four and quite a husky little man. One morning we heard a knock at the back door just as day was dawning and who was there but the little fat Grady. He had "slipped into my shoes and come to see you all while d'ose others are taking care of that baby."

Rationing made Christmas quite different. We could not buy any greeting cards so we cut out pictures from old ones and pasted them on two-cent postal cards. It took a hundred to be enough for the family and close friends. We couldn't go to the city to shop for anything special for the girls. In fact, we never even drove the ten miles to town more than once a week unless something drastic was needed. We gave the girls each a heifer for Christmas.

Arthur gave me a beautiful floor vase to add to my collection, and one of the carpenters knocked it over and broke it. Lydia and Pena came to see us that Christmas and rode back on the 27th to San Antonio when we followed a truck load of rolling-fat calves which we sold for the then fabulous price of thirteen cents a pound.

We closed the year with thankful hearts — despite the storm. Arthur was still with us, and he might not have been for he had had to register for Army service on February 16.

Learn To Adjust To Changes

September 1943, the tension had not eased in the world picture. At home we were thankful to be allowed to go to Beeville to have our car tires re-capped with rubber. Both girls were attending school in town this year, and Carolyn was playing a horn in the band. School consolidation made so many changes that it would take a book alone to write about the reactions, the way neighbors began to feel toward each other — depending on whether one was for or against the consolidation issue.

The school ran a bus out from town for the Fant City community's older children, but that did not help us as we lived a mile down the Schulz lane where travel was out of the question when it rained. It was not like in former days: then when it rained and the bus could not make the rounds there was no school, and classes stayed together. Now classes went ahead, and country kids just missed — period.

So we moved both our girls to Furlows for the year. It was their second home, so to speak. Bob and Wilma were as fine parents to our girls all week as if they were their own children. It was very lonely on the farm without the chatter and rush-rush of two lively girls.

In San Antonio to get eye glasses that September, we rode the escalator at Joske's for the first time. We naturally wondered how in all the world they ever managed to have steel to build such contraptions. I surely was thrilled as I hate stairs. On this thing, I thought, I can just get on and shut my eyes while ascending. Good thing that I thought to open them just in time as my big feet were scooted onto the landing — quite automatically. How we could have enjoyed this back in public school!

It rained a lot that fall, and on September 28 Arthur went to George West to sign a permit for the purchase of a new tractor. H. D. House and Sons delivered it the next day just in time for the truck to get back to town before a cloud-burst came.

The government also allowed us one new tire that year. We felt real privileged. After all, it surely was an inconvenience to live ten miles from a doctor and sometimes have to change flats twice in that distance. Too, our dear neighbor was very ill and I liked going over to see about the Gregorys. I needed her cheerful spirit more than any help I could be to her. The couple was so brave and self-supporting, they neither one would let us do for them as much as we would or could have. I sewed some for the children and tried always to take some fresh-baked bread and kaffee-kuchen to help out with the cooking.

Arthur worked as hard as ever, but it seemed with so many rains there was such an endless amount of field work. Too, screw-worms were about to ruin us. Every day he and the Compos boys would have to rope and wrestle with calves and even many of the larger animals.

Again, we were lucky to get a deferment for Erasmo, one of the hands on the farm. Production records on our place were well kept. Thank goodness, we had gin tickets to prove our right to a farm helper's deferment from the draft.

We were thrilled to have the Hornungs and the Schweikerts for friends again. None of us would ever admit today that there ever was a period of rift between us and fortunately so. Least of all will our children admit it. With our interests all so mutual, it was most nigh impossible to remain cool to one another in our neighborhood.

We all got busy making adjustments to the many changes since we no longer had our own school activities. I helped with the Three Rivers Parent-Teacher Association and was elected as one of the room representatives, often called Room Mothers. Also, I was doing more news-writing now. I was asked to write several area stories, which gave me something of a thrill and, too, a change of scene.

One of these articles which I particularly enjoyed writing about was a gathering called the J. Frank Dobie Game Preserve Barbecue on October 14, 1943, on the Holman Cartwright Ranch near Dinero. Doris and A. E. Bay went with Arthur and me, and we met many fine people that day who have become lasting friends.

Ruth played the piano for the P-T.A. meeting that month and did exceptionally well. As I was complimenting her the next day, Saturday, while we were busy laundering their clothes for the next week of school, Ruth took advantage of the good mood of her mother. She told me she had made up her mind to accept Lee Roy's proposal of marriage. I made her promise to not mention it again until "tonight after Carolyn goes to sleep and you and Daddy and I can talk — just the three of us."

166

It just made me sick, for I had planned for the girls to go to college after high school. That being my only real objection, it was soon set aside with her promise to do just that. Arthur cried like a baby but never once tried to persuade her to change her mind.

"Guess after all I can't say anything against it for your mother was just a little kid, too, when I proposed to her. I do hope you and Lee Roy will do as we did — wait a couple of years. Now, with the war and all, is a poor time to be married. Your mother will want you to have a nice wedding."

"How did you know that? Have I ever complained about our not having all the frills?" I sobbed.

Our pastor, Rev. J. W. Leggitt, and Jack Gurwitz, a Three Rivers merchant, came the next day to enlist our services to collect for the War Fund. We had to go to training meeting the next week. The John Stendebachs came from Palestine to see us. Dr. Gipson put me on the new drug — sulpha — and I got sicker than a dying calf, the likes of which we and several neighbors had at that time. The diary records the community gave almost $100 to the War Fund.

Mrs. Albert Huegler and Mrs. Zeb Furr and I gave a bridal shower for Ruby, my dear friend, who was now Mrs. Sam Huff. Sam was in the service, too, as were so many of our young men. We had no school on October 22 that year as the buildings and staff were used to issue new ration stamp books.

It gave a group of senior girls the day to dream up some foolishness. They paraded downtown Saturday afternoon to advertise something they were having the next week at school — perhaps a P-T. A. carnival, which in those years was a dilly, no less.

Ruth and Hazel Van Cleave were cigarette girls, Mildred Smith a clown, and Maxine Shumate drove a donkey — or rather, she attempted to and did after Georgia Faye Coquat (dressed like a coy old dame) whispered into the beast's ears. The fact that the beast got going just then was quite co-incidental. After this, the girls always said Faye could move a jackass with her soft talk . . . even a jackass!

Maybe it was the first year our church held the Week of Prayer service. Anyway, I have needed to pray about the attitude I took. It was a program designed to the theme of fasting and praying. Very few women came for the morning session. Yet when time came for the lunch, to which I had taken only a small bread and butter sandwich, the whole room was jammed full of women

167

and the long table groaned and creaked with bowls of food and fancy cakes.

To keep from exploding (that temper of mine), I left. As I spent the rest of the day and far into the night decorating the W.S.G. float for the parade of the annual P.-T.A. festival, I prayed. Mostly I thanked God that I had left without expressing my opinion.

When the school band played in the Beeville Stock Show and Rodeo parade, we took the day off to attend. Beeville is only 30 miles away but to folks even much farther (and tires and gasoline were rationed) it is a special event. Supt. and Mrs. Larkin had asked us especially to go so we could see Ruth strut with that big drum. There we met W. H. Gist, a shutterbug who has a treasure of pictures he takes at all youth events in the whole area.

We counted this day as our anniversary trip. Yet when the 20th came on the next Saturday, it was Arthur who remembered. He came in from the barnyard and sat down in the kitchen, just looking at the clock.

At exactly 8:30 a.m., he got up and came over to where I was mixing bread and coffee-cake dough and said, "That's for seventeen wonderful years" as he kissed me until I could see the yeast beginning to raise bubbles in my mixing bowl.

Sadness reigned for a long while that fall and winter. We had a good friend, Virginia, who was Dr. Williamson's secretary. She had married the year before and now she died in child-birth. Her father is our neighbor, and we went to do our bit to console him and his wife. Bill Furlow and many other young men were shipped out for overseas duty. Some never returned. Yes, sadness reigned.

Several of the mothers were determined there must be Christmas joy, war or no war, and it was the thing the sad world needed. We borrowed a truck for all the band students to ride on while they drove all around the town and suburbs singing carols, Everyone was cheered — whether they were this or that denomination — and children whose parents sing best in Spanish sang along with ours whose forefathers came from Europe.

"The Lord does provide!", I said over and over that winter as we gathered vegetables. Even at Christmas, with no killing frosts having come, we had radishes, tomatoes and English peas in our gardens. We sold them (tomatoes brought 15c per pound) ate them, supplied every preacher and every teacher and canned a few.

With so much food to spare and a nice fat deer, it was the time best for entertaining all our daughters' teachers and their husbands and wives. We missed Miss Roby. We never knew what happened to her. She had just called to say goodbye and that she would write someday. Mr. D'Arvil was now the band instructor. The Larkins, Dr. and Mrs. Drozd, Mr. and Mrs. Nichols (he was the Ag teacher), Coach and Mrs. Robert Blake, Miss Henslee Fox, and Mr. and Mrs. Herman Woerndel came.

The next day, C. B. (a daughter of the Mexican family then living on our place) and I were doing the linens we had used. By now, C. B. considered herself quite educated. She felt it safe to recall the time she had come to me asking for a billy-goat . . . at least, that was what I thought she had said.

"Do you remember how you laughed at me when I say billy-goat that time I want a petticoat to wear to school?"

"Yes, I remember, C. B. But then you did not say billy-goat, I just thought you said it." I meant to encourage her to speak English and to continue to improve herself even though she now was out of school, married and expecting her second baby.

"Why do we have to iron these nastyins when you peoples just going to wipe faces with them?" she asked.

"Napkins, C. B., not nastyins! And really you do have a point there."

She looked and looked at the one she was just then ironing and replied, "Miss Biola, I no see no point!"

I explained we needed the same linens for another dinner party. This time, it was the Haaks, Miss Diana Mae Edwards, Luther Haak (a cousin of Lee Roy's), and a pal of his, Lester Williams of Oakville.

And Lee Roy, Fredwill, Eunice and Frank were among our holiday guests. It was a real consolation to know that they loved coming to our house, and we enjoyed our new home very much. Another year had raced by. Lester returned to service after the holiday — never to come back alive.

Roy G. Knox was teaching the first few grades left in our school and the community spirit was at a dead stand-still. It was the year of the coining of such words as "ceiling prices." One night when we were six hours coming six miles from the end of the pavement at Suniland, Carolyn asked A what "ceilings" really meant anyway.

Good thing, Loretta Curry Bridges, a classmate of Ruth's in senior class, was along. This was back in January but roads never got good that year; we were often pushing to get to or from town.

Four days later, we got the girls back to school, Tuesday

169

morning. Then we got stuck in town at the grocery store. We were crib-feeding over forty calves that winter and finally had to catch a week when the roads were passable for trucks to get them to sell them just because the feed lots were too boggy to keep them. One would never have dreamed a drought had ever been here or could ever come again.

I was named chairman of a committee to start a youth club in Three Rivers. They named it Teen-Town, reported later to be the first anywhere. Good, I thought, as I read the little motto that night. I may keep some boy or girl off the streets this way. Mrs. James Coquat, Mrs. Sam Huff, Mrs. C. E. Walker and several other mothers were with me in the new endeavor. Many were not, I assure you. But the youth were! They were most cooperative in cleaning a big building and raising funds for furnishings by work, pledging, and saving from their own allowances. After a while even many of the men pitched in with volunteer help such as the Rotarians, who bought tables.

When we couldn't get a nickelodeon at first, Clarence Adamietz played boogie-woogie on the piano until the kids danced themselves to national publicity. Of course, none of the preachers thought the idea was so hot. They just knew there would be no youth in the Sunday Schools the next day after the big opening night on February 19, 1944. But there they were. My class was present 100% for the first time in months.

I'll admit I finished the lesson early so they could talk a few minutes, and naturally they talked about the good time had by all last night.

I received a letter from the Baptist minister, Rev. Holt. I was afraid to open it for several blasts had come our way. He asked me to come to see him, and I went. After I told him all about the Teen-Town, he offered to chaperone any time we wanted him. It was a great turning point in the support the idea received after that.

It was also the year that Ruth Hornung suffered encephalitis. For many weeks she lingered in the hospital, then began a remarkable recovery seemingly by sheer force of will. It was the spring Lee Roy bought Ruth's diamond ring; the spring our Methodist Youth Fellowship sent a cheerbox to Billy Leggitt, who was in the Naval Hospital in California. Ruth had an appendectomy; and Dr. Gipson set Carolyn on the foot-stool so she could watch the operation.

It was the spring that I had to go to the district conference in McAllen, my very first trip to the Texas valley. The Wesleyan

Service Guild met there on Sunday, March 11, and I caught the bus that night to return home at 1 a.m. I had spent the night in the parsonage with Miss Mendez, a teacher in Valley Institute, and the Rev. and Mrs. Haver were our hosts. Many things were new to me on this trip. There were Mexican members in their churches. I first spoke of them as Latin Americans, but Miss Mendez corrected me.

"We are not Latin Americans. We are, of course, Americans, but if you have need to distinguish for any reason then call me — and others like what we are — Mexicans. We are not ashamed of our heritage anymore than are you. I presume yours is American Indian, judging from your high cheek bones. Yet, the hair is too blond," she laughed as she guessed everything except the German, Dutch, French and English that they say is back of me.

When I got home, I visited again with Mrs. D. E. Bomar. She was always so interested in our church and community affairs. She had, previous to her marriage, lived in Beeville where she was as active as I hope some day to be. It was not long after this visit that she went away to her mansion, like Papa always said. She had been sick over two years. She told me someday we would have a new church and she really would like to stay to present her gift to the building. As it was, she did leave a fine gift — a stained glass rose window for the front loft.

Mrs. Fred Churchill, Mrs. Gray and I attended the annual conference in Corpus Christi this spring even though I knew I should stay home and work in the garden. "What would Papa think of us? Here, it is way past Washington's birthday when every right-minded gardener plants Irish potatoes and I am traipsing off to one church meeting after the other," I said.

"Your Papa would be right there with you since it is church," Arthur reminded me. "And now your Mama since Papa can't be there."

It was the year when once again the crops froze off on March 30; the spring Jack Mang died in the service; the spring Uncle Willie was operated; Arthur and Ruth took the measles; the year colored piece-goods returned to the store counters and everyone bought ten times as much as they needed. I bought red net by the armful to make Ruth's senior prom dress.

I was a room representative so Arthur insisted I, too, must have an evening dress to wear to the dance at Teen-Town after the banquet. It was royal blue satin fashioned princess style, and

171

with it I wore white rose-buds in a waistline corsage. It was the very first evening dress I had ever had.

We gave a tea in Ray's dining room on Saturday afternoon before Mother's Day for Mama. Ruth and Betty planned the party and invited fourteen ladies from our neighborhood and church. Mama looked so surprised. She thought it was odd that we were going to town Saturday afternoon just for supper in the cafe.

On May 16, I organized the Wesleyan Service Guild in Kingsville. I had to go on the bus and return by train as Mama insisted on going along and also insisted on not staying overnight. Mama wouldn't let me out of her sight on her visits these years. She stood by the hour to read over my shoulder as I typed news articles or features.

There were poor connections, but we finally made it back that same night at 2:15 by train via Robstown. I was too excited to go to sleep by then so I baked cakes for the senior day. I thought to myself that anyone in the Kingsville church could have organized them better than I. Why do we track here and there when actually home-folk can often serve better in the same capacity? I was asked to go, and so go I did! More new friends were my treasures: Dr. and Mrs. E. R. Bogusch had us on their patio for a lovely supper and saw that we got to church. The Reverend Donald Redmond came as far as Alice for us when it was discovered the bus schedule had been changed without the Three Rivers' office having been notified.

Today Dr. Bogusch is still teaching at Texas A. & I. College, and Dr. Redmond holds a high position with our mission board.

Graduation exercises for Ruth from the Three Rivers High School were the high-lights of our lives. She had missed so many days because of an appendectomy, measles and the flu that we were satisfied that she still graduated among the honor students. Supt. Larkin made a few comments about her as it came her time to approach the stand to get her diploma. It was a good thing there was a double door to the auditorium, or Arthur's head would never have gotten through. He beamed with pride as the audience applauded. I imagine I glowed like a birthday candle, too. But then thirty other papa's heads were a little out of shape that night and an equal number of mamas were glowing beautifully. We parents understood each other.

She got many lovely graduation presents. She showed them all to my sisters who visited that summer after her graduation. When he showed them to C. B. and other members of the hired help on the farm, C. B. said "Me go house and bring you present, too." In a short time she and several others returned, walking across the field like ducks in a row on the new earthen terrace we had built that year. Erasmo was carrying an animal, and they gave it to Ruth for her graduation present. It was a baby Bob-cat he caught in the field that day.

The girls kept the kitten and made a pet out of it, but very soon it had grown to be a vicious cat. Leaping one day from a tree trunk, it caught a grown hen in the back of the neck. I had to knock the cat out as cold as the hen before she released her jaws.

"Now, see, that could have been one of you or Grady," I said. Grady and the Schweikert girls played a lot with the cat as did our girls.

Arthur phoned the Brackenridge Zoo in San Antonio after the cat came out of her konking I gave her. They were glad to get her, so we crated her and shipped her. The Zoo sent us a life-time pass to visit the animals, but we lost it some place before we ever used it. We were sure when we went to the zoo next, however, that we could still recognize that unique graduation gift.

On June sixth, Ruth was sixteen and what should have been a most joyous day was very gloomy. It was called D-Day, and our troops were sent into France. We kept the radio on all day. Ruth and I went to San Antonio the next day to enroll her in nursing school, but they would not take her as she was much too young. She had thought this would be a fine career, and she could always squeeze in the music and journalism later. Betty Paul enrolled in business college that week in San Antonio, and Ruth felt like a real bum that summer.

Lee Roy came to see her one summer night after it had rained so much that the sunflowers almost hid all the fields and farm gates. He had a young cousin with him from San Antonio. The cousin asked, "Wee Woy, how did you ever find a girl out here in all these weeds?"

It was the year A had to begin serving as a member of the Tenant Purchase Act Committee, a government idea to assist tenant farmers to buy their own places. He needed this diversification from the every day grind; learned the county and many of its people; and I am sure served the committee well. Several of the families he helped to be selected have through the years expressed their appreciation to us with cards at Christmas and hearty hand-

173

shakes when we chance to meet at gatherings such as football games and county fairs.

With all that rain, we made such a bumper corn crop that we had to buy some more shoats to glean the fields. Arthur started the project in the summer after cutting out some of the patch which was wired for hogs and feeding the green corn to the cattle. Prices were shaky. We bought nice large shoats for five dollars each.

On June 28, Carolyn stopped breathing during an appendectomy; Arthur was scared so badly, he still talks of it. Dr. Gipson massaged her chest without slashing her, and in a few minutes he was whistling softly through his teeth again. When he did that, everyone looking on relaxed and knew the patient was fine.

Pearl was home that summer for the first time in six years, and I hardly knew her. She was here while Carolyn was in the hospital and was disturbed that Carolyn looked so bad; the hospital was so inadequate. We were amused because she expected to find a Cincinnati City Hospital in Three Rivers, Texas.

"I sure am glad the Bartletts are moving West instead of turning into Yankees," Carolyn said after the criticism. Carolyn felt Drs. Williamson and Gipson were unmatchable anywhere in the world. She defended them against any comments. The R. E. Bartletts were very good friends of ours at church and in school affairs, and we were heartsick when they moved to Denver, Colorado.

Arthur accused the girls of being disturbed because we had so often said we hoped Carolyn could catch their teen-age son, Bayly Boeck, for her husband. Carolyn was the dumbest person we had ever known about housework and could not even boil an egg properly. Bayly Boeck had baked the best cakes at the church suppers or school parties ever since he was about nine.

It was also the year customers returned waste fat such as bacon drippings to the stores, from whence it was gathered to be used in the manufacture of ammunition; tin cans were opened from both ends and flattened and taken to the war materials committees; the people gave to the American Red Cross War Fund with tens and twenties in our community; the summer we found a fawn in the millet patch and got a permit to keep him; the summer Ruth Hornung's lapse of memory ceased and she was learning to talk again; the summer Ruth passed her tests in George West and got a driver's license; the time of the family gathering when we took Bambi, the pet deer, along in the car; the year we saw the

174

movie, "The Sullivans" (a true story of five brothers lost on a ship in the Navy the previous year); the year Live Oak County's Agriculture agent R. H. Mason was lauded for his fine work — and we, too, were most appreciative of his help on our farm, with our new hog business and in advising us about terraces.

It was the August when someone stabbed Calvin Jones as he ran out into the back yard of Teen-Town to see who was calling him; the all-night watch at his bedside and the many visits in the following months. So it was when that September came and Ruth left home full of hopes and afraid to dream . . . were not we all afraid to dream? Wars are not the times for dreams. Only the stoutest can even hope, it seems.

The September Ruth Left Home

Does anyone ever forget the day his child leaves the home-fold for good? It was September 11, 1944, that we took Ruth to San Antonio to enter Trinity University. What a day! There was no time for tears. It had been very wet that week, and we almost got stuck getting to town. We brought Carolyn to Three Rivers to school; Ruth played the piano for the opening assembly just for "old-times' sake," and we all four ate lunch together. Of course, not one of us thought of it as a sad occasion for we all wanted the girls to get a college education.

We picked up Georgia Faye and her things in a car that was already as full as I thought one could get. She and Ruth were roommates. We had two permits for new tires; so after taking the girls to their dormitory, we searched all over San Antonio and found none to buy. On our return trip, we found two for sale at Struve's store and station in Campbellton.

I breathed a sigh of relief . . . just one though . . . as the rush of the year which had just passed that I thought was over was not. Like a fool, I had agreed to serve as president of the P-T. A. for next year. Of all years, just when I had started a new manuscript!

The whole year just gone by had been head over heels with issues that made me look up again and again to the little motto over my desk. It reads:

"I sought my soul
But my soul I could not see.
I sought my God
But my God eluded me.
I sought my brother
And found all three."

The year had begun in an atmosphere for all the world of substitutes, rations, and tensions! Even a simple diary such as I used could not be found in Three Rivers, George West or San Antonio. I used an old ledger which had plenty of blank pages left.

We made 125 bales of cotton that year and paid off all the notes we had signed for money to pay hospitals and surgeons. It

176

was a good feeling, and I was content with the results of the year of hard work. Arthur thought there should be something to show for the whole "kampft," as German people call an endeavor. So he bought seven lots on Murray Hill in the northern part of Three Rivers. Just what possessed him to do that I don't know except the remark he made after walking six miles several times with groceries on his back in a sack after the car just sunk to the axle somewhere along the way.

"Someday, I will be too old to carry groceries in here; and someday when you are sick, they won't even find us out here in this mud."

He meant they, the doctors. I hoped sicknesses were over for us. For surely we had paid our share of bills for a long time to come. Rains ruined about 20 bales of cotton that September. We had planned a real vacation trip with the money after debts were paid; but as it turned out, it was just I who went any place. I went to Hebbronville to visit Ruth and Bill Hornung and their two children and would have stayed a bit longer, but Grandpa Menking died in Gonzales. And we went to the funeral.

That was on October 8th. We saw all the kith and kin we had not seen since the golden wedding, and the male quartette sang the same beautiful German hymn, "In Dem Himmel Ist Wunder Schoen" which I had not heard sung since Papa Adlof's funeral and since my father died with it on his lips.

My year as president of the P-T A will long be remembered. We raised more money than we should have with the annual carnival and school queen's race. After all, P-T A does not sanction voting for candidates with penny votes. In our enthusiasm, committees often started another good idea before the executive committee even heard of it.

People had plenty of spending money this fall, and everyone and his hired help turned out for the big Hallowe'en carnival. It kept the youth so busy there wasn't an upturned little-house in the town the next day, and there was money in the bank for every project.

With money to buy a few things the kids had so wanted for their youth center, the interest suddenly fell. I think it was that the loss of the challenge of having to work to "make do" killed their zeal. Mr. and Mrs. R. H. Napier were my right-hand assistants, but by the time the carnival crown was on Peggy Wheeler's head, the last child checked out for home, and the doors were locked, I was guilty of saying "Teen-Town is really just for kids."

177

Luckily, my treasurer Maxine Hutchins knew a party is not over when the guests leave and a profit is not counted until every nickel and penny is rolled and in the bank. It was the first time I had ever rolled money. It was the first time for many things for me that year, seems like.

I got on the train November 7 and went to Ft. Worth to the State P-T. A. Convention. One car was reserved for delegates all along the line so everyone was mutually interested in each other all the trip. It was my first time to sleep in a Pullman. Two of the presidents had failed to make reservations so I shared my room in the hotel. There were over 1,500 attending. Mrs. Scuddy, Mrs. Early and I attended every hour of the session that lasted until noon on the 9th.

It never occurred to me that the car in which we were riding would be over a mile from the depot when we stopped in San Antonio for a half hour. I had promised Ruth I would phone the college to talk with her. Now this was not possible. By the time I got home, she had called Three Rivers to see if something had happened to me. It had. But not what she feared. I had talked with many mothers who would have given "their eye-teeth to trade with me." They just couldn't see why I should worry about a daughter's being away from home at sixteen. They said to be glad she was engaged to a nice boy who worked and that she was willing to go to college.

Alas! The P-T A convention was simply nothing compared to the uproar that next transpired on the home front. We were in a mess now. Carolyn had to prepare eleven luncheons or suppers for her Home Economics credits. The first one she fairly slaved over was on our wedding anniversary. She would ride the bus home every day she could as she did not like staying in town without Ruth. Rainy days, she stayed at Furlows. Many nights she was caught at home and so missed many days of school. It was on these days she caught up on her cooking assignments.

"Today you had better cook supper so you will have all day," her Dad advised one rainy morning.

That afternoon Mr. Mason, our County Agriculture Agent, telephoned to say their baby arrived. They named her Marynell. Carolyn told him she was cooking supper and invited him. They couldn't come, of course, and Daddy said, "That's good as he might have wanted to help with the dishes, and it looks like that will take all night."

Once as the day progressed, we laughed until we cried: Carolyn's recipe called for six beaten eggs. So she put an egg in each of six cups and beat each.

"How else can you tell if one refuses to beat and maybe spoils the rest?" she insisted on knowing. She wished we had a microscope. We wished she had selected another course.

The year ended with people still fearing a repeat of Pearl Harbor, which was three years ago; livestock prices dropping every day; Ruth making good grades in college, including German. Mama had stayed a few weeks again, and again she had suddenly gotten too homesick and would not stay another day. Christmas "came" early so she could get on back to Gonzales. It was just as well, for when the holidays got here it rained and rained. We had a wonderful rest. Arthur read Time Magazines that he had stacked up and a couple of novels.

It was something good to write to Lula who always worried that we were working Arthur to death.

The Teen-Town building was sold in December. What next? Dr. and Mrs. Gipson loaned us a huge rock building which they later used for the hospital.

What next? Ruth and Lee Roy decided they would be married in February. They told us at Christmas while Ruth was home for the holidays from Trinity. Why the rush and now when it was nearly impossible to get sugar with which to bake a wedding cake?

"If only I had known this when last September, I bought all that yard goods. I would have bought some of it in white for your wedding dress," I said. That was what I thought.

White, for some reason, was the material hardest to find in the stores. I went back with her after the holidays and we walked miles and miles afternoons after her classes from store to store before we found white materials for her dress and the huge slip under the dress. Money was as scarce as the proverbial hens' teeth; but somehow we managed to arrange a lovely wedding for February 12th in our home.

Of course, couples would never get off to such pleasant starts if it were not for the lovely and useful showers they receive. Ruth's was given between semesters when the girls of the beauty shop shoved all their equipment aside and set long tables down the reception room to hold the gifts.

Aunts and uncles sent gifts from far and wide. When a letter came special delivery from Uncle Hot Shot, Ruth was quite excited. She need not have been for he was thoroughly disgusted with her idea and told her so in no first-grader's language. Words as long

179

as your arm finally spelled out the story "here's ten dollars and if your marriage lasts, I will send you a real wedding present five years from now."

At first, it made us angry. Later, we referred to it as a challenge. We would tease Ruth and Lee Roy when they came to visit, asking them if they were still bound to get "that real wedding present."

If necessity is the mother of invention, I should be called Necessity. To arrange a setting for the wedding vows, I turned the china cabinet's back to the living room and draped it with three fully gathered white bedsheets. The edges did not show after pushing the gathers together. I had ironed the sheets until they fairly shone. This stood just back of the arch-way that separates the dining room and the living room.

Guajilla brush was just then coming out fresh in the woods and it made beautiful arrangements for either side of the archway. Lee Roy brought some white carnations from San Antonio that afternoon; and to save us a trip up there, he also brought the wedding cake we ordered from a bakery. He brought Mama, too, from Teeler and Charlie's house, where she was presently staying.

We used artificial sweetening in the punch; tiny colored sandwiches were made that afternoon from home-made bread.

Betty Paul played the wedding music. Carolyn was the bridesmaid. She looked real grown-up in a full length dress of coin-dotted green organdy. For her flowers, she held a long stemmed rose out of the yard. Ruth had the standard white, florist's bouquet. My! everything was pretty. The room was full of guests and in all the excitement, Bob Furlow and the preacher got to be real chummy.

Not that Mr. Furlow dislikes preachers but he doesn't walk across the street to "bother any of them at their thinking and studying." He said it was sure good to have such a real-person to marry "my kids." The Furlows approved of the marriage and that meant much to all of us, for we appreciated their views.

It was during the next week while helping to get their things to San Antonio that I fainted out again . . . colder than a mackerel. This preceded a siege of diarrhea which was referred to in fun (by me) as the annual spring track meet. I'd have it every year, more or less, at the time of the county interscholastic meet which I enjoy seeing but often miss because of my own private track race. Maybe those old-timers with their spring tonics and sulphur and molasses know more about spring than we think.

The September Carolyn Left Home

Carolyn graduated from the Three Rivers High School in 1947. By that time she was so definite in what she planned to do and so engrossed in studying that the lack of Ruth's company was much easier to bear. Grady was going to school, too, and she looked forward to his coming across the fields each morning to meet the school bus with her. Bambi and the dogs would go to the bus with them. Then after they left, the animals would come back to the yard and snooze until time for the bus to return.

One did not need a clock to tell the time of day . . . the deer knew. Furthermore, the deer never came to the yard gate to run to the road and meet the bus on a Saturday or Sunday. Bambi knew that was a school holiday. The dogs maybe would rouse up to go but not Bambi.

I felt sorry for Carolyn as the whole year preceding her senior high school days I had been a victim of some type of intestinal infection. It seems I took a wheelbarrowful of medicine. She and Arthur carried the load of housework along with school and field work, never complaining, and so I tried to hide how badly I really felt.

Rev. H. H. Washington visited with me many times and helped to keep up my courage. Yet, he had a hunch I was playing off and needed some outside interests. He knew I missed Ruthie very much.

"Outside? What do you mean outside interests? Many days she cannot even go outside much less to town and to church," Arthur protested. He stammered a little as he added to the preacher just what he meant by going outside. We had no plumbing inside on the farm. We had the usual pit-type accommodation and a cement walk for an all-weather trail.

Later I did manage to help Rev. Washington organize the Youth Fellowship again. In studying the materials, it was I who benefitted the most. I ordered a book entitled *Christ and the Fine Arts* by Cynthia Pearl Maus (Harper Brothers) which helped me through many hard days. This book is now worn from the hands of youth and other adults who have participated in MYF since that day.

181

Arthur said he knew I must be sick — bad sick — when I did not make it to church, and several days at the time are blank in my 1946 diary. It was almost a tragedy when on May 5, I was too sick to go to see Margaret Walker and Billy Campbell get married. Margaret had visited with us very often and is such a cheerful person that we have always adored her. The same week, I missed the district Guild conference in Pharr.

Ruth had finished her freshman work at Trinity, and Lee Roy was now working for Halliburton Oil Well Cementing Company in nearby Kenedy. I went to stay a day with them for a change of scene while Arthur went to Victoria to get a new pickup truck. We had sold our car to Joe and Dorothy Ligon, who needed one and could not find a suitable buy. Cars and trucks were hard to come by at that time.

When our school closed on May 14 because another child, Verlene Kuenstler, had polio, the doctors warned me to stay put closer than ever because of my weak condition. Just thinking about the sick children made me worse. Arthur suggested I quit thinking . . . imagine that! From one who thinks and schemes and studies far in advance every year and every day.

I got busy again on my novel. I worked hard at it for over six months, hoping all the while to get it done "before I died." There was no money left that fall to even think of having a book published, and, too, when I read it over in September of 1946, I cried. It was a sobby sort of story, and I thought the world did not need any more tears. So I burned the whole 300 pages.

"It just is not like you at all . . . no jokes . . . no cheery little bits of life to tell about . . . you would not recognize it was even you," Arthur said.

He began to talk more about trying to move to town. "Why, a person can just push a truck so far in this black mud and that's all."

"Yep, I could die out here, and you would just have to bury me in the pasture; couldn't a hearse get out here to haul me off!"

"Don't say 'haul' when you refer to people. That's ugly. One hauls cattle and trash and such things, but people one carries."

We tried to plan many little cheerful things to do to make life for our family and friends brighter. On the first anniversary of the plane crash which had killed Lt. Earl Randolph (of our church) in Oklahoma, we planted a pine tree in his memory. But, when A insisted on planting it on our town lots, I knew what he had in mind.

I sewed eight picture hats with matching net gloves for the girls of the community to wear in the Huegler-Benham wedding. Jo Beth and Mr. and Mrs. Benham were so thrilled with my work that it made me feel happy to be able to help.

When Arthur's brother came for a visit on July 26, Carolyn took the opportunity to pack up and ride back as far as Kenedy to spend a few days with Ruth. Charlie had brought a big package of steaks, and Arthur had helped me cook a feast. There were several others "who just happened to know Charlie, Elmar, Erwin and Otto were coming and wanted to be here, too."

They were amazed that Arthur could cook so well. He was only amazed that they did not all stay out of the kitchen while we were working. "I don't like unexpected company, especially not in the kitchen when I am cooking," he growled at them. Charlie just roared with laughter. It was good to hear him belly-laugh again. There had been quite a bit of tension among the three brothers because Arthur had said he was going to sell our farm. Not that it was any part of theirs, but he worked their lands which adjoined ours. I am sure they could tell from their rental checks that they'd surely miss him.

In the middle of August, I got it in the middle so bad that Arthur took me to the hospital in Three Rivers to be cared for while he gathered what little crop there was that year. It was a hard time for him which was made even gloomier by the sudden death of M. T. Buckaloo, his banker. Mr. Buckaloo had a lot of confidence in Arthur's ability and had often loaned him funds when I frankly did not see why . . . considering payments were based on what the weather would do for the farmer.

It was my first encounter with penicillin. They shot me so often that I began to feel like a tea strainer. When I got out of the hospital, Arthur took me straight to the beauty shop where I had Ruby cut bangs for me.

"My goodness, are you sure you really want me to cut you some bangs?" she asked as if she thought I had truly gone nuts.

"I do, for I have to look nice when I get home."

"What's going on at your home after you have been in the hospital all week?"

"The Pedro Ruiz crew is leaving, and we always give them a party with homemade ice-cream and lots of ice cold soda-water when they have finished the crop. Besides, this year several of them brought me crepe-paper flowers they made for me, and this year, they have piled up and burned all their trash and stuff, Arthur

183

said. I just have to look nice for them. They love pretty things so much."

Poor Ruby! So she was to make a pretty thing out of me. What miracles we women expect from beauticians when we spend a couple of dollars. It did make me feel better, no folly! I even looked pretty.

We voted for Governor Beauford Jester that August. It was the summer of the long wind-storm. We had never known such a thing could happen. For three weeks the wind blew up so much black loam from the fields south of the house that each night Arthur had to shake the beds, put on clean sheets, and water-mop the floors.

Just like clock-work around six in the evening, the time we normally begin to have the best gulf breezes, it got very calm and hot. One had to wash and hang out the clothes in the night or it would be as dirty as sandpaper and no one could wear it. There are hundreds of acres of row-crops to the south of the farm-yard. "Never again will I burn any stalks or trash. Look, the dirt isn't blowing away where there's trash," A observed.

When it seemed we were about to be covered over with the dust and silt, we had a cloud-burst rain of almost seven inches one day. The next day, it rained four more inches. Schweikert's and Kelm's stock water tanks broke. Arthur's back almost broke when he walked the two trips back and forth to the pavement at Suniland where he caught a bus to town for medicines and flour.

Earl Gregory was in the same fix. They trodded the miles together and no doubt both were worried about illnesses. It was good to have a telephone in times like these. The girls would call each other to console themselves about being caught in "this boggy jail."

So the September came when we left the farm. Max Gottschield came over from Cuero with his huge moving truck as soon as the roads were dry enough to travel and lifted up the house. He did this on the twelfth so that he would not start the job on Friday, the 13th, the day he hauled our house to Three Rivers. We placed it on the lot next to a four room house we had bought the year before when Uncle Sam decided to sell all the government houses out of the Nueces River Valley project.

Fortunately, the four-room house was rented to the happiest people in the world. It was like a tonic to hear them chatter and to hear the mother, Mrs. Ollie Herring, laugh. The children,

184

David Lee and Barbara Ann, and Mr. and Mrs. Herring welcomed us to the "hill" as though we were royalty.

It was hard to leave the farm, though, and I would never have consented to go if we had been able to get some farm-to-market roads. A few years later such a road was built to within a mile of our place. Though it was then too late for us to return there to live, it did make it possible to go there now more easily on rainy days to tend to the cattle and do machine-shop work.

Arthur commutes to the farm to work, and many times I am right there in the truck with him at daylight.

"Are you on a committee today or do you have to cover something?" is a daily question in our morning coffee chat. "Are you going with me?"

The farm is where one can think more clearly, where one looks over to the northeast and remembers the sweet face of Mrs. Gregory, who died of cancer . . . (which makes me also remember there is a cancer drive to help with in the county this month.)

The farm is where one can almost see the footprints of the many children romping with our two for birthday parties and 4-H Club meetings that always ended with recreation and where it seems Lena and I must have sewn up at least a bale of cotton dresses for our four girls.

The farm is where the little Mexican girl died before a doctor could get there. It is where the dog Lubber is buried under that huge mesquite tree which still has two short ends of rope dangling from when hogs were hung out to cool over-night. The farm is where the water is fine for stock-water but rose bushes curl up and die after a few drinks of it. The farm is where one pours his entire bank account and all he feels safe to borrow into the rows that once had to be as straight as a bullet shoots and now are so crooked from contours that one can't tell if the tractor is heading this way or that.

The farm is where town people flock on Sunday afternoons and where folks always have a couple of extra cakes on hand. The farm is where the government has given non-farm folks the impression that all one has to do is "sign up and you've got it made another year."

Three Rivers folk are all more or less dependent on the earth — whether it is the surface crops or the oil and gas beneath the surface. So we found there was a welcoming attitude in town toward us and toward Carolyn in her senior year at high school.

We missed the community closeness brought about by giving

parties for our community girls as they married, by looking after each other during long illnesses such as Dora Gregory had, and by loaning each other tools, dress patterns and recipes.

It was hard to get used to the larger community life. It was even harder to become accustomed to highway noises, and it seemed very odd that folks living within a few blocks of one another drove their cars to each other's homes. (So soon after rationing, I thought!)

We were so thrilled with electricity that we snapped on every light when they finished wiring our house, tested the irons and toasters, and soon bought more gadgets than we really have any use for. We had both helped to get rural electrification to our community; but since there were no permanent dwellers on the brothers' farms, the R.E.A. could not see building a line down the ranch road just for one customer for what we could pay. So it was in September of 1946 before we had electricity, running water in the bathroom in the house, and heating with natural gas.

One day when I felt extra good, I spent the whole day enjoying my new convenient kitchen by baking every neighbor a pan of coffee-cake. They had all been so kind to us when we were jacked up on the trucks for a few days that now I had the chance to repay them.

Moving was really funny the day that the crew had come back to let the house down onto the foundation blocks. The carpenters had then finished. The manager, not knowing that I could understand him, was cussing a blue streak about Arthur's insistence on the way the foundation should be. He was using his own version of German.

I was peering under to see how they were doing, and when he paused to catch his breath, I spoke to him in German, "Ist das so?" Poor fellow nearly knocked his head off as he raised up in surprise. The other men just shook with laughter. When he was all done, he came to me to apologize; but I made a joke of it as I, too, often am provoked at the delay caused by Arthur's insistence on thoroughness.

"Do you not remember Miss Ora always said whatever you do, do well?" he says on many such occasions.

Ruth and Lee Roy returned to college that fall to get their degrees. He wanted to be a football coach and wanted to badly enough to make the sacrifice of leaving a good job and working his way through. Texas A. and I. College had leased the Navy base at Kingsville and was offering married students housing in the officers' trailers parked there. It was a September of real joy for me. Now I had two children in college. I knew they would be glad they went. I counted two — Lee Roy and Ruth!

Lula spent a few weeks with us after recovering sufficiently from major surgery which was a cancer. During this time, the Three Rivers School let the Methodist youth use a bus on a Saturday to go to San Antonio to a youth rally. There were 25 reservations and when it came time to leave only five came. I went along with them and though the five sang all the way home, my heart ached to think of what the others missed. I just could not seem to let Dr. Baxter's message take full possession of my thoughts.

"Please, Mother! Remember the message the speaker gave us. What is the matter with you, Mother? It was always you who reminded us to see the good, no matter how small it is. It is you who says, 'Eat that and be glad you have something to eat.' Can't you get hold of yourself?"

It was a desperate battle, but I fought to get back to my full strength. I sewed Carolyn's high school prom dress all by hand while sitting up a few hours at a time in bed. I learned to iron while sitting on a stool and arranged my cooking and shopping so well that Carolyn managed most of the evenings after school.

When she had a button missing or some minor little repair, she always brought it to me to do.

"When are you ever going to learn to sew your own things?" A asked her one morning when he was in a hurry to get the morning devotional "over-with" and get on the way to his farm work.

"I don't intend to sew except square stitches. By the way I have decided to go to A. & I. for my first two years of pre-med."

Another golden September for us! Carolyn started on her pre-med studies. I was happy; yet I could not choke down my supper that first night she was gone. I missed her very much. She is a real chatter-box and never seems to worry about a thing. In fact, sometimes we wished she would worry about us . . . about herself . . . and about other things we thought seriously needing attention.

Arthur had an electric motor put on my sewing machine so I could sew again, not being able to tread the foot-pedal. I managed to get Carolyn's clothes ready with Mrs. Herring's help and by buying much of them ready-made. We were fortunate to make almost a hundred bales of cotton. Pedro Ruiz had brought his crew to gather the whole crop. It cost over $5,000 just to gather the cotton.

Arthur decided I should have a car as he was away most of the time with the farm truck. It is a mile from our home to the post-office and stores. He bought me a Ford V8, paying $2,000 cash for it.

Carolyn's first room-mate was also named Carolyn. Ruth and Lee Roy were digging away at their classes and both had part-time jobs in Kingsville. Lee Roy was ushering at the theatre with a book propped on the ticket-take box. We visited them late in September when *The Egg and I* (Betty Smith) was a hit film.

"You see, she wrote a very simple story about just plain people and look how cute it is," I commented as we were returning home.

"That's right! You can also write such a story if you will tell the truth. Tell what a battle you have to keep going; how you bake the cake for a church supper anyway even if you have to sit to do all your chores, how you have your right leg elevated in bed while you prepare the youth studies; how you can laugh through your tears; and how you are always blowing your top!"

Just suggesting how I can blow my top usually blows it another time. There is a brown spot, left there for a reminder, of chocolate cake dough on our kitchen ceiling from one of those blow-outs. I cannot remember what mite of friction set the blaze, but I like to blame my illness for the build-up.

I am crazy about festivals, parades and community gatherings. Maybe, because I have so much fun with all the people on all the committees that have to work together to stage these events. So this September a golden opportunity came to me to assist with plans for the first annual Live Oak County Fair, 1947.

The Junior Chamber of Commerce of George West and the American Legion Post and Auxiliary were the sponsors. I had written many news articles about the two and somehow won recognition with some of their members. It was real fun, and I even felt much better.

When it came time for the big day, I was in surgery at Scott and White Hospital. It had nothing to do with the work or the excitement. It was a tumor, and I was lucky to have it test out benign. Dr. Williamson had told me a couple of years ago that I should see a specialist. Now he was gone. He had died this fall just a few days after Carolyn had visited with him and he had reminded her she had promised him to be a good doctor.

When I was in Scott and White this time, my favorite nurse was Miss Mary Mikeska. She was a corker—full of wit and tease.

She told me she really didn't see why she was so careful with my stomach tubes, my transfusion, injections and all.

Looking up at her in amazement at such a statement, she gave me a gentle pat and said, "Cos I sure love you hosebund." She had an accent from having spoken Czech, she explained. I recall hearing her and Arthur talking all day long as I came and went out of and into a doze from the anesthesia.

In the next few days Mary was a life-saver, not only with her actual nursing care but with her good cheer. She made me forget myself by telling me such true parts of her own life as the fact that her blind sister actually did the housework for the two of them.

Buddy, mostly I called Arthur that now since the little Stendebach girls had started it, was thrilled that Dr. Terrell Speed allowed me to get up early . . . just a few steps the third day . . . more steps the day after . . . and soon all the way down the hall. Soon, home again.

We especially appreciated this doctor because he took the time to explain what all and why they had done so much more drastic surgery than had been planned. We were over $400 poorer, but then what is money for if not to use when needed?

While in the hospital, I remembered the little doily I had made while in the Santa Rosa a few years ago. So I got busy again with something to pass the time away. From the ribbons tied on the flowers A had brought me and the jar of sachet powder out of my bag, I fashioned little sachet pockets for every nurse, scrubwoman, and aide that came to my room. It gave me a feeling of real joy as their surprised faces turned to say thanks.

When I got home, I could hardly wait to make a sock-doll for little one-year-old Margaret Ruth Lee, our next door neighbor. It was certainly a day for celebrating that November 11 . . . Armistice Day for the nation, and my first tub-bath since surgery. Wonders never cease, I thought as I bathed my bony old frame with its road-map of scars on my abdomen.

We needed a vacation. We went to the valley for two days. It was Buddy's first time there and he enjoyed it very much. He especially enjoyed staying at the Casa de Palmas in McAllen. We stayed the second night in Kingsville in the Ricardo Hotel. There, too, tall palms fascinated him. It was the start of the landscaping idea which has made our home-grounds a copy of many of the valley places: large shade trees, palms, bright colored roses, and waxy evergreens. The trip was good for us.

189

We visited briefly in Premont with his sister, Ella, and her husband. In Premont we also bought some palms to take home.

By this time I was beginning to be strong enough to drive the car, so it was I who bashed a fender on the side of the garage. I was upset over Lee Roy's having to have an appendectomy with them on a shoe-string budget. They had not asked for help, but now his parents and we did pay the doctor and hospital bill.

In our church we always give our preachers a pounding. This is the word used to describe a shower of foods. It originated, perhaps when people brought pounds of butter and other produce for the minister and his family's Christmas. Mrs. John Stendebach and some of the young people invited me to come to watch them decorate the tree in the church. We placed a large box in the foyer for the people to put in the pounding the next night for the Washingtons.

Brother Washington cried. He thought it would have been much better to have taken these things to some folks who had no salaries.

Ruth said, "What a preacher! Maybe he knows something about the battles people have getting through life on a day to day basis."

This was the holiday season that I got Aunt Nora Humphries' (Lee Roy's aunt) recipe for Chess pie. It turned out in later years to be the pie that our Mayor Jack Montgomery became famous for baking. I tease him at social functions when folks all want some of his pie, that he stole the recipe from me. He says, "You published it in your news column, you got it from Aunt Nora, she got it from England, and they got it from where?"

We went to the Baptist Church for Watch-night services. It was quite coincidental that it poured down rain and sleet and hail that day. For all afternoon the girls had sung the popular song, "I Had a Little Talk With God," by Mann Curtis and Vic Mizzy. The chorus still fascinates me with its message, "I begged the Lord to send down some rain, to give me strength to stand again. Right there my heart began to smile, and I had a little talk with God. And the Lord spoke, And the clouds broke, And the thunder crashed around, And I knew the Lord had blessed me . . ."

I knew the song did not mean only water from the sky, which we surely needed once again. An Indian Chief in full regalia was the guest preacher. He, too, reassured me that life has much to offer if one will only accept it. I began to ponder on how I could be of service to my community now that the girls were away to school.

190

Many of Carolyn's friends who were still in high school and who were members of the Youth Fellowship would visit with me after school. True enough, they often only came to sell tickets to some school functions or maybe sell magazine subscriptions. I always enjoyed them and tried to have them tarry a bit to visit.

On Tuesday, February 17, I invited a number of the girls to come to my home just to see if they would like to form a little club to sew, study etiquette and dating problems, cook and bake a bit and just plain have fun. The girls seemed to really enjoy the idea. At first, Patsy Montgomery, Alice Brown, Sylvia Kolodzie, Anna Maria Moser, Betty Jo Casey, Leatrice Garrison, Ann Hathaway, Bessie Biddle and Bettye Stendebach came. We decided since our house was small we would limit the membership to 17 and the girls said they would just call their group Seventeen Sisters.

They may not have learned very much in the following months, but they formed a close fellowship which had to bear sadnesses as well as fun in bringing them together for their monthly sessions. All of the girls and others that joined later are now happily married except Bettye. She married, had a baby son and died shortly afterwards of cancer. It was gloom in our lives that had no glow.

Before her death, though, she lived a full and exceedingly happy life. She had only recently been elected Queen of Live Oak County for the fair.

Now that it was September again and Carolyn was back to college, I was again faced with too much spare time. I could not do the heavy work. Like the old darky used to say, "Too light for heavy work and too heavy for light work" was I.

The Herrings had built a new home south of Three Rivers, and we missed them very much. Even Mr. Herring would tap on the kitchen door and call to me in bed when I had been ill to ask, "Are you all right today?" Pat and Bob Collins moved into the rent house and they, too, were wonderful neighbors.

We had a new pastor this spring, the Rev. William Parrish. He loves to hike, and soon he discovered the Tips State Park on the Frio River, which was not even cleared of under-brush. He brought this to our attention and was pleased that the Three Rivers Civic Club had started a project to get it developed. It is a beautiful site, consisting of thirty acres of land shaded by immense moss-draped elm and other trees.

We knew of its beauty, for we often ate our Sunday lunch there when we still lived on the farm. A small area was cleared out from the days when another group of women in a club had

191

strived to make it what it can truly be — a beauty spot to compare with any anywhere.

Buddy fell in love with this preacher. He was interested in the community here and now, as well as off in some distant future referred to in songs as the "up yonder." He and Mrs. Parrish even helped us with the Queen's race that netted $4,496.59 for the fair and the clubs. If it were not a matter of record, one could not believe such a thing.

Never let a community know that you are willing to work on committees unless you are willing to work overtime. For if you "do" for one group, you'd better be ready to "do" for the other. I helped make the queen's float, which was sponsored by the Three Rivers Lions Club, and the Civic Club's float. Mrs. Stroman Harris, Mrs. David Davis, and I were working on it when we decided we needed more air.

We were in the Bartlett machine shop in George West. I pulled a door back, which made a ladder fall and hit me squarely on top of my head, sending me to the Gipson Hospital in Three Rivers. Little Ross Harris saw me a couple of years later at a football game and he asked his mother if I were not the "dead lady." Mrs. Harris had taken me to the hospital in her car while I was unconscious.

I think Buddy was vexed enough with me for being so careless that he might have wished I were the dead-lady, I recalled a few times afterwards. Times like these, I would get busier than ever and write more news articles so I could partly, at least, earn back some of the money.

He really did feel sorry for me. We had for years said we were going back to San Antonio for a second honeymoon. Now in 1948, after all the trying days, we went. I wore my wedding hat and dress, but, alas, my shoes would not even begin to go on my feet. Buddy could not wear his suit because the trouser styles had changed so much, but he could still wear them for fit. He could even have worn his shoes if he had had them, for he was fully grown when he married; but I had grown several inches in height.

One of the biggest comedies in our lives are the days for trying on last season's clothes. Used to when the girls were small, they would invite Betty Paul and Marie over for that day; they, in turn, would watch Betty and Marie's trying-on-day. Usually Carolyn would tire of the foolishness in a very short time and wind up by saying, "Mother can add a ruffle."

I added many a ruffle; let out many seams; turned many

aunts' dresses into nieces' clothes; but this time there was no solution to my wedding shoes' problem. So I decided just to wear the things that fit for the heck of it under my new coat.

The Live Oak County Herald had put in an office in Three Rivers and hired me to work in it. I liked the work but missed the spare time which I had come to use for many community interests by now. I dared not think of giving up the job, though, as it was extremely dry, and we wondered if it would ever rain again.

Septembers Decide The Future

September, 1949, was sufficiently optimistic to get us into a lot of trouble. Ruth had taught the past year in Alice while Lee Roy finished earning his degree which was awarded on August 26. They moved to Nixon for his first coaching position, and Ruth taught the second grade. For several months we had planned on being grand-parents; but, by now, it was just a false report.

Arthur had suffered severe headaches much of his life. Now he had had them again for many days. Yet as we went into the fall plans, he assured me all would be well. Pedro had not gathered our crops this year as they were so miserably scattered.

When we went to Nixon to see Lee Roy join the Methodist Church as a transfer from the Three Rivers Baptist, it was a joy to have Rev. and Mrs. Washington to be their pastor there.

Carolyn could hardly wait to see Ruth to show her new shoes. They were Carolyn's first high heels. Carolyn had worn braced shoes for many years and later special arch-supported shoes. Arthur teased and said it was as high up as that year's whole cotton crop had gotten him to see the thrill on her face when Mr. Reyes at the Guarantee Shoe Store in San Antonio brought out this pair of slippers. (Now she says high heels are for the devil to take a peep in on his competition.)

"When they came in, I thought of my little girl Carolyn and I almost mailed them to you," Mr. Reyes had said.

We had made 77 bales of cotton but had paid three dollars per hundred pounds of bolls to have it pulled. We could just as well have plowed it all under for fertilizer, I thought. But I dared not say it. Even so, Arthur allowed Carolyn a checking account that fall, and he finally decided she was a grown lady.

We were all excited about her branching out all on her own. (While she had been at A. and I., Ruth had also been there.) The night before we took her to Austin to transfer to the University, we would call back and forth to each other after we were in bed.

"Did we pack my . . . ?

"Shut up and go to sleep," A would yell.

In a moment, he would holler out, "Did you all pack her . . . ?

We took Marie Schwiekert along to Austin as she was also

attending the University. I got a lead on a feature story so we went to Corpus Christi that weekend to dig it out. It was the first time in 25 years for Arthur to stay at the hotel near the bay. He told all about the first time he had stayed there when Uncle Willie had brought him and his own boys down for a look at the coast country, hoping they would love it as much as he did.

If we had not taken Marie along, I would not have known of this story. One never helps another but what he helps himself if he does not expect it. When you expect a reimbursement, what you get seems too small, I have found. It was now twenty years since we had moved to our own farm in the coast country, and we loved it as much as Uncle Willie did.

Carolyn wrote that a lady came forward in the University Methodist Church to tell her, "I am so glad to know you for I used to be your father's girl friend, and I just knew he would have a nice daughter and . . . " On and on she talked right there in front of God and the pulpit, Carolyn said.

On September 21, President Harry S. Truman announced in Washington that we had evidence that within the recent weeks an atomic bomb had been released within the U.S.S.R. Therefore, we knew they had now developed atomic bombs. We always allowed for this possibility. I was just writing my diary when the words came on the radio so I recorded it.

For Christmas that year, we sent homegrown cotton to the mattress factory in Kenedy to have mattresses made for Ruth and Lee Roy and many nice large sofa pillows for my family and closest friends. This was done mostly after we came to realize how lucky we were that the predicted gulf storm had taken another course.

By next September 1950, I was one major surgery farther along and Arthur was one big headache worse off. In the months that had just passed, we had gone to see Teeler and Charlie in Sanderson, and we had had a wonderful time. Carolyn had joined us during the Easter weekend for that trip. The bus driver forgot to leave her bags; and, of course, she didn't bother to see that he did. She was studying a new book while riding on the bus and had not even realized they were in San Antonio until Arthur stepped on the bus to get her to join us there.

So with one change of clothes, we left for Sanderson for three days vacation. Why worry? She figured she could borrow night clothes, and somebody would surely assist with washing and ironing her day clothes each night. It was a thought. I agreed we would all be much happier if we had less clutter. The next week, I'd pack up most of my clothes and give it away. But the next week, I'd be in the hospital for removal of my gall-bladder. It "just rose up in my throat and stuck there when we were up on the Davis Mountains," I told Dr. Gipson. I almost did not make it this time.

Mr. V. D. Wellington, my boss at the Herald, thought to cheer me by writing that I had had major surgery nine times and yet always more than did my share to keep it a secret. When a couple of weeks later I read this, I was furious. If I had kept it such a secret, people would say, how did he find it out?

But now it was September again and a golden one. For the first time ever, we attended the Menking Family annual reunion at La Grange. My mother was the honoree that year. Each year, they selected one to be the honoree. We saw many cousins, aunts, and in-laws (and as Arthur says out-laws) and ate enough to kill us.

We went on to Temple for complete check-ups, and for the first time I was told to reduce though I only weighed 130 pounds. Carolyn's doctor thought she needed more physical exercise and noted that was typical of all students. Arthur liked Dr. Hammond very much, mostly because he did not nag about his smoking. He said Arthur just does everything "TOO" much: too much work, too much worry, too much smoking and too much looking ahead.

Arthur leased a large acreage in the vast Schulz Ranch that September and after getting a good report from the clinic, worked harder than ever. We even gambled to buy some more cattle and to have a large stock-water tank built; repaired fences; put up the cattle for security at the bank. Seemed everyone was optimistic. The students moved into the new Three Rivers High School building that September.

The Methodists had opened a new church building on March 12 and everyone was thrilled over the town's growth. But the gloom of communism into Korea over-shadowed all the glow. Our new preacher, Rev. E. F. Kluck, was very serious as he warned us that only through Christ could dictators be brought to their defeat. Even in families it sometimes needs to be remembered that there is no place for dictators.

That September while I was at work in the Herald office one afternoon and no one was paying any mind to Carolyn at the ironing board, Arthur's brother Paul told him "just exactly what he ought to do."

He meant it well, but one does not tell Arthur just exactly

"what" at any time. He has a mind and uses it. True enough, he was very thin and worked very hard. It was extremely dry and folks were scared stiff. Yet, why should they again bring up this idea of our moving to Houston to work for Max?

"We will make out. Viola earns more with her typewriter than you do with your service station or I did this year with the tractors. And besides, she does not want to leave the country life and so I don't either," Carolyn told me her father had said. "And a lot of other stuff!"

It was her growing-up. She decided the next summer she would stay on in college and take a business course. We laugh about it many times now, eight years later, as she types with two fingers on medical charts.

C. B. and Leon had another baby that September. We had some neighbors named Dunn, and they had a six year old, Mike, who just couldn't be consoled that the new baby was taken to the Mexican house instead of to theirs.

"I wanted him for a long time and they've got too many babies. They are stingy and won't give him to me," he wailed when we brought Mike home from the farm where we had taken him along to feed the cattle that September evening. Feeding cattle in September? It *was* terribly dry.

We listened to every news report and pondered over every "sign" of rain. One evening our next-door neighbors were not cleaning their yards but were even over into ours.

"Just trying to make it rain!" G. T. yelled at us through the thick dust his rake was stirring up. There was no rationing of water for yard watering but we could not afford the water bills three lots took. (We have that much yard so that we can feel we are still country.)

Septembers mark the under-ground moisture for the next year's crop, my father used to say. In Live Oak County, most folks are ready for rains by then. The over forty inches of rainfall in 1949 had brought on a good cotton and grain crop, but the extremely dry 1950 summer had really been long; cattle were already lean.

So the spring of 1951 found us hauling water to the leased land and ironically fighting to keep from drowning. It was the days of the Corpus Christi interests' law case trying to build a lake at Oakville which would inundate Three Rivers. J. F. Gray, our state representative, and many others were battling the issue.

We even went to Austin one night to hear the arguments in the Senate Chambers in the State capitol.

Naturally, my string receipts were good those days, and I began to pay all the expenses incurred with newswriting: car, gas, telephone and such things. I felt much more important. I was feeling much better these days and I enjoyed rushing about visiting and committee-making. Then suddenly our neighbors had a son, Robert William Lee, celebrating his birthday, and I forgot to make him a doll like his sister's.

I cried over that until I actually was sick for days. Arthur and I both knew something was wrong — something more major than the doll's oversight. What was it?

I had lost loved ones. I had missed Bettye as much as even her family missed her. I had been sick almost to death several times, but never had I so completely lost interest or been so forgetful of others.

Was it the drought? I doubted that it was, for to me money is not the most important thing in life.

Buddy suggested I visit oftener and work less. He even promised he would do the same. So I started the next day by going to take some roses to Mrs. Albert Cobb, the high school coach's wife They had lived here about two years and now were expecting a baby again. She had lost their first one a year ago.

The wind blew dust as thick as ever that evening, too, but as we sat on the terrace after supper, I told all about my pleasant afternoon. How was I to know that Mrs. Cobb had been very blue and lonely and that she was so happy that I came, the tears came freely to her eyes?

"Good! You just keep that up and every day go some place a little while. Go over to Lee's and see their baby once in a while, too. He does not know you forgot to make him a doll."

I tried and tried. Many days, I was so depressed that it was just all I could do to bathe and dress. Luckily, we have to go to the postoffice for our mail. So each day, able-bodied people do go to town and there one greets and sees folks. I hope we never get house delivery.

I soon found that lots of folks like snap-shots as much as do I. So I would usually take along my camera. Many times, later (on birthdays or other occasions) I send them a snapshot. Sometimes it is of a loved one who has suddenly gone away soon after I had just happened to take his picture. It's come to be quite a little joke: "Don't shoot me like you did Mr. John Doe!"

198

Mary and Pappy Wellington sold the "Herald" and the new owners, Alma and Owen Phillips, were also country-loving people. They kept me on as their Three Rivers correspondent, and I enjoyed working for them.

September '51 found Arthur with little crop to gather and a promise he would also do some community work, just like he thought was good for my depression. He helped with clearing the park. Many of us fairly slaved at this until it was really nice. An elderly couple moved there to run a little concession made out of a used school bus. The Lions Club built a miniature golf course, and the firemen assisted with stringing lights under the beautiful moss-draped trees in the picnic area. Mr. and Mrs. George Tubbs, the caretakers, loved their new location.

It was an interesting project to take one's mind off of the dry weather and the family troubles. Ruth and Lee Roy moved to Natalia for better salaries. Carolyn enrolled at Southwestern Medical College of the University of Texas in Dallas. We had to haul water to the cattle from town every day so we could not take Carolyn to Dallas. We did take her as far as the rail-depot in San Antonio.

That September, I interviewed the first woman doctor I had ever actually known. She was Dr. H. H. Reissmann from Germany, who came to live in Dr. Gipson's hospital. Many interesting things were taking place to write about and to hear from Carolyn and Ruth.

Carolyn had a room-mate from New York, Miss Aileen Young, an American Chinese — or does one say a Chinese American? She was studying medical art. At Christmas she came home with Carolyn. They went, one afternoon, to get some meat from the locker plant downtown. Carolyn introduced her to Mr. Lee.

"She can draw just about everything about anybody," Carolyn told Mr. Lee.

Thinking to trap Carolyn, whom he called "Sister," he asked, "Can she draw me?"

Miss Young, soon to be Doctor Young, replied, "What will you have me draw, Sir? Your insides or your outsides?"

It was Aileen who, very modestly and apologetically, suggested during the holidays that Mr. Adlof seemed to be ill. We told her we knew he did not feel well and that normally he was a very jolly person. We took the girls to see the Magic Valley, and it was during that drive I realized something very serious was wrong with A. He had a lot of trouble with his vision, seeming

199

not to be able to keep the car aright in the road although it was a new Chrysler.

The afternoon after we took the girls as far as Kenedy, where they joined other students going back to college, Arthur suffered a subarachnoid hemorrhage.

Following on a year of crop loss, the doctor at first thought it was only a headache of tension. But as three days and nights passed with no relief and partial paralysis setting in, with him raving with pain, we knew something had to be done. Luckily, Ruth and Lee Roy had moved to Natalia, for there a fellow-teacher recommended Dr. Lewis M. Helfer, a neurological surgeon in San Antonio.

When September next arrived, 1952, we looked back on a night-mare having passed. By then Arthur could walk real well again and was filled with his usual foresight for the future. We had a good flax crop that spring, had made 175 bales of cotton and a nice crop of corn. I had driven the truck across the rows to tend to anything he wanted to see, and we had learned to herd the cattle entirely by the honk of the truck horn and by Arthur's calling them.

Dr. Helfer was kind but firm. He warned against hard work but also against just sitting idly by. He told us not to eat animal fats of any kind and was amazed that I was up and about, considering my physical report. He also made us take a long vacation . . . a whole "cotton-picking" week the fall of 1952 . . . the first time we were either one out of the State except briefly into Nuevo Laredo. Some of the night-mare began, at least, to fade. But the year had ground on day by day into further drought.

When September 1953 arrived, we had word that Uncle Frank had burned to death in New York. Mama was extremely excited about it. Why? She certainly never lost any affection on him when he was alive. But then Mama loved quietly, and who am I to judge her affections?

We learned of this on our way home from Temple where A had had major surgery in late August. Carolyn had stayed the summer in Dallas to work to help finance her next year's schooling and now she was coming back to spend a few days before the new fall term. While he was in the hospital, seems a hundred doctors came to see him. Dr. Speed said if he did not mind they just wanted to see a patient who was so strong after having had a cerebral hemorrhage.

How we ever lived over all the excitement of that fall I will perhaps never know. The day we got back to Three Rivers, it rained. We first ran from window to window looking at it; and then after Buddy did, we all went out into the rain and stood there shouting, "Praise God from whom all blessings flow."

I felt he would take pneumonia, but he was fine. We all slept like dead that night. The next day the girls and Lee Roy helped me, and we brushed the drought out of every nook and cranny.

Carolyn, Mama and I were very busy for a few days making white linen doctor coats and skirts, for Carolyn was required to wear them now. Ruth and Lee Roy moved to Hardin where Lee Roy was the head-coach and Ruth found a good position in the Texaco office in Liberty. Ruth began to notice that Carolyn was worried about financing the remainder of her college days if we didn't get rains and so she saved up enough to really help later on.

It was the first time for Ruth to be in the deep piney-woods and Lee Roy tells with glee how she made him promise at first to go back to the brush-country at the end of the term; instead, in only a few weeks she was hopelessly in love with the area.

When we visited them, we drove up to the only Indian Reservation in Texas at Livingston. It is a most interesting experience. There at first some of the people preferred to live out in the yards, using their modern homes as storage places.

We can now look back at the days of drought with a bit more understanding. The wee bit of good that is supposed to be in even the worst of things was the leisure time forced upon us. Arthur was not to lift or strain himself and so it was that he made the most of the days and days when there was no farm work.

Yet, we lost time, the most valuable thing we all are ever given. All goes well until one runs out of time. We had to give up the leased pasture, sell most of our cattle and let the hired hands move away. Many times, A had said they were not "worth the salt in butter-milk soup," but now that they had to leave, it hurt him deeply.

I got him to go with me as often as I possibly could persuade him when I went to cover a new story. One that he enjoyed very much was an interview with Mr. and Mrs. Edgar N. Langley, a neighbor's son, who was now stationed in Asuncion, South America, with the agriculture department. We wrote about them while they were home on vacation.

It was as if the government had not heard of the Texas drought when we received notice that the dead and dried cotton stalks that only made from eighteen acres a bale still had to be plowed out. Uncle Sam did not know they were as dead as a door-knob and probably did not want to risk driving out in that dust to see.

With all the hands gone and Arthur not able to drive a tractor, we got a man from Pawnee to come over and plow them out on September 27 to the 30th. As he plowed, the dry dirt would roll back into the furrow so that when he finished, it all looked the same except the sticks were missing.

It felt that same way to me that night in late September when at the official church board meeting, the pastor announced I would step aside from the youth class as a teacher. I had taught almost six months without missing except the Sundays we were in Temple. It was the first class in our church school I had come to feel was my very own; all others I had only substituted teaching without any previous notice most of the time. I was so crushed, my chest actually felt it would squeeze me to death.

I did not have time to stay grieved over the hurt and insult. The next day we were called to Max's bedside in Houston. We commuted back and forth a few nights from Hardin, and then we just had to come home. We could have stayed on longer as there was water for the cattle, but Max was too sick for company and we were too tense to stay. It helped to relax us when on Friday night, we did go to see Lee Roy's team play and they won in the last three minutes of play. I was shocked at A for jumping up in the stadium and cheering as wildly as anyone. He would never have done such a thing at home where people knew us, I thought.

Again, his sister Lula had asked him if we couldn't move to Houston. She always felt so sorry for Max because "he is so all alone." Now just what she meant by that, we could not understand. He was married. True, he lost his only son and that was tragic. Yet he had the best opportunities to have friends; and he had many friends.

Again, Arthur explained we would not be leaving the farm unless it became a matter of life and death. He does not consider living in Three Rivers as being "off the farm" actually for all Live Oak people are truly rural.

That fall, October 11, we opened the new Foster Memorial Building for our church. As I was debating whether or not to do so, Rev. Jimmy Stone telephoned me and asked me to bring my camera and take pictures of the first church-school exercises there. I did. We also attended the regular morning services; but instead of going that afternoon to the open-house, I spent the time crying and running back and forth to the bathroom.

Having been so bluntly told I was not needed at the church, not by the pastor, but by a few others whom I should only have ignored, I set my time on helping again more than ever with the county fair. The Future Homemakers of the two schools were interested in the new exhibit hall. We built a 45 by 12 foot replica tableau of Live Oak County which took the better part of a week. That is spare-time.

Owen went to Kentucky that week to bring Alma home from the hospital, and so I edited the paper for him. It was an exciting experience. We stuffed the paper so full of local news that we forgot to put in the story about the opening of the new educational building of the Methodist Church in Three Rivers. It taught me a lesson: editors are human. Rev. Stone was nice about it, saying he supposed we just did not have room with all the fair publicity.

"Besides, the church should have bought an ad. Churches should not expect to get everything free from the whole community," the young preacher said.

1953 was the year the Parent-Teacher reorganized in Three Rivers. To keep my membership continuous, I had paid it to the State office. Mrs. Bob Boudreau was elected president.

That fall, Buddy decided he would just do what farm work he could and let the rest go. There was no money for hired help. It rained a little so he gambled on some spinach seed. I was more and more on my own now, so I kept as busy as possible.

I remember one frightful experience. Way back when we still lived in the country, Mrs. Matthews had submitted my name for membership in a study club. Now, this many years later, I was invited to be a guest speaker and on, of all subjects, journalism. It pleased me to know the new club had not inherited the knowledge that I was once rejected for lacking education. Yet I was so scared I could not stand up when I got to Mrs. Roger Frank's home that night.

She did not seem to know anything about my fright but suggested that I remain seated as the floor lamp made queer shadows on one's face when one stood in her living room.

I was about to get "big-headed," for that same week Henderson Coquat complimented me in front of all the people gathered for the formal opening of the beautiful new building that houses the gas company, the drilling company offices, and rents to the power company. My diary records that I had worried all this time about being voted out just because I had spelled cantaloupe "canteloupe." (Many times, Ruth and Carolyn had reminded me that I made this natural error because "e" is pronounced "a" mostly in German, and though I said "ta" I probably thought it was "te.") At any rate, the cantaloupe had returned after many days to be a most pleasant experience, after all.

The Home Stretch September

September 1954 found us in the home-stretch so to speak. It was Carolyn's senior year in medical college and like A said, our last one to farm unless something came along to finance us. The flax crop which cost us almost $2,000 in seed and estimated possible yield left us with a large stack of beautiful burlap sacks which I stitched with heavy wool of Spanish colors into drapes for the dining room. That's all we made.

The Phillips had sold the paper, and I was not sure that I could continue to write for the new owners. Even with all the crop losses, some new people came to Three Rivers. Among them was a new young doctor, Dr. Elmo W. Muecke, a graduate of Texas University School of Medicine in Galveston, and his pretty wife and son, Michael. When Carolyn was home for a few days in early September, we asked them over for supper.

That September Smitty Smith helped me make up a list of a couple of thousand names to send to the State Tuberculosis office in Austin to boost the Christmas seal sales. Tuberculosis is a deadly force in the southwest when dust and below average incomes set in for a few years stay, as was the case then.

The Davises moved back to Oakville. They had been perfect neighbors for quite a while now. Mrs. Davis had cooked for the hospital but had fallen and broken a leg. They owned a little place in Oakville so now they had decided to move there. I almost envied them. It is such a tucked-away little retreat near the Sulphur Creek valley.

The Rev. C. M. Nyquist was our pastor then; seems none of them stayed very long with us. Rev. Kluck had died suddenly, bringing Stone for a short stay and now Nyquist. He held a Blessing of the Tools service for the Sunday of the Labor Day weekend. He asked everyone to bring some article representing his work and lay it on the altar rail to be dedicated.

We thought it a very thoughtful service, but many people thought it was rather sacrilegious and did not bring anything. Pena was with us for her birthday, and so we put a Bible on the rail for her work.

"You should have put a cake, judging from the way Pena is working at it," George teased. "What did you use, cement?"

On the ninth we took Carolyn as far as San Antonio again for her trip to Dallas to start her senior year. We came right back home as it was teachers reception for the school's P-T A program. I flat blew my stack when Buddy refused to go along. He said he just had to stay home to think.

Later, he admitted he was worried about Carolyn's being a doctor. There is so much responsibility to being in charge of a human life. True! But it was too late to discourage her now. He seldom wrote letters to the girls but this night, when she was just arriving in Dallas for her senior year, he wrote a long letter . . . "things," he said, "I should have said when she was at home."

Mattie Black phoned to ask why Carolyn had not visited her while she was at home. Mattie is Mrs. Raymond Black, and she is blind. She is interested in everything good that goes on in the community, and I often marvel that she knows much more than those of us who are constantly on the watch for news stories. I was now writing for the Corpus Christi Caller, too. Often Mattie telephones me news tips.

One just had to keep on that year. There was now no turning back with over $10,000 notes in the bank signed against crops. Everyone was cross and tense. When I suggested to the commissioners court one Monday while covering the session for the papers that it was time to start plans for the Centennial celebration of the county, they looked at me as if I were afflicted with some rare disease.

Drouth or not, young people fell in love and married. We had a shower-party for Darlene Woelfel who married Larry Goebel. After all, we had known the kids since the year one. Darlene went to school with our girls, and Larry's parents were the Otto Goebels who have always been very hospitable. They were married in the Lutheran Church in town.

It was the September I realized my first more or less heart attack, not that the doctors would call it exactly that. But suddenly, pains squeezed me down to nothing and the next thing I knew I was gasping for breath seated by the clothesline. I thought to myself that it was good that I was alone, and I would not tell a soul. Arthur did not need any more worries.

Carolyn won a telephone call at the State Fair so she called us. My, it was good to talk to her (remembering how awful I had felt just the afternoon before.) It was also good to be able to tell her it was raining — not much yet but anyway, every drop was wet. We did not tell her we had had to ship the calves including the two pets — Bench Legs and Alfredo — for we only had $28 left in the bank. Arthur never wanted the girls to know such harsh realities. But life does not protect one always.

On Hallowe'en, Arthur built a big bonfire for the MYFers to enjoy when they returned from trick-or-treating for cash to send through Christian Rural Overseas Program. With money as short as it was, the Three Rivers people still gave almost $50. This is used to pay transportation lines' costs for taking surplus foods to other lands.

On Sunday afternoons, to get over the loss of not having the MYF to sponsor, we would drive some place. One Sunday we went to Tynan to see Eunice and Frank's new baby, Maureen. Betty Ann was now five. We discussed the need for rain and I reminded A it was time to go, for we were having special prayers for rain at the church that night. Frank said we could pray for that any-place.

On the way home from Tynan, when it was the time set for the church services, Buddy pulled to the side of the road all of a sudden.

"What's the matter?" I asked.

"Nothing! You said we were supposed to pray for rain tonite at seven, so let's pray."

We neither one said anything aloud. After a few moments, he started the motor and we proceeded to go home. That was on Sunday, and on Tueday it rained 2.30 inches. Downtown it rained four inches, and at the Nueces River the Williams gauged five inches. It was the biggest rain at one time there in 13 years, she said. It came in a severe electrical storm that knocked out all the telephone fuses and struck in several trees about the town.

Rains don't bring immediate cash to a farmer, but it puts dollar signs in the bankers' eyes; so we managed for a government loan. We paid off the remainder of the debt on the farm, and Buddy branded the entrance gate with his cattle brand irons — A A. It had been 28 years since he bought the place. Mr. Mc-Claugherty had just brought him a wandering Indian man; with his help, the whole place was cleaned and looking nice . . . and then put on the market.

"Now when it is finally ours?" I asked when he told me of his decision.

"Yes, now so we can buy the section we have leased all these

207

years. That is some wonderful land, and it does have the pavement coming to one of its corners."

Just when I thought he would be ready to call it quits, he planned to launch in deeper.

September 1955 found us a year older and a lot wiser. I now had taken a job with the Three Rivers News. The owners said I was to be the editor, but they never got around to putting that in print. Perhaps, it was a good thing as lots of folks find lots of faults with their local newspapers. Many of them want stories in the paper, seemingly like some sort of magic. It never occurs to some people that when a column is full, it just is full and there's no way to heap it up or round it.

Buddy took an agency again to sell cotton seed for Kasch Company at San Marcos.

Many things had happened since the September before. While we were in Dallas for Carolyn's commencement, Arthur's brother Paul had had a stroke. I was always afraid that would happen to Arthur these hot days as he burned the thorns off prickly pears and then cut, loaded and hauled them to the farm to feed the cattle we had managed to keep.

We do not have the pears out there; so he would get permission from people with vacant lots here in town to get theirs. He also burned them from fence-rows along the streets and highways. It was what he termed his year in hell.

The morning we were to go to Dallas for the commencement, he first had to burn some pear for the cattle. He got started at one a.m. and by seven had finished — besides having a flat and killing three big rattle-snakes. Just before we got to Pawnee, the water-hose broke on our almost new car — after all, we thought it was still new.

Ruth and Pena came to the exercises. Lee Roy had a summer job and could not leave. Pena flew over from San Antonio; that's what we should have done. But we had to bring back all of Carolyn's things as she was to intern at the Robert B. Green Hospital in San Antonio.

There were ten women doctors in her class with "Pid," Dr. Mary Bone, winning the top honors for the whole class and the $1,000 cash gift. Mr. and Mrs. Zink with whom Carolyn had boarded gave a reception for her after the exercises.

Paul died a few days afterwards. All his nephews were the pall bearers, including Lee Roy. We went by to see my two aged aunts, Louise and Freida. Lou had been bedfast now for a long time and was just skin and bones. One almost wished she could have passed away during a deep coma.

Joel and Shirley Casey were now our new tenants. Shirley helped unpack Carolyn's text books and gobs of other stuff. Shirley said, "Books, books and books! All about worms, germs, sperms and lawdy mercy look at these terms!"

Carolyn had to study some more even though she had graduated, she explained. "In fact, I intend to study all the rest of my life. I only wonder where we will ever put all these books."

Buddy was cross this summer. It bothered him for me to have to go to work every morning. Yet, he knew we needed the income and the $150 monthly would help out "just until I make a crop — promise!"

One September night, we went to the hospital just to sorta' observe what emergency duty really meant for Carolyn. One time was enough. There were three men brought in hand-cuffed together by police.

After they were sewn up, suddenly two other jail mates were brought in with huge slashes on their arms. They had been allowed to shave; and when the guards had momentarily looked aside, they had cut themselves.

"Why did you cut yourself?" one of the doctors asked.

"We all done swore we would protest in some manner until we got new mattresses. When you all get tired of having to fix us up and haul us around, you will see that we get new mattresses," the big burly fellow told the policeman who had hand-cuffed him to the stretcher.

Near morning a suicide came in. Before that a little boy had caught his arm in the wringer of the washing machine and literally ground it out of socket. "If this is doctoring, no thanks!" Arthur said as we journeyed home in time to burn some more pear for the cows.

Carolyn's medical license came, and she wrote a prescription for me for diarrhea — the first one she wrote for me. I kept the bottle for a souvenir.

I was elected as a member of the board to put on the centennial celebration next year. It was an interesting experience as I interviewed people who had lived here many years. I worked like fury to build up the paper, for I felt it was a need in the town. Yet, all the time, I knew I could not keep up the grind. Carrying my own typewriter back and forth to work was getting to be a nuisance. I dared not complain for A did not like me to work as it was for such long hours.

It was my pleasure to write stories about Mrs. Mary Ann Hinnant, who was 100 years old and was named Queen of the Live Oak County Centennial.

I gave the boss notice that I would leave his employ on October 20; but just two days before that, Arthur accidently got a piece of steel in his right eye. So after first aid in Three Rivers, I drove him to see a specialist. When we returned, the co-owner gave me time to pick up my stool, my table and my typewriter — and my pay check for the month.

We laugh about it all many times these days for it was once in my life-time that an upset didn't make me sick. I was far too excited over the plans Arthur had for us to open an office supply and stationery shop all our own to give a second hoot about the newspaper, I thought.

But I was wrong. I missed it. I had enjoyed the work, and the Cunninghams are the finest of people to work alongside at the printer's table — or folding and addressing papers each Thursday afternoon.

On November 7, we opened the shop, The Write Shop. Even from the very first, it has been successful. We let it serve as the headquarters in Three Rivers for the centennial celebration as I worked to help with publicity and sold souvenirs for the event People were very kind to trade with us, and we continually had to add new stock.

The Caseys who had lived next door to us, had been transferred. Now the Topes with their three darling daughters — Sharon 9, Darnell 7 and Nonie 4 — were always out in the yard in good weather to greet me when I came home. The first year, we kept the shop open only in the afternoons.

Ruth and Lee Roy were moving to Bellville, where he had chosen to go to a new coaching job. They had so wished for children and had had no luck. Even the adoption papers made out now two years ago had not produced. Ruth planned to teach the next year while they waited and to work in the summers as vacation relief in the Texas Company office.

We chose the name Write because much of my income and work was from writing for the San Antonio Express and the Corpus Christi Caller. New people thought it was my name, and I began to hear "Is this Miss Write?" when I answered the telephone, "Write Shop."

By this time, I was writing a by-line column for the Beeville Bee-Picayune of which I was, and am, proud. It is called "Leaves From Live Oak" with stories fluttering about from obits, bridal showers, rain-reports, car wrecks and most anything which could be interesting to the thousands of readers this prize-winning South Texas paper has.

During the early days of my shop, the owners of the radio station between Kenedy and Karnes City came over to get me to write news for their programs. We went to the Chamber of Commerce meeting suggesting a direct tie-in with Three Rivers, but the directors took no action on the matter. The station K A M L did employ me to write for them, and we called the news "Live Oak Peckings" because, like a wood-pecker, I could just peck a bit of this and that using as many person's names as possible.

Soon folk dropped in to tell me how much they appreciated hearing some item today "on Henry Howell's W O A I program" or on "Chuck Martin's K A M L news" . . . several came in to tell me they kept up with my column . . . and soon, I started sending news items to the Alice Echo and the San Antonio Light when the stories happened to fill their needs and interests.

Among my treasures are thank-you notes from the Tilden Lions, the Three Rivers Lions, from W. C. Luce who has the store in Tilden that sells "everything except a goose yoke," and from the many readers in the Dinero area. All was not praise, by any means, and often I had to count to ten to keep from cussing when the telephone had rung and I had gotten "a piece of somebody's mind." People often forget the newspapers belong to the people who work hard to pay for their businesses and try to please their public.

All Glittering Is Not Gold

Looking toward my fiftieth birthday, I decided I had surely been blessed. Many times when all was gloomy, a ray of bright gold had come bursting through as beautiful as the sunset of that first Thanksgiving Day in Live Oak County.

September 1957 marked the beginning of my fiftieth year since first my parents started the whole idea. I looked forward to celebrating a fiftieth birthday. It had been a full and tumultous year since 1956.

Ruth and Lee Roy were now sunk in teaching work in beautiful Bellville. Carolyn had gone back to Dallas, where she was a resident doctor in the great Baylor University Hospital. She loved her work and trusted her fellow doctors, who had introduced her to a young technician whom she had married in early June. I had been rather opposed to the idea of a hasty marriage, but then this was 1957 and not those good old days in which I grew up. She had persuaded him to come to see us, and he was to get acquainted; but in all her excitement, she had done most of the asking, telling and talking.

Ruth had sewn and sewn on a gorgeous white satin and lace wedding gown all the weeks she had had before the wedding date. Friends in Three Rivers had insisted on a shower and given her the nicest ever. We went to the wedding, which was in the hospital chapel as she only got two days off.

Luckily, it had rained and rained that year and there was farm work galore again. The shop was beginning to be more than I could handle alone, especially when it came to packing and unpacking shipments.

For the first time in the seven years I had written up the news releases about the wild and wooly rodeos held on the Labor Day weekend in Tilden, we went to see a performance this year. Buddy balked at the idea — what could be so interesting about that? — but when he did go, I almost had to have them rope him and drag him to the car to get to go home. I had a busy day ahead of me and knew I needed to get some rest.

"I will stay and help you tomorrow since Mondays are always

so busy. Why don't you stay closed for the day? It is Armistice, you know."

"Now it is no longer called Armistice but Veterans Day," I said.

Mrs. Harry Hinton came to see me the next day at the shop. I was anxious to hear about her newest son, Byron. The Hintons had become true friends during the centennial work as he served as president of the board. A new son is happiness to share.

It was a September to learn again and again that all that glitters is not gold; and thank God, it is not. For many things came my way down at the shop that glitter in my memory which are much more valuable than gold. Friendships such as Ann Hinton's; afternoons when little Glenna Jo Jones would come in to get me to let her type just a few lines on my typewriter or to "help" me gift wrap. She loved the glitter used to decorate packages and came to be quite good at using it.

Then, it was the September that Larry Taylor, one of our neighbor babies now grown to be five, came in for his kindergarten supplies. He beamed up at me with a dollar bill in his hand and said his Daddy had said to spend it all since it was at Mrs. Adlof's store.

Even the sad tale Buddy told at the supper table was to me a treasure. It made me feel warm and loved to know my husband is so kind-hearted that when he cut a rabbit to pieces with the stalk cutter in the field, he stopped to bury it. He almost cried as he told me how it had ruined the day for him.

Another treasured memory of that year was the almost perfect attendance we made at Sunday School. Later, I heard Buddy tell Ruthie and Lee Roy it was easier to go than to hear ma preach about it all week. Story teller! He enjoyed going. I could tell from the many funny tales he would come back home to tell.

I was elected secretary of the Three Rivers Garden Club on September 9, a new club which will surely make itself felt in the future. One cannot work with plants very seriously and not come to appreciate God's creation. I had served the first year of the club as the program and yearbook chairman.

Once again, some people proposed we no longer have a P-T A in Three Rivers and the school heads asked me to come to speak in favor of continuation. This I gladly did, being a staunch believer of facing one another with problems of common interest. That is what P-T A actually is meant to be — a meeting place between the teachers and the parents.

213

I served the Live Oak County Tuberculosis Association as executive secretary. Mrs. Elbert Brown, state field worker, came to help me and to train me. By the time we got all the extra things done and worked in the shop and on the farm we were perhaps good candidates for tuberculosis. It was after my feet "gave way" and my head grew terribly faint-feeling each time I had to get something for a customer from a low shelf, I knew I must slow the pace. Postural hypotension is an embarrassing condition, to say the least. Fearing one will fall flat on his face is an uneasy thought.

Perhaps, we should have kept the shop and hired clerks. Yet management would have taken up about the same time; and my real desire was not to make money, though during the worst of the drouth that had been a necessity. The shop was a good income as it had no competition locally.

It gave me more contacts for news-stories and more opportunities to meet new people; and I learned, firsthand, to keep tax records, to go to market in Dallas and San Antonio to buy, and to imprint cards and other social supplies such as party napkins. I kept dictionaries, etiquette books, references, and Robert's Rules of Order, Revised, handy for folk to read and check out.

There was now another case on trial in George West concerning the new lake. This was to set the value of the Reeves Brown land to be inundated someday when the lake was raised. I enjoyed seeing all the Lagarto and Dinero folk. Mrs. Cartwright expressed her thought that perhaps "before this is settled, many of us will be dead." I asked her what to do about the shop now that A had his farm work again.

"Sell! Be with him as much as you can and do write the rest of your book." I took her advice. There's nothing more interesting than writing.

Asiatic flu was rampant. Arthur was positive he had it. But one day a letter came from Carolyn saying she had finally rented a suite for her private office. A nice rain came, too, and within the hour, he was completely cured. Marvelous what a bit of joy can do!

Added to the long list of work done on an average Friday, my diary tells of the cricket invasion. Crickets were so thick that fall that they covered the walls of buildings two stories high. Toward morning, it seems, they grew weary and came tumbling down in great heaps. Each day Alfred Guerra would sweep the walks of the Rialto Building, in which the shop was located.

Glowing in my thoughts of that year is the fine sermon our

district superintendent preached that fall when on his regular rounds — "How Wide Is Your Church Door?" It was just what I felt the whole nation needed to hear. In Little Rock, police were trying to make people tolerant. Should this not be a business of the church? As we discussed it, Arthur agreed. But he loved to recall other things in the past on the same general subject.

Again he retold the story of the Negro preacher who had gotten a real loud "Amen" from a dear old sister seated on the front row each time he blasted some sin of which she knew her neighbors were guilty. Then when he started in on the sin of women's gossiping, she nudged the sister next to her and said, "He done quit preaching now and started meddling."

"That's the way it is when we blast the other states for their sins. We done started meddling."

The Wesleyan Service Guild gave the annual social honoring the public school teachers, and we had a fine time. It was inspiring to have so many fine persons gather together for an evening of fun and fellowship.

The Christmas seal sale campaign was now done from our office, and one of the duties of an executive secretary is to get as many volunteers as possible interested in the work. One evening, Mr. Black invited us to come to Mattie's room, for she has a wonderful memory of names. She helped us for hours to add new names and to withdraw cards of the deceased.

Richard Arthur Adlof was born that winter to Elroy and Mona in Alta Loma. This was number six but their first boy, and he was the first to carry the name Arthur. It was a proud moment when the news arrived that he was named for my husband.

I had so much Christmas business I needed two assistants. Promptly at four on Christmas Eve, we closed. It is traditional in our two families to cease work early on that day. We even tried to milk the cows early back on the dairy farm on Christmas Eve. We waited and waited for Carolyn and her husband. They did not come. The next morning, Carolyn called very early to wish us a Merry Christmas and explained she was out on calls all night. That's the life of a GP.

Many people claim one can predict the whole year's weather by the first twelve days of January. Others say to count by what the last six days of a year are and the first six days of the new year. Although I never believed that nonsense, I always write it down. After all, what the weather does is what we do. Everything hinges on the weather when one farms and ranches.

215

Things were looking up for us. At the beginning of the year, the first twelve days or the last six and the first six had seemed to predict a bright future to Buddy. He insisted on buying the ranch next to the farm which we now had sold. This we did on March 10. Coming home from San Antonio where we had gone to sign the final papers, I remembered it would have been Miss Ora's birthday were she still alive.

"She always said whatever you do, do well!" Arthur reminded. He told again of how he planned to turn this native brush-land into a model small combination farm and ranch.

"With the help of the Lord," I reminded him.

"The Lord probably is saying with the help of me and the weather-man and the banker," he replied. This could have led to an argument, for to me the weatherman is none other than the good Lord.

"Does that mean that if I write a good book this year, you are in favor of my trying to get it published?"

He agreed it did.

I reached my golden anniversary birthday that June and also sold the store. I was happy about the birthday, but I truly missed all the people who came in or just tapped a friendly hello as they went by each day.

I had promised myself that when I reached this birthday I would take the time to write a novel about myself. What's so novel about me? This I asked myself again several days and nights on end that summer.

Soon, however, things were in order again; I felt better with more rest, after having given up the TB job and having sold the store. I spent more time on the farm again. Long walks in the quiet helped me to get back on my feet. I wrote the book but lacked the title and wondered just what good could come of publishing it.

I was invited to Beeville one day to meet with city and county officials to plan their centennial. I recalled now as I worked on this manuscript how the County Judge had wished that more people would write more just plain everyday stories about Texas.

He said many people think Texas is just a wide open space with a few cow-pokes propped against fences watching the tumble weeds roll by. Off in the distance, oil wells of Oklahoma are seen, and down at the border the usual picture shows some pretty women in bright skirts and blouses dancing on a Mexican som-brero. Couldn't anyone write about cotton picking, rabbit hunt-

216

ing, cat-fishing and how many of our men and women have died on battle-fields?

For days I thought on what he had said. No! I cannot write about heroes going to battle in wars, for one cannot write such things from second-hand knowledge. One must feel that as it comes right into one's own circle.

But about cotton picking, rabbit hunting, cat-fishing — yes and silo filling, church suppers, youth organizations, taking petitions to the county court to get a public health nurse, P-T A, M Y F and consolidation of rural schools — I could write and more.

The telephone rang. Now who in all the world would be so stupid as to call at eleven o'clock on a September evening? Surely all our kith and kin knew we went to bed with the chickens this time of the year.

"Gracious! It is Ruthie and they are going to the Home tomorrow to get a baby girl," I shouted to Arthur as quickly as she told it to me. Many hours later that night after discussing all the differences a granddaughter would make, I suddenly said, "Now I have someone who will someday be interested in knowing just what her ancestors did. After all, she will be truly ours from this day forward."

We called Dallas to make sure Carolyn knew of the wonderful event.

"Hello, Doc. This is Grandpa Adlof!" he muttered sleepily.

After a short period while he listened to Carolyn's telling that Ruthie had called her, too, I heard him say, "Lisa! That is a beautiful name. We were wondering what they would name her and in all the excitement, we forgot to ask. Lisa! Lisa! That is a beautiful name. Do you suppose she will like us, too?"